20

BILL DEVER

BILL BEVER

Great Stuff! I can't stop reading your new book and turn the lights out. Thanks for all the great memories you're stirring up for this lifelong DJ. Learning more about the lives and careers of the jocks I looked up to all these years is making this a memorable vacation indeed. Anxiously awaiting your '70s volume!
~ **DJ Warren Garling**; aka Jesse James/Chris Warren
Blast from Your Past! 1960s and 1970s

LinDee captures the marvelous magic of the airwaves. The Swinging Sixties *is a great trigger for memories of the best Rock and Roll decade. It's fun reliving Philly's WIBG radio history of my youth, through the DJs' eyes, and learning what they were really up to when we called in for a dedication. As a nonfiction "storyteller" Rochelle makes facts and history fun, weaving them together to bring us the great stories of these pioneering disc jockeys. A welcome reminder of their contributions and legacies to radio.*
~ Enjoy often... **John F. Harnish**
Author, retired VP small press publishing company

This book has so much information on the DJs of my younger years. Just like the movie American Graffiti, *it brings back so many memories. Since I'm from the San Francisco Bay Area, it was interesting to find out about all the other DJs of that time in the rest of the country. My favorites were "The Wolfman" and of course, "Dr. Don Rose."*
~ **Ron Connelly**; retired mortgage broker

Congrats on Book 2 Rock and Roll DJs...the '60s!!!!!! Thanks a million for your contribution to the history of radio!!!!
~ **DJ Kent Burkhart**; retired
Blast from Your Past! 1950s and 1960s

Blast from Your Past!™

Blast from Your Past!™ series

Book 1
Rock & Roll Radio DJs
The First Five Years 1954-1959

Book 2
Rock & Roll Radio DJs
The Swinging Sixties 1960-1969

Book 3
Rock & Roll Radio DJs
The Psychedelic Seventies 1970-1979
(Look for it late 2018)

Blast from Your Past!™
Book 2

Rock & Roll Radio DJs
The Swinging Sixties™
1960 ~ 1969

aka Rockin' Rochelle ~ your California BFYP 84.8-FM DJ
BlastFromYourPast.net

Copyright ©2017

LinDee Rochelle. All rights reserved.

The text contained herein is comprised of biographical vignettes based on actual occurrences as reported from research and/or through participant interviews, and the author's editorial perceptions. The publisher and author disclaim all liability in the use of the information contained herein. The Internet is unreliable, memories are fallible, and perceptions are subjective.

Unless otherwise identified all images are from the author's personal vintage and/or contemporary collection. Individually owned images are used with owners' permissions or fall under fair use for commentary and reporting. Please contact publisher for authorization to quote.

eBook edition first published 2017

Print edition first published May 2017; 2nd printing September 2017

Black-and-White Edition ISBN 10: 154579624X

Black-and-White Edition ISBN 13: 978-1545796244

Library of Congress: [TBD]

Special appreciation: Wolfman Jack Licensing per Lou Lamb Smith ("Wolfwoman") for excerpts authorization from *Have Mercy! Confessions of the Original Rock 'n' Roll Animal* and Wolfman's "Rufus" signature character.

Original *BFYP* (Book 1 cover) design logo from which all others are derived: Christopher Master Designs; TheMasterdome.FolioHD.com/all

BFYP Book 2 cover design: LinDee Rochelle

Radio Consultants: DJs Bill Gardner, BillGardnerOnTheRadio.com; Shotgun Tom Kelly, ShotgunTomKelly.com; and all *BFYP* DJs.

Published by Penchant for Penning™
(Through CreateSpace.com)
4203 Genesee Avenue, Ste. 103-439, San Diego, California 92117 USA
PenchantForPenning.com
Signed print trade paperback available: BlastFromYourPast.net
eBook and print editions on Amazon

BFYP Book Series dedicated to

Wolfman Jack
The Original Rock & Roll Radio DJ

"Who's dis on the Wolfman tel-e-phone?"

Wolfman Jack—Robert Weston Smith—summed up our generation and the dawn of unconventional Rock & Roll Radio, in "*Have Mercy! Confessions of the Original Rock 'n' Roll Animal.*"

Alternately glorified, vilified and memorialized, Rock Radio DJs personified the turmoil and tremendous strides of three decades of society in the United States.

The Blast from Your Past! series is dedicated to Wolfman Jack, and all of the pioneering Rock & Roll Radio Disc Jockeys, 1954-1979, who were often fleeting sounds of our youth, but remain locked in our memories, still spinning the music of our souls.

Trippin' Through the Years

Turntable of Contents

Copyright ©2017 iv
BFYP Book Series dedicated to v
Trippin' Through the Years vi
The DJ was "The Man" ix
Idiosyncrasies & Idiocies xiii
Why DJs Do What We Do … xv
Rockin' Legacies 1

Forrest "Frosty" Mitchell 3
    Best known KIOA/Des Moines, Iowa
Joey Reynolds 6
    Best kown WKBW/Buffalo, New York
Rich "Brother" Robbin >Part 1 10
    Best known KCBQ/San Diego, California
Bill Gardner >Part 1 13
    Best known WIBG/Philadelphia
Have mercy! >Part 1 of 3 15
    Wolfman Jack
Kent Burkhart 20
    Best known KOWH/Omaha, Nebraska
Lee Gray >Part 1 23
    Best known WTRY/Albany, New York
Tom Donahue >Part 1 25
    Best known KYA, KMPX, KSAN/San Francisco, California
Burt Sherwood 28
    Best known WMCA/New York City
Norm Prescott 32
    Best known WBZ/Boston, Massachusetts
Rick Snyder >Part 1 35
    Best known WTRY/Albany, New York
Ken Chase 40
    Best known KISN/Portland, Oregon
Sandy Deanne 47
    with Jay & the Americans "Come a Little Bit Closer"
Cousin Bruce Morrow >Part 1 51
    Best known WABC/New York City
Mitch Michael 56
    (Terrell Metheny) Best known WOKY/Milwaukee, Wisconsin

Lee Gray >Part 2 61
    Best known WTRY/Albany, New York
Alison Steele 66
    Best known WNEW/New York City
Mike Rabon (Founder).. 71
    with The Five Americans notify "Western Union"
Bill Gardner* >Part 2 78
    Best known WIBG/Philadelphia, Pennsylvania
Billy Bass... 82
    Best known WIXY/Cleveland, Ohio
Ed Sciaky 86
    Best known WDAS & WMMR/Philadelphia, Pennsylvania
Ron Riley... 90
    Best known WLS/Chicago, Illinois
Have mercy! >Part 2 of 3 94
    Wolfman Jack
Jim Higgs... 103
    Best known WKMI/Kalamazoo, Michigan
Dave Mason 107
    Best known WSAY & WBBF/Rochester, New York
Shotgun Tom Kelly 111
    Best known KCBQ/San Diego & K-EARTH/Los Angeles
Jack Vincent... 117
    Best known KCBQ/San Diego, California
Neale Blase 121
    Best known at too many to mention
Rick Snyder >Part 2 129
    Best known WTRY/Albany, New York
Bill Bailey 133
    Best known WKLO & WAKY/Louisville, Kentucky
Jim Stagg 138
    Best known WCFL/Chicago, Illinois
Rich "Brother" Robbin >Part 2 143
    Best known KCBQ/San Diego, California
Neil Ross 146
    Best known KCBQ/San Diego, California
Warren Garling.. 151
    Best known WGNA/Albany, New York
Tom Donahue >Part 2 155
    Best known KYA, KMPX, KSAN/San Francisco, California
Raechel Donahue... 158
    Best known KMPX & KSAN/San Francisco, California
Cousin Bruce Morrow >Part 2 163
    Best known WABC/New York City
Don Rose... 167
    Dr. Don best known KFRC/San Francisco

William F. Williams 170
    Best known KMEN/San Bernardino & KPPC/Los Angeles
Have mercy! >Part 3 177
Wolfman Jack

Is That All There Is ... ♪ 183
    Epilogue
Save the Last Dance for Me ... ♪ 185
    Acknowledgments
What'd I Say? ... ♪ 186
    Glossary
Sources & Resources 187
    Bibliography
Book of Love ... ♪ 189
    About the Author
Psychedelic Shack ... ♪ 191
    TOC ~ Psychedelic Seventies

[*Image:* Wolfman Jack & Lonnie Napier, friend, advisor and business partner from 1970 until Wolfman's death, July 1, 1995. Photo c. 1976, courtesy of Lonnie.]

The DJ was "The Man"

Foreword by Lonnie Napier

Some people grow up wanting to be rock stars. Some people grow up wanting to be doctors or lawyers. And then there's that unlucky bunch who dream of being a radio DJ.

For the latter, it usually starts at a young age and is more than a dream. It's an obsession. The reason I say "unlucky" is because the job is never about money and, more than likely, not about fame. It comes with a passion to play music through a small radio speaker and excite the listener.

But once-upon-a-time, occasionally *both* fame and fortune came to that rare breed of personality who rose above the mere mortals to become the Zeus or Apollo of radio. In *Blast from Your Past*, LinDee Rochelle has put together an insight into the endangered animal known as the Rock & Roll Radio DJ.

Her request to the industry for fun, old-radio reminisces, especially about Wolfman Jack, to whom she's dedicated the book, struck a memory chord and of course, I answered.

It was fun to recall ... I must've been barely eleven or twelve years old listening to "Happy Hare" on KCBQ, San Diego. Harry Martin was just that, *"Happy."*

A whacky DJ who made you laugh. You hung on his every word and then he'd slam into a hot platter of wax from the Beach Boys or Del Shannon.

I laid under my covers at night, not thinking of carnal images of Ann Margaret or Natalie Wood, but trying to pick up San Diego's KGB-AM on my transistor radio. In later years, I became friends with Buzz Bennett, the program director from KGB. And I met my idol, a production God in my eyes and ears, Bobby Ocean.

Then I found a Los Angeles station, 93 KHJ on my radio and I heard the incarnation of the Boss Jocks. Robert W. Morgan. Bill Wade. The Real Don Steele. Sam Riddle. Later on it was Charlie Tuna. Humble Harve. Rich Brother Robbin.

And then there was the Mexican station. The Mighty 1090, XERB, where this strange voice emanated every few hours claiming to be "Wolfman Jack." Little did I know at the time, but my life was on a direct path to a twenty-five-year career of working with the Wolfman.

Radio has changed a lot since then. The DJ was "*The Man*" back in the Golden Age of Rock & Roll Radio. I began working for Wolfman Jack in 1970 and one of the first things he passed on to me was his love for radio. His passion for the art of broadcasting.

Wolfman taught me that you didn't go home just because you'd worked your eight hours with an hour lunch. You worked until *you felt* your job was done. Until you *knew* that what you'd produced was the best it could be and that everyone who heard it would be blown away.

Probably no one would ever know you'd created that ear candy and you probably wouldn't make a lot of money. But *you'd* know. And if you loved radio, that was enough.

Wolfman was my best friend. A confidant. I loved him like a brother. Over the final ten years of his life, I probably spent more time with him than I did my own family. And now, nearly twenty years since his death, I still think of him every day and wonder what he thinks of the radio productions I'm putting together now. Even though we live in a digital age, all of the lessons I learned from one of the masters of radio, are still inside of me. The passion and the art of radio has never left.

I hope LinDee's fun collection of stories will remind you of the innocence that was the excitement of radio. Or for you young'uns, sneak a peek into the lives of your parents and grandparents—something they refer to as "the good ol' days" when great radio was "live."

Maybe *Blast from Your Past* will take you to a fond moment in your childhood or have you wishing you had been there "when." Regardless, radio *is* and *always has been* a conduit between information and entertainment.

And the DJ—that guy or gal with the gift of gab was the flamboyant master of ceremonies. Read. Enjoy. And learn about a time of innocence. A time of frivolity. A time when radio was "cool" and the Rock & Roll Radio DJs were gods.

Lonnie Napier
Nashville, Tennessee
Associate Producer
    American Country Countdown with Kix Brooks
VP Wolfman Jack Enterprises
Forever friend to Wolfman Jack

Idiosyncrasies & Idiocies

(Preface)

We're Rockin' now!

Blast from Your Past!™ series is a twenty-five-year tribute (1954-1979) and legacy to those behind-the-microphone icons of our pioneering Rock & Roll Radio days—the deejays who brightened our mornings and capped off our nights. You are reading **Book 2**: *The Swinging Sixties!*

These mini-biographies are lively vignettes of just a few brief peeks into their lives that barely do them justice. Written from a radio fan's POV, most of the book is in layman's terms and generally focuses on the positive side of life.

In addition to research, quotes and fodder for your enjoyment were gently hoisted from the depths of thirty- forty- even fifty-year-old memories. Though hopefully at a minimum, we beg your tolerance of discrepancies, ambiguity, and perhaps a little ... *ahem* ... "enhancement."

While working on the 1950s, it became apparent that the original thought of one large, twenty-five-year tome would take forever. There were just too many great stories!

Book 1 was subsequently published to introduce the series and reflect on the importance of those "*First Five Years*," 1954-1959 (2010; 2012). Breaking down the project into three dynamic decades was the only way to go.

- o BOOK 1: *The 1ST Five Years 1954-1959*
- o BOOK 2: *The Swinging Sixties 1960-1969*
- o BOOK 3: *The Psychedelic Seventies 1970-1979*

Regarding radio stations and DJs' careers—due to length restraints, not all the DJs' radio stations and/or related jobs are presented in *BFYP*; however, some of the great stuff "left on the cutting room floor" will be posted when possible, on BlastFromYourPast.net.

If you're reading the eBook edition, you'll find links throughout that take you to historical websites and coveted broadcasting airchecks.

Please note, *BFYP* DJ books are pure nostalgia. I don't pretend to know the broadcasting business. Any radio tech-talk is related to how it pertains to a particular DJ, or learned through cursory research.

Many of these interviews took place between 2008 and 2011. Delay in writing and publishing was a by-product of life. But because they are historical/biographical, they are relevant until the end of time.

[*Image:* Back when gas stations were "full service," they even helped us find radio stations while on the road! *BFYP* Collection; c. mid-1960s.]

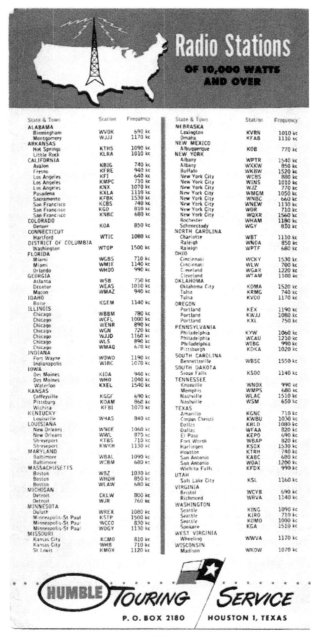

[*Image:* Veteran Rock & Roll radio DJ, Bill Gardner at KLZ/Denver c. 1965. Bill is the eldest of a trio of radio DJ brothers. Al & Andre Gardner followed big "brutha" Bill into radio in the *Psychedelic Seventies.* Photo courtesy of Bill.]

Why DJs Do What We Do ...

It's for YOU!
Special Introduction by DJ Bill Gardner

I'll never forget it. One morning in the mid-1990s, while hosting my KOOL morning radio show in Phoenix, Arizona, I answered another of my ringing studio lines. The caller said something that's permanently etched in my mind.

"Good morning Bill Gardner! I just figured out what makes your radio station my absolute favorite, anywhere in America. What makes you different from the rest of the voices. Each spring I drive my mother from Arizona, several thousand miles back to her home in Florida. Along the way, I listen to many, many radio stations for countless hours on end, all with virtually the same music as yours. But it's *you guys* alongside the music that separate your radio station from the rest!"

I thought, "We did it. We *broke the pane of glass.*" Have you ever, when you least expected it, turned toward the radio and thought "My god, he was talking to *me*!" That's what I've always called "breaking the pane of glass."

When you're listening to a radio station, and we are "live" inside, talking between songs, if it's easy for you to ignore the voice on the radio, we haven't gotten through to you ... we haven't *broken the invisible pane of glass* that separates the people on the <u>inside</u> of the radio, with those <u>outside</u> who <u>listen</u>.

If someone calls our studio lines and after any short conversation says, "... and what was your name again?" I know I haven't gotten through to that person. We haven't formed that radio bond. But if I hear, "Bill Gardner, I love waking up with your morning show on the radio," those are the listeners who make my job worthwhile. And they've made it worthwhile for me each morning since I began as a radio DJ in 1965, at America's very first rock and roll station on FM, KLZ-FM, Denver, Colorado.

LinDee Rochelle and I have that bond. I know her name well, and she knows mine. Through that wonderful miracle known as "the radio," we *connected*. When I first heard of the Rock & Roll Radio DJs project, I was glad for LinDee, and glad for the radio industry on a number of different levels.

Many times I've heard spoken words over the radio and thought *that was brilliant!* Maybe even said a few myself that I thought might qualify. But I knew full well that unlike live television, or live music, or live performances of *any* kind, the likelihood was extremely low that what I'd just heard or said over the radio airwaves would be saved or preserved.

People do record television, live concerts and other performances, but the evocative, daily creativity on (terrestrial) radio almost always just *goes away* after one real time, right now airing. That was especially true in the early days of rock & roll radio. Although radio airchecks abound on the Internet, they're most often of "celebrity" DJs. But there are countless moments of thousands of DJs across the country devoted to their listeners that were not recorded. What I'd heard in one fleeting moment that made me smile would evaporate into thin air and be gone forever.

LinDee's Blast from Your Past! book series preserves a bit of the magic, a bit of the bond that keeps radio personalities like me doing and enjoying what I do, for as long as you'll listen ... it isn't just the blah, blah, blah, it's the link between people, between you and me ... and it's our reward.

Blast from Your Past! preserves some of the spirit of thousands of hours of radio broadcasts that will never be heard again. But maybe the spirit, and the connection between people who don't really know one another yet feel a genuine link, makes it worthwhile for all of us.

BRAVO, LinDee Rochelle.

Bill Gardner
Las Vegas, Nevada
BillGardnerOnTheRadio.com

Rockin' Legacies

(Author Introduction)

Whoohoo! Hula Hoops and beehive hair-dos! From the get-go, the Sixties challenged our staid Stepford lives languishing from the 1950s.

The strange but dynamic 1960s decade began with a leap year and we leapt into love songs on our tinny transistor radios. Think, Marv Johnson's "You Got What It Takes" (up to #3 on WIBG/Philly's Top 99 Records of the Week, January 31, 1960).

The next nine years our music transformed from Bubble Gum Pop, full of hearts and flowers, to doom-and-gloom guitar-heavy protest tunes.

"Eve of Destruction" (Barry McGuire; 1965), a prediction of our apocalyptic future, is as relevant today, as the 2000s mirror the Sixties. "And When I Die" (Blood, Sweat & Tears) is full of societal angst that hit #8 on the November 5, 1969 KHJ/Los Angeles Boss 30 survey.

At the same time, Peggy Lee asked the haunting question, "Is That All There Is?" No, Peggy, there was and is a LOT more. Take heart and ignore alarmists in the media. We've survived this long, let's have a beer and sing along ...

Were you there? Did you call your favorite DJ and request a happy, sappy love song to wash your blues away? Let's remember together, as we skip through the 1960's true, behind-the-microphone, Rockin' Radio DJ stories.

Ready to peek into the personal lives of pioneering broadcasters? You'll remember from the good ol' days, or meet anew, thirty-plus disc jockeys and three bands who dug deep and dredged up their best memories to share with you. Good—bad—and holy-moly!

Swinging into Action

In the second week of 1960 at Philly's WIBG, we find Ricky Nelson looking for a girlfriend. He didn't have Match.com, so "I Wanna Be Loved" had slipped from #10 to #19 on their Top 99 Records of the Week. I was only eleven, but was sure that he sang with those beautiful baby blues, just for me.

Guy Mitchell felt the burn as he slipped a little, counting his exes in "Heartaches by the Number" at #15; and flaunting her patriotic colors, Connie Francis landed with a proud version of "God Bless America" at #29. We were all over the charts in beat and genre.

Though still a little tame, by the end of the year, we were twistin' with Chubby Checker, bumpin' 'n' grindin' with Elvis, and the West Coast waved a howdy-do, hangin' ten with new "surf music" by the Ventures, and Jan & Dean.

Of course, era aficionados claim "real" Rock & Roll died in 1959 with the last decade, marked by the tragic deaths of Buddy Holly, The Big Bopper and Ritchie Valens; aggravated by Elvis' stint in the Army, Little Richard's calling to the pulpit, and the scandalous antics of Jerry Lee Lewis. (During a 1958 British tour it was learned that twenty-three-year-old Jerry had married his thirteen-year-old cousin—busted!)

Musically, we tried to keep the mood light—for a while. It wouldn't last. The Vietnam War dug in and took its toll on moods, faith, and lives. We had no clue it would ultimately define the decade and devastate a generation. Soon, Berlin and Cuban Missile crises would add to our angst. So, we turned to music.

Radio's payola woes finished off Rock & Roll's "phase I." Payola Congressional hearings dominated much of 1960, ending careers of several key DJs and quite possibly changing the course of music history.

Let's see what else ... and in some cases, *who* else ... was turned inside out, as we delve into the Sixties with our disc jockeys. We begin with those fun-lovin' guys who ventured forth from the Fifties, in *BFYP* Book 1, and watch them change the course of Rock & Roll history.

BFYP DJ Neil Ross, hit the proverbial Rockin' nail on the head with these words of wisdom:

"I tell my daughter, the difference between 1960 and 1969, is as if a hundred years had gone by ..."

Flip on the mic ... and on with the show!

Radio's Rockin' Rochelle at BFYP-FM 84.8 is serving up the tunes in sunny Cal-i-forn-i-A. Plant your tush <u>down</u>, Baby, and stay awhile!

Crank up the radio and ask me dear, **Why?** ♪ Because I love you!

Forrest "Frosty" Mitchell
Best known at KIOA/Des Moines, Iowa

In late 1959 DJ Frosty Mitchell was running listener contests around his kids' births at KIOA in Des Moines, Iowa. The new decade brings a fresh baby story from Frosty and his very open-minded wife, Joan.

DJs are dedicated dudes you know, and Frosty was no exception. I could have finished his story in the Fifties, with a quick nod to the new decade. He soon ditched the DJ gigs for station ownership.

But this story is too good a lead-in from our Stepford Lives into the ultimate Age of Aquarius, to leave it behind.

Emceeing shows was a fun break for Frosty, and as often happened. one night. a very pregnant Joan joined him.

[*Image:* Courtesy of Frosty. "Joan's a saint," says Frosty; read on to learn why he's right! They're enjoying life off the air in this 2008 photo.]

Frosty's self-deprecating humor teased his audience on the lively night in 1960, as Joan watch and took mental notes of his rights and wrongs. He recalled it with a hearty laugh, as if it were yesterday ...

"I'm off-mic for a minute and this waitress comes up and says, 'Your wife broke her water.' My mind is on the show and I said, 'Get her another glass, fool. I'm doing a show.'

"I finished my show and strode over to Joan's table to get my usual critique, and here she is with her legs wrapped around a chair!"

Yes, you guessed it—*her water broke*—and *this* water doesn't come in a glass.

"We carried her and the chair out of the ballroom to the car and told her not to move. My twin girls were almost born at a teen hop!"

No wonder women soon began to burn their bras. We needed to make our men aware of a thing or two.

But to give Frosty his due, back in "the good ol' days," we simply did not discuss these things in public. It didn't occur to him what she was going through, while he grabbed the glory on stage.

[*Image:* Fresh-faced Frosty c. 1962, helped promote Tony Bennett's new song, "I Left My Heart in San Francisco." A karaoke favorite today, it still sounds great about 1:00a.m. Courtesy of Frosty.]

We were barely past the "with child" whispers as opposed to shouting, "she's pregnant"! Guys had a lot to learn about gals in this decade. The Sixties was a new universe of change for all of us.

Frosty is still in Iowa, but winters in Florida and recalls it took three decades to get him off the radio. Although he didn't exactly "DJ" after 1960, necessity is the mother of invention, says Frosty, and as a radio station owner, sh*t happens, and there you are on the air again.

You may have heard him too, as the voice of the Iowa Hawkeyes for a mere thirty-five years.

Frosty owned fourteen radio stations over the years. He bought his first station in Grinnell, Iowa. Why there? "I had signed a life-time contract with KIOA that I could never work within fifty miles of Des Moines (a practice since thrown out by the Supreme Court)—Grinnell is fifty-one miles. Gotta love a smart man.

Today: Frosty and Joan are traveling through retirement, enjoying frequent visits with their three daughters, their spouses, and six grandchildren in Iowa, Florida, Oklahoma, and Illinois.

🎵 📻 🎵

Waxin' the '60s: Late in 1960 yours truly turned twelve. And discovered boys. Puberty is not a pretty sight for us girls.

Dramatic sighs typically alternate with annoying squeals at the sound of practically every teenage boy's voice. Is it any wonder why we swooned over the silky sounds of Elvis and Ricky Nelson?

Around 1959-'60 a couple of Gordy family record companies mixed it up around Detroit musicland, forging Motown Records. And we all discovered luvvvvv, like "The One Who Really Loves You" (Mary Wells 1962).

How could Motown go wrong with velvety smooth frontliners like Smokey Robinson ("Shop Around"), and The Marvelettes ("Please, Mr. Postman"), sweetened by Marvin Gaye ("How Sweet It Is [To Be Loved by You]") ... and oh, so many more.

I slid into the Sixties, following my older brother and his friends around, not really knowing why. It would soon become apparent, we mature quickly and intensely between thirteen and eighteen. Sigh.

In the meantime, I bounced between KXOA and KROY/Sacramento on my trusty transistor radio dial, and sang along with Chubby Checker, Frankie Avalon, and The Shirelles—while the disc jockeys who spun their platters became celebrities in their own right.

Like a tenacious bulldog, KROY's General Manager, Dwight Case, is often cited as the reason they overtook KXOA in the early 1960s ratings race. They traded DJs back-and-forth, but KROY always seemed to come out ahead.

Let's see what they were doing on the East Coast about that time, and then, follow Route 66, Pike's Peak Highway, or discover your own Rockin' route, back to the West …

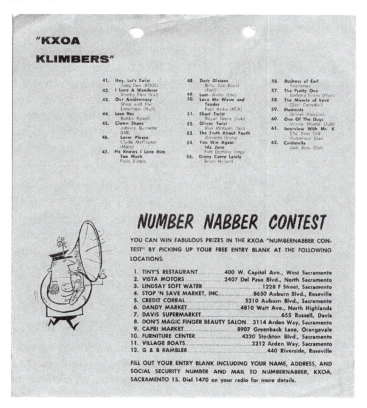

[*Image:* It's March 1962—did you visit Sacto's Vista Motors or the Dandy Market looking for KXOA's Number Nabber Contest entry blanks? *BFYP* Collection.]

Come on along and we'll cozy up to keep warm, while your fave BFYP-FM jock spins some cool tunes on the ra-di-o!

Pop on another stack of wax! Let's head northeast, Baby. *Uh! Oh!* ♪

Joey Reynolds
aka Joey Pinto
Best known at WKBW/Buffalo, New York

Before there was Howard Stern, there was Joey Reynolds!

"The beginning of Rock & Roll was two guys who sounded like they were black," said Joey. "Alan Freed (aka Moondog) and George Lorenz. George was in Buffalo on a 50,000-watt station, WKBW. We didn't have FM yet. Well, we had it, but it was on in doctors' offices."

So began the lively interview with Joey Reynolds, at times known as Joey Pinto. We talked about Alan's move to WINS in New York. "The game was to play 'race music.' Sound Black, get the audience, and play music that was written by Black people and sung by White folks." In essence, Rock & Roll swept the nation, in disguise.

Joey's fond of saying "I've lived the entire history of Rock & Roll so far," and that history has taken us through some of the most tumultuous culture clashes of our country's young life. In music, however, the lines have always been slightly skewed – it's the sound that counts.

[*Image:* Joey gets excited about an upcoming show; c. 1965. *BFYP* Collection.]

"I had a good conversation recently with Mel Carter* about this—you know, the 'Hold Me, Thrill Me, Kiss Me singer'—Mel and I were on-air talking about it and he's going to do a CD of music originally written by Blacks that became hits by Whites. Now, he's a Black guy who's gonna reclaim them." (*Mel-Carter.com)

Joey, with only a few years on this ol' bird, had more energy than a peacock on steroids. Good thing the tape was running and I didn't have to write down his seemingly endless and hilarious stream of memories.

"I loved Mel Carter. When I was a kid, I danced to Mel's music in my basement in Buffalo and gave myself a hickey! I would prime the pump ..." Whoa, Joey! This is a family book! Well, sorta. So, do you get the Howard Stern reference?

"I gotta tell ya somethin'. I hated Rosie & The Originals. Hated 'Teen Angel,' I thought 'Who Put the Bop in the Boppity Bop Bop' [sic] was %@$&#, and all those songs that when the public liked them, you *had* to play 'em whether you liked it or not."

In those early days, DJs, with the power of the people (their listeners) often behind them, sometimes felt the compunction to force an issue. In the early Sixties when the stringent Top 40 took full hold, the formulaic radio format drove innovative stations to pull FM out of the doctors' offices. Some DJs took matters into their own hands and said, "*This* is what I want to play."

Such a time came for Joey. "I'm an outsider, a street guy. So is Frankie Valli (The Four Seasons). I broke the record (first to play it on-air) and made 'Sherry' a hit. In Hartford [Connecticut], 1962, I locked myself in the studio (WPOP) and played it for four hours."

Always grateful for the hit record, The Four Seasons later produced a special radio jingle for the introduction of Joey's daily show.

Joey and I chatted about radio in general, his DJ buddies and the youthful love affair with his lifelong habit.

"There are a lot of different levels of insanity, you know, in this [radio biz], and I respect a lot of levels, whether it's Larry Lujack in Chicago, or Shotgun Tom (Kelly) in San Diego; and I lived with Robert W. Morgan when I was in L.A. (who I think emulates a bit of Don Steele, Boss Radio)."

Joey tried to put it in perspective. "I was a poor kid who wanted to get laid and have records. I was in the neighborhood in Buffalo, in a $30-a-month rental on our house. I wasn't going anywhere. Nobody could afford college. So the way to get out was to be popular and *be* somebody."

Joey not only listened to his favorite childhood disc jockeys ... he *learned* ... as well. Tom Clay, popular in Buffalo and Detroit, taught Joey how to make a name for himself. "He was brilliant," said Joey. "Ahead of his time and quite a promoter." Although, brilliance plus revolution can come with a price.

Buffalo's popular Shelton Square was once the sight of a Tom Clay "happening." Joey described the scene one day in the summer of 1955. "He got up on a billboard [yep, climbed onto a huge sign], took a microphone—with a wire, 'cause we didn't have wireless yet—and started playing Rock & Roll from the roof of the station."

Of course, he caused a traffic jam in the central "roundabout's" busy intersection. Even though Clay was arrested (and fired), Joey exclaimed while I laughed, "I was off to the races on how to get famous."

Flamboyantly famous in the Sixties

Perhaps trading on that flamboyant lesson, by 1960 Joey figured a way out of his old neighborhood. He entered a television-sponsored "Announcer of the Future" contest. Which he promptly rigged.

"I got on the air and did my commercial, and voted for myself with a mimeograph machine—many times—and won. Then they found out that I'd fixed it. They saw it was all the same signature."

Obviously, receiving the prize money wasn't an option, but he did win them over with his chutzpah. They offered him a job in sales!

Joey held out however, and on his way to professedly becoming our first Rock shock jock, made himself the pain-in-the-ass kid who hung around at WWOL/Buffalo. Unofficially interning, he schlepped for "Purtan's People" host, Dick Purtan (aka Guy King). "He was very smooth. And a decent person, good family guy."

Admirable inspiration for an impressionable kid. His malleable young mind mashed the best of his mentor DJs into his own on-air personality.

Like many DJs Joey soon skipped through a series of towns and stations: WKWK/Wheeling, West Virginia (late 1950s), KQAQ/Austin, Minnesota (1960), WNDR/Syracuse, New York (1961), WPOP/Hartford, Connecticut (his favorite, 1962), WKBW/Buffalo (1963). Phew! And that's just gettin' into the mid Sixties!

By this time, Rock & Roll ruled the nation's musical psyche and he ambled over to Cleveland's hot stations, WDOK and WIXY (1966), then floated over to Detroit's WXYZ-AM.

Few Detroit stations played much Beatles in the early to mid-Sixties. There, he found the other side of Rock & Roll—Motown. While he loved the sound and spun those platters 'round, Joey listened to other stations and knew the Beatles' sound was in town.

"We listened to CKLW across the border from Detroit, in Windsor, Ontario." The 50,000-watt blaster had his childhood mentor, Tom Clay, on staff. "Tom had what was called the Beatles Booster Club, and he was the only one who played Beatles records. Some DJs happened to be better promoters than on-air jocks. Tom happened to be both."

For this California girl, he answered the question why vintage Canadian radio surveys are so popular on eBay!

Joey Rocked in place for a while and wound the decade up at WDRC/Hartford, Connecticut. When it stopped being fun, he quit radio. It's true!

"I once retired at a young age," he said. "When the control was taken away from the jocks, I quit. 1967-68, I didn't want any more of it, I hated it."

Joey detested strict formats and loss of freedom behind the mic. He couldn't deny, however, the connection to his listeners. His hiatus from the airwaves lasted only a couple of years. He dons headphones again as he heads into the next decade.

Today: Between then and now, Joey continued to enjoy his place in radio, in various capacities. Most recently, he was known and loved in a fifteen-year overnight show for WOR/New York. After another short hiatus, you can now hear Joey joining the fun on the airwaves for Cumulus News-Talk WABC.

[*Image:* Joey's boy-next-door brooding good looks connected with WXYZ listeners, June 1966. *BFYP* Collection.]

BFYP-FM is bookin' 'cross country to balmy weather, blue water, and shirts designed with little palm trees, to ask ... how did he get here?

A brother is *family*, man. Bros love a *Surfin' Safari!* ♪

Rich "Brother" Robbin >Part 1
Best known at KCBQ/San Diego, California

He may be in San Diego now, but Rich "Brother" Robbin (in truth, Richard Werges) first discovered the lure of the microphone at a Minnesota golf course. Before we yell "Fore!" ...

His mother an avid radio listener, Rich gives her initial credit for his career. Though they lived in Minneapolis/St. Paul, the family traveled often. On the road, said Rich, "The minute we would get within fifty miles of her home town she would say, let's see if we can get WJMC [Rice Lake, Wisconsin] on the radio."

In radio he found great comfort, when his mother fell ill in 1956 and never recovered. It left him with his father, sister, grandmother—and a love for radio.

WCCO/Minneapolis, Minnesota, landed a new listener in twelve-year-old Rich. Probably not a stretch, since they were such a dominant force at the time, with huge variety and ratings.

Tickets to the St. Paul Open golf tournament a couple of years later proved providential for young Rich. With every intention of enjoying the fairway action, he stopped short on his way past the WCCO tent.

Preparing for a day of remote broadcasting, "A small guy, about 5'6" was unloading, stopped to mop his brow, spotted me watching and said, 'Geez kid, you gonna stand there all day with your thumb up your ass, or you gonna come and help me?!'" So errand boy became his first inglorious radio job.

Fate and opportunity dealt another helpful hand to Rich, while still in high school. University of Minnesota's "carrier-current" station, WMMR—which stood for Women's and Men's Minnesota Residences,"—broadcast weekdays only. No one manned it on weekends. So Rich and a buddy (who is also still in radio, and they're still friends!) snuck downtown, commandeered the studio and filled the weekend air with their own style of radio DJ magic.

Rich thought about attending the university but his enthusiasm disappeared when a teacher who was fired from a radio station and, says Rich, was a complete dweeb, showed up as a speech instructor. He knew at that point, college was not for him.

After some unexciting copywriting work for a TV station in Rochester and KCUE/Redwing, Rich's dad suggested he might be too young to handle the "real world" and pointed him toward the Army. So have you ever wondered who the real-life guys are who filled the air in Saigon with *Good Morning, Vietnam?* (Robin Williams, 1987.)

Rich manned the mic in Saigon (now Ho Chi Minh City) for over a year. Relegated to music for the mostly over-forty listeners, he managed to sneak in an hour of Rock & Roll on Friday nights—without permission. Of course, he was caught, but he cajoled and they relented.

Rich left the Armed Forces Radio Network about four months before Adrian Cronauer arrived (on whom the movie is based).

Surfin' for a living ...

By the mid-Sixties Rich kicked around civilian life at a succession of stations. One day he blew into KUSN/St. Joseph, Missouri, where he picked up *part* of his professional name. The general manager wanted to spruce him up as "Rock Robbin." That was a firm NO from Rich, so they settled on Rich Robbin.

Then it was on to KISN/Portland, Oregon; KABL/San Francisco; and KRUX/Phoenix, Arizona—where he fiddled around with his name some more.

"I remember reading the back of a Gary Puckett & the Union Gap record album," said Rich. "It showed the guys, and one was named 'Gary "Mutha" Withem.' So I came up with 'Rich Mutha Robbin' and used that on air in Phoenix." But he just couldn't leave it alone ...

Rich followed the Beach Boys' sound to hang out in Southern California, but a serious question plagued Rich throughout his travels.

How does a DJ distinguish himself from the guy who left the air before him, in a business filled with sound-alikes? "I never tried to copy anybody," said Rich, "until 1965 when I heard the Real Don Steele on KHJ/Los Angeles. By the time I got to KGB/San Diego in 1969, I thought I had it down." Sincerest form of flattery? We shall see.

Sneak preview, Part 2: A consultant for KGB felt his on-air name was too coarse and the program director hated "Rich Robbin" by itself, so, "Before I went on air for the first time, a bunch of us from the station were sitting around a big table in a restaurant. Buzz Bennett, the program director said, 'So, before you go on the air, what are we gonna do about your name?'"

Rich chuckled with the memory, "We all were a little bit high. And it just fell out of my mouth, 'Why don't I be Rich "Brother" Robbin? I'll be everybody's brother.' All the people around the table, musta been eighteen or twenty, stopped. Like you'd frozen a frame on a movie. They all turned toward us and applauded. We knew we had it."

Having a great name and enjoying new kid on the block status, doesn't mean you know it all, as Rich Brother Robbin was about to learn.

Three weeks into his gig at KGB, Rich was summoned to the big guy's office. "Buzz said, 'I've been trying to figure out why I hired you—you *can't be* the Real Don Steele.'" He pointed out the difference between Rich's audition tape (the "real" Rich Brother Robbin), and his current on-air voice.

"I corrected it immediately," said Rich and understood, "the worst thing in the world is to copy someone else's act—if it isn't yours, people aren't going to buy your act. When I stopped being Steele and became myself, I exploded and became famous. A lot of people have had that experience [in radio]."

Don't touch that cell phone! Rich will be back ... you'll find him eyeing the beach bunnies and Rockin' on, through the late Sixties ... [*Image description in Part 2, 1969.*]

Meanwhile, back in the jungle, or ranch, or hoppin' diner, while Rich learned the DJ ropes in California, we'll cross the country for the next budding DJ, testing his pipes, preparing for his broadcast debut.

Waxin' the '60s: At the top of 1961 the foundation for Camelot in America began with the inauguration of John F. Kennedy as our thirty-fifth president. Moods were light and the country was robust.

Motown is coming up strong as it signs The Supremes to contract and in February, The Miracles' "Shop Around" sold its first million-selling hit. But I see the swinging light of Paul Revere's lantern—chant with me! "The British are coming! The British are coming!"

Well, they're at least tuning up their muskets, as The Beatles make their first appearance at the Cavern Club in Liverpool, England (February 9, 1961).

Siblings ... rug rats ... ankle biters ... BFYP-FM knows they're pests, but it's kinda cool when they follow your musical footsteps on the ra-di-o.

Short little ditty 'cause we've been *Tossin' and Turnin'* all night! ♪

Bill Gardner >Part 1
Best known at WIBG/Philadelphia, Pennsylvania

♪ ♫ ♪ ♫ ♪ ♫ ♪ ♫

Special Intro: *My path and Bill's crossed when he arrived in Phoenix, Arizona, in 1999—well beyond the timeline for this book series. However, you may not be reading this if we hadn't met.*

I recall my shock at turning on the radio for my morning commute and my favorite top 40 KOOL DJ was gone! (It pains me to say, I don't recall his name.) In his place was a guy who sounded pleasant enough ... but we all hate change, right?

By the time I slid into my parking space at the office, new morning guy, Bill Gardner, had me laughing and ready to start my day with a smile. I recall thinking, OK, I can listen to him.

Fast-forward to 2008 after several years of enjoying Bill's special connection to his fans, meeting him at various events, and establishing a friendly rapport. Whether I called for a prize or just to chat, Bill made me feel valued. I had no clue our meeting would someday lead to a radio disc jockey book series. Don't believe in kismet? Think again.

Back in San Diego for a year, I sought unique thoughts for a magazine article on Rock & Roll memorabilia. I called my Rockin' radio friend Bill, for tips. That conversation brought us here. You're welcome. ☺ *Meet Bill Gardner ...*

♪ ♫ ♪ ♫ ♪ ♫ ♪ ♫

"I grew up in Philadelphia and the radio station I grew up listening to I eventually worked for," said the jovial Bill Gardner. "And I have WIBG's Issue #1 'Top 99 Records of the Week' survey from 1958. (Coveted by collectors!)

"Somebody recently told me that I may have the last surviving copy, 'cause whoever kept them, other than DJs?"

Search for "WIBG survey" on eBay and you'll know who kept them and how much they think they're worth now—IF you find any at all. Pre-1960 surveys are disappearing into private collections, as more Boomers wax nostalgic.

Many former teen collectors are funding their retirement on eBay. Our youth is up for sale, folks, and we ain't cheap!

Young Bill listened to "Chantilly Lace" by the Big Bopper and Kingston Trio's unique sound in "Tom Dooley." But move over, 'cause "Beep Beep" soon raced up the charts. (Playmates)

[*Image: WIBG, November 15, 1958 survey (No. 7) graces BFYP Collection!]

Who played the platters for you and Bill at WIBG? Tom Donahue (the DJ who later put freeform formats and FM radio on radar, with wife, Raechel), Hy Lit, Joe Niagara, "Humble Harve" Miller (he won the hearts of KHJ/L.A. fans), were a few of the pioneering DJs Bill emulated.

Lovin' the surf sound, "I still have a copy of 'California Girls' by the Beach Boys, 'cause it's the first song I ever played on the radio."

Still hanging on to the best, "I've got about two to three hundred singles (45rpms) and a couple albums around somewhere. But I don't think I have the first record I ever bought—Richie Valens' album with La Bamba on it." Pity. We won't tell him that pricing guides list a near-mint copy at around $525.

There are two other "Gardners" in *Blast from Your Past*. You'll meet Al and Andre coming up in the *Psychedelic Seventies*. Big brother, Bill, began the family's DJ legacy in the Sixties and set the bar high for his younger brothers. [*Image:* Bill coming to you in BG Part 2, 1965.]

Bill chuckled, recalling his brothers trailing after him into radio. "Andre says I used to tell him it's a tough business. And I'd tell him on a post card from Acapulco. 'You oughta stay out of it, I cautioned him.' Both of my brothers said, if *that* son-of-a-gun can do this for a living, how hard can it be?"

So, which station was "the very, very, very *first*, Rock & Roll station on FM"? Bill share with us in BG Part 2.

Don't touch that dial! Keep it on BFYP-FM 84.8 for Rockin' Rochelle's Hits 'n' Misses of the decade!

Next thing I know, I *Turn Around* ♪... and ... did you hear that?! His distant, raucous howl floats on the night wind, reaching for the stars.

Have mercy! >Part 1 of 3
aka Robert Weston Smith
1938 ~ 1995
It's Wolfman Jack ...

Although the Wolfman has not yet emerged, there's a guttural howl heard low on the horizon!

Troubled teen, **Bob Smith**, headed out of New Jersey around 1956, toward the big white Hollywood Hills sign. Like many trekking West, he dreamed of fame and fortune.

A side trip however, proved life's penchant for unpredictability, and it would take a few more years for him to reach the land of glitz and glamour. It was time needed, however, to shape his destiny.

Bob and friend, Richie, slid into Alexandria, Virginia, in a 1949 Buick "big bamboozle that you could use to mow down trees," he described in his book, *Have Mercy*. Their original intent was to spend a night with his sister's family, on their way West.

As Bob put it, "... two young, prowling New York types with ducktail haircuts and slick, wild-colored clothes invading a serene, sleepy family suburb ... We brought with us a couple of case-hardened attitudes."

Nevertheless, Joan and husband, Emile, welcomed them for a night ... or two or three ...

After a tumultuous childhood, Bob thrived in his sister's loving home with hubby and kids. He fit the "fun uncle" picture perfectly and revived his arid sense of family.

For all the Jersey boys' enthusiasm to live the California dream, the soothing family atmosphere quelled some of their restlessness and they settled in for a week.

But as life does, another twist saw Richie heading back up north and Joan asking Bob to show some responsibility.

Many eighteen-year-olds even today, have no clue what career or path of interest to follow. Not so, for Bob. He "grew up" in his sister's home, pitching in with chores, attending night school, and ... building a killer DJ system.

"The playroom became my bachelor apartment. We soundproofed the ceiling so I could do my DJ thing until all hours without disturbing the rest of the family." So there ya are ... and there he was ...

California still floated through the back of his mind, but for now, Bob was content to revel in his family's affection and find out who he was. Shades of Wolfman Jack began to emerge.

"I loved being around all the kids," he wrote. He was "... somebody who played music and stirred up excitement all the time. Every day I tried to come up with something new to win those kids over."

Uncle Bob's bedtime antics resulted in Navy man, Emile's, stern command, "All Stop! All Stop!" But not before Bob's nephews squealed in delight at his blanket-caped figure chasing them down the hallway. He menaced them in a deep, throaty voice, "The W*ooo*lfman is coming to your doooooor ... Now he's coming to GET YOU and *EAT YOU UP!*" followed by his soon-endearing "*Awooooo*!"

A job ensured his room and board while Bob rounded out his youth. Did your parents or grandparents have a set of *Collier's Encyclopedias*? Could be Bob Smith was their Alexandria door-to-door salesman.

The '49 Buick soon gave way to a spiffy 1954 Ford convertible. Always flashy, Bob's "lipstick red" ride with wide whitewalls and dual exhausts made a splash in the staunch town along the Potomac River.

From Collier's to Fuller Brush, Bob was naturally *good* at sales. A trait that formed his basic approach as a disc jockey and radio businessman. It would be enhanced and honed many times, over the years on his way to Hollywood.

Alexandria was a life-changer for Bob in more than maturity. He soon discovered the nearby National Academy of Broadcasting. With a little convincing from Emile, Bob's dad, Weston, invested in his son with the first year's $3,000 tuition (hefty for the late 1950s).

"I was positively the only one in the whole school that wanted to work for a rhythm and blues radio station," said Bob. Beethoven, Wagner, or "How Much is That Doggie in the Window" simply wasn't his style. Bob grooved to Clyde McPhatter and the Drifters' 1953 "Money Honey." (You may recall the more widely played 1956 version by Elvis)

A chance meeting with United Broadcasting Company's Richard Eaton sealed the deal on Bob Smith's radio career. "Mr. Eaton's stations are aimed at Negro audiences," the school president said as she introduced them. Bob stepped right up, eager for the challenge.

Beginning of a lifelong passion

"WYOU, the Newport News station," recalled Bob, "wasn't much more than a peanut whistle ... the gig would have to do just about everything from sweeping the floor to selling advertising, plus take over half of the airtime." He went in as the second of two DJs.

It would stretch Bob's patience, work ethics, and creativity, nearly to breaking, but he declared, "Radio wasn't a hobby anymore. Once and for all, it was my life."

Bob opened the mic of his first job in 1960 with his résumé promo personality name, "Daddy Jules."

[*Image:* WYOU, Newport News, c. 1960. At this point, he was hooked. From *Have Mercy.*]

Tex Gathings, his on-air co-worker, was a big black man who spoke "like a Harvard professor." (Bob later learned Tex really had attended Harvard.) To balance the team, Bob, well, he gave Daddy Jules a smooth, southern-colored drawl.

It was the perfect first gig for young Bob, playing tunes he loved in a format full of soul, jazz, and rhythm and blues. But along with his jock duties, came the advertising sales that paid the bills and taught Bob the business foundation that would sustain him through life.

"It didn't take me long to figure out that hustling on the side was gonna be my lifeblood," said Bob. "As soon as I got more connected in the community, I got all kinds of action working. Some of it was even legal."

Bob felt fortunate that the owner and Tex let him have his head behind the mic, setting up his own playlist. It didn't hurt either, that he brought in several boxes of classic and current rhythm and blues records, to help augment WYOU's meager music library.

His record collection endeared him to station management (saving expense dollars), as well as his predominant black audience. Tex took the young buck under his wing and taught him the finer points of black diction, to add realism to his personality. Daddy Jules took on character, and Bob began edging toward the Wolfman.

Robert Weston Smith also learned that to some, "illegal" is a point of view. He began delivering packages between nightclubs that he hit up for advertising. He soon learned he was transporting marijuana.

The bewitching Mary Jane hadn't been popularized long at that time, and when curious Bob asked about the packages' contents, the club owner was only too happy to help him explore a new life experience.

"The music was speaking to me in a little different way than before, easing its phrases into my ears," Bob recalled, as he tested the contents. Weed became a lucrative, long-time sideline.

By the time Bob created "The Daddy Jules Dance Party," for his young audience to enjoy, everything was swinging his way.

At this time of his life, cool cat, Robert Weston Smith lived life large at every stage. You wouldn't think it would be the right time for love. But the heart wants what it wants ...

While visiting a Fred Astaire Dance Studio hawking an ad, he watched the love of his life walk through the door. Long blonde hair and "a vision of innocence—like somebody out of a dream," he walked away from a sales conversation, and approached her.

"'Yes, ma'am,' I said with a big, friendly smile. 'Can I help you?'" The shy girl from rural Tidewater, Virginia, thought she had met someone who would take her application for a dance instructor.

Bob admitted to waging a "full-scale assault" to get young Miss Lucy "Lou" Elizabeth Lamb, into his life.

Despite her naiveté, Lou wasn't immediately smitten by the smooth talkin', fast-walkin' Bob. She was wary; but Bob was persistent. He had learned, a great salesman never takes "no" for an answer ...

This time, this place, and these people began to mold Wolfman Jack.

Look for Rufus and the next Wolfman Jack break in the mid-Sixties.

Waxin' the '60s: Every boy-crazy girl ... ok, that was all of us girls ... knew every word, voice inflection, and music note to songs like "The End of the World" (Skeeter Davis, 1962), "... *'cause you don't love me anymore.*" (Cue the tears, and where's my handkerchief?)

Or 1960's "Angel Baby" by Rosie & The Originals. "*It's just like heaven, being here with you ...*" Ouch. You've never heard such high-pitched screeching! Although teenage girls are known for shrill voices, not everyone can carry a tune at that altitude.

We didn't care. The intro chords blasted from the radio speaker and whatever was handy became an "air" sing-along microphone. Coke® bottles were great. Hairbrushes were handy. We warbled our little hearts out.

Think our "vintage" songs are too old for today's young'uns to enjoy? Think again, Boomers. Check out your ringtone lists. There are plenty of Classic Rock and Old Time Rock & Roll tunes to choose from; which proves we're still relevant!

"With the arrival of iTunes and video games like 'Guitar Hero,'" said one such site, "a whole new generation of fans are beginning to discover the music so many of us have loved for two, three or perhaps even four decades." (Try five or six!)

[*Image:* How many songs on the KUTT/Fargo, North Dakota, hits chart can you still sing along to? *BFYP* collection.]

KUTT's Top 10 songs August 18, 1962 (displayed as listed on sheet, errors & all):

#1 Breaking Up is Hard To Do ~ Neil Sedaka

#2 Devil Woman ~ Marty Robbins

#3 Yesterday's Champagne ~ Bobby Helms

#4 Limbo Limbo ~ Kai Ray

#5 Locomotion ~ Little Eva

#6 Boys Kept Hangin' Around ~ Dorsey Burnett

#7 Vacation ~ Connie Francis

#8 Toy Soldiers ~ Strangers

#9 She's Not You ~ Elvis Presley

#10 Sheila* ~ Tommy Roe

Rockin' Rochelle here, coming to you another day on BFYP-FM, in super-sunny Cal-i-forn-i-A. We be Rockin'...

We were driving Hoopers numbers up, all the way to *Route 66!* ♪

Kent Burkhart
Best known at KOWH/Omaha, Nebraska

In the late 1950s Kent made the most of every DJs dream job. Though pulling double duty as a DJ and program director at WQAM/Miami, by one in the afternoon, his top floor high-rise office provided the perfect perch for watching beach babes.

Showing an early flare for management, his PD style reflected the fresh, emerging role of Rock & Roll DJs, as opposed to staid "radio announcers" of the previous decade.

"Everybody wanted to come to work for us," said Kent. "My job was to find the right guy, put him in the right time slot, and give him some *personality* rein, not just more music."

As killer as that was, rather than itching with the nibbles of summer mosquitoes, Kent was bitten by the ownership bug. He borrowed a few dollars, and bought a little station in San Angelo, Texas.

A great small town, but with small-town problems. The locals' advertising dollars were sheared off when their sheep died and the wool production took a dive. He stuck it out a couple of years, then headed north.

Kent's reputation as a radio turnaround specialist followed him. He spent a few months bouncing around, helping other stations. His drifting ended with a call from *Esquire* magazine in Spring 1961. Their new Atlanta station, WQXI-AM 790 needed his expertise.

"This was possibly the worst radio station that I've ever heard in my life; and I knew I could turn it around," said Kent. It was up against a formidable rival and many a fella would have turned tail at the daunting prospect of facing the competition's PD.

"A guy by the name of Bill Drake at WAKE was their program director." Yes, the very same Drake who would later develop the legendary Boss Radio format from Storz and McLendon's Top 40 programming innovation.

"But I knew I had a facility advantage," said Kent. "I had 5,000 watts, he had 250 watts, and I thought that we could take him—which we eventually did, with a tight Top 40 rotation. Drake left just about the time we beat him, and went to California. You probably know the rest of that story."

♪ ♪ ♪ ♪ ♪ ♪ ♪

Bill Drake, aka Philip Yarbrough, chose his personality name from family and liked that it rhymed with Atlanta's WAKE. In California, he and partner, Gene Chenault, are credited with "Boss Radio" and perfecting the Top 40 format which revolutionized radio music programming.

♪ ♪ ♪ ♪ ♪ ♪ ♪

Early to mid-1960s at WQXI proved providential for several up-and-coming DJs. "I met a couple of very good guys who worked for us during that time," said Kent. "As manager, I appointed Paul Drew program director [1963]; he later became head of WRKO radio."

Personalities were shaped under Kent's tutelage in Atlanta, honing the DJ skills of Sam Hale (1962-66) soon to be better known at WOKY/Milwaukee; Ken Dowe (1962) skipping on to KLIF/Dallas and beyond; and "Tony the Tiger" Taylor (1965), who after his WQXI gig beguiled Boston and New York radio listeners.

One quirky guy needed no honing. "I believe I hired him out of Fargo, North Dakota, or Duluth, Minnesota, and this guy stood out tremendously. He was highly recommended by Bill Gavin's wife, Janet." Bill of course, was the originator of radio's Top 40 tip sheet, the *Gavin Report*.

"I listened to this guy and he was *great*. I brought him to Atlanta … and his name was Don Rose.

[*Image:* WQXI's Top 30 Survey, week ending February 5-12, 1968. Dr. Don Rose top row/left, hummed along to French composer Paul Mauriat's chart-topping instrumental, "L'Amour Est Bleu" ("Love is Blue"*). *BFYP* Collection.]

Don went on to do huge ratings for us, but there came a day when he walked into my office and said, 'Hey, a larger market wants me to move.' I asked which one. He said, 'Philadelphia.'"

Though fighting hard to keep Don, Kent knew he was outmatched by WFIL's massive market. "He was #1 in Atlanta, went to #1 in Philadelphia; he was absolutely spectacular with all sorts of voices, and one-liners ..." And anyone in 1970s San Francisco Bay Area knows Dr. Don Rose also became #1 at KFRC.

Kent has reason to be proud of his role at WQXI. As an Airchexx.com visitor said, "'QXI' set the bar high for all other top forty stations all over the nation."

About this time WQXI's owners merged with another company and Kent became president of the emerging Southern Broadcasting (radio). It kept him entertained until around 1971, but his urge to consult rose again, and his basement business—literally opened in the basement—flourished.

An amazed Kent soon found himself working with twenty to thirty accounts offering him prestigious titles with open arms and similarly open pocketbooks. His days behind the mic and mixing with upstart DJs were numbered.

Though no longer behind the mic, as a consultant, Kent boosted 1970s stations battling their bobbling ratings, under the unrelenting scrutiny of Hooper Services and Arbitron ratings. Ahhhh, the good ol' days of format radio.

Today: Kent's DJ days became marvelous malt-shop memories without end. Thinking they'd retire, he and wife, Pat sold the radio consulting company—sort of; keeping in touch with the industry, they spent a lot of time with family in Texas. His brother-in-law soon suggested picking up a small station near Dallas. With a group of friends, Kent soon found himself back in biz as owner/operator.

Says Kent, "It is a delight to create new formats and hire people to teach the radio biz. I still hang out at some radio conventions ... looking for new ideas ... and they definitely have them. Who knows what's next? I do, but I am not telling. The fun will continue!" Love it when someone is still so excited about their life and times. [*Image:* Courtesy of Kent, c. late 2000s; a happy guy!]

* Paul Mauriat's easy listening love song seemed out of place at the top, but it held the #1 spot at many Top 40 Rock stations across the country for five weeks—beating out heavy hitters like Otis Redding's "The Dock of the Bay.".

Visitors to the BFYP-FM studios are reminded that when the On-Air sign is on ... don't just stand there ... dance!

What am I ... s'posed to dooooo? *Blame It On The Bossa Nova* ... ♪

ℒee 𝒢ray >Part 1
aka Lee Darling
1936 ~ 1996
Best known at WTRY/Albany, New York
(Interview with son, David Darling)

David Darling wasn't around during his dad, Royce Lee Darling's heydays in radio. But "Lee"—who chose his on-air personality name of Lee Gray in 1962—captivated David with his many radio stories and passed on a living legacy that David cherishes, and shares with us.

This brief introduction sets the timeline for Lee—who truly blossoms behind the microphone in the late 1960s.

In 1959, Lee was stationed in Germany in the military during the Cold War, just as the Vietnam "conflict" was heating up for the U.S. "He didn't really have an interest in radio, but found himself recruited for the AFN (Armed Forces Radio Network)," said David.

According to his dad's stories, David recalled, it's a wonder Lee got past his first on-air experience. "He was in the studio and watching the big old-fashioned clock with the sweeping second hand," his dad recalled to him. The clock ticked away the moments when he would open his mic and debut as a DJ.

"About fifteen seconds before he was to go on-air," recounted David, "his superior called him and said, 'Don't let the fact that there's millions of Europeans listening to you, bother you.' Lee froze. He botched the entire broadcast while his supervisor laughed at the radio rookie."

Perhaps a shaky start, but Lee got over it and found he liked working in radio.

After the military, since he liked to sing, Lee briefly considered a warbling career, but was urged by others to find another public venue for his voice. Family and friends applauded his choice.

In 1962 Lee's short gig at WKRG/Mobile, Alabama, provided an important stepping stone to the mighty WOKY in Milwaukee. There, he met Terrell Metheny (aka Mitch Michael) and the two became lifelong friends.

We'll cut back to Terrell's story soon, to see how that friendship played out and later, explore Lee's role in the British Invasion. Don't touch that dial!

Waxin' the '60s: By summer 1962, President John F. Kennedy's enchanted reign burst into full swing; and the music world reflected the love ... WOKY/Milwaukee's fans boosted Bobby Vinton's soulful "Roses are Red" to #1, followed by Ray Charles crooning, "I Can't Stop Loving You."

[*Image:* A prized *BFYP* Collection survey with three *BFYP* DJs pictured! Lee Gray (bottom/right), Jim Stagg (top/left), and Mitch Michael (Terrell Metheny), bottom/left. Other DJs: (l.) Bob White, (r.) Sam Hale, and Don Phillips; June 2, 1962.]

Wait! Don't touch that dial! BFYP spins your mind at 84.8-FM. Let's unwind with a little jiggle in our wiggle.

Let's Twist Again, like we did last summer ...♪ and defy *Too Many Rules* ... ♪

𝒯𝑜𝑚 𝒟𝑜𝓃𝒶𝒽𝓊𝑒 >Part 1
aka Thomas Coman; "Big Daddy"
1928 ~ 1975
Best known at KYA, KMPX, KSAN/San Francisco
(Interview with wife, Raechel Donahue)

Everyone agrees. Tom "Big Daddy" Donahue was a larger-than-life kinda guy who could persuade a pet rock to follow his booming voice.

Raechel, his wife and ground-breaking female DJ in her own right, admits to having had absolutely no interest in joining her husband on-air ... but ... succumbed to his persuasive and persistent ways.

He ultimately won her over in the mid-Sixties. But before we tell Raechel's story there is more to know about Tom's early journey that brought them together.

His lifetime love affair with radio began at WTIP/Charleston, South Carolina, in 1949. He called WIBG/Philly, home in 1951, and hosted the daily "Danceland" show. As the '50s ended with a payola bang, Tom made a quickie stop at WINX/Rockville, Maryland.

Long about this time, Tom looked for a change of scenery and following his buddy, Bob Mitchell, he hopped across the country to San Francisco's KYA in May 1961.

He slid right in to the Bartell Broadcasting station's Top 40 format. Correctly assuming his East Coast popularity would dutifully follow to California's balmy seashore, every Donahue show began with his trademark line, "Here to blow your mind and clean up your face." The listeners went wild and KYA hit the top of the ratings.

♪ ♫ ♪ ♫ ♪ ♫ ♪

What makes a record a hit for one artist, but not another? We listeners are funny and fickle ... Do you know "The Twist" by Hank Ballard popped up on the KYA Official Hit Parade as a "KY-Aces in the hole" tune to watch, May 18, 1959? Yup, 'tis true. But it didn't catch on; fast-forward a year and we wriggled wildly to Chubby Checker's hit version in July 1960, after his American Bandstand *performance.*

♪ ♫ ♪ ♫ ♪ ♫ ♪

Tom never gave up on Hank Ballard, though. He still preferred the earlier tune and after playing it in December 1961, said, "Now, of the three hundred or so records we receive every week, I'd guess about two hundred and fifty of them are 'Twists.' Most of 'em *baaaad!*" (*Listen on ReelRadio.com.)

With more energy than a wildcat, and not content to simply sit behind a microphone, Tom produced record hops and concerts with buddy DJ Bob Mitchell (Tempo Productions), started a record label (Autumn Records), and opened Mother's, a pioneering North Beach/San Francisco psychedelic nightclub.

Was that enough to keep him busy? Nope. He and Bob followed the ponies, and enhanced their brand with Tempo Stables, populated by prancing thoroughbred race horses.

[*Image:* KYA Official Swingin' 60 survey #218, July 31, 1961. Note *BFYP* DJ "Stag"—Jim Stagg—drove you to work and Tom Donahue got you through the afternoons. *BFYP* Collection.]

Were you in the San Francisco Bay Area in 1961? If you listened to KYA, did you win in Bob and Tom's on-air "Jockey Races"? The jackpot galloped all the way up to $15.00—whoohoo!

Tom stayed at the popular San Francisco station until 1965. "Big Daddy for the Boss of the Bay!" Bouncing between his businesses for another year or so, his industry name grew as big as his DJ personality, signing the Beau Brummels to Autumn Records.

More success followed in 1966, with his coup to produce The Beatles' final fabulous concert at Candlestick Park. In the late 1960s, Tom, forever linked with the Top 40 formats, grew restless for music with a message.

His revolutionary radio destiny would soon pave a new path to a whole new ocean of underground airwaves.

"Top 40 is dead," Tom declared in San Francisco. "And its rotting corpse is stinking up the airwaves."

Stay tuned and check back with Big Daddy Tom and the lovely Raechel, in the latter half of the decade when we'll have details, Baby, details!

[*Image:* KYA ruled the airwaves in L.A. with powerhouse DJs Tom Donahue and Bob Mitchell (right, middle/top). Bill Drake, soon half of Drake/Chenault radio history (left/top) joins jocks Russ Syracuse, Peter Trip, Johnny Hayes, & Tommy Saunders. Survey no. 282, October 22, 1962. *BFYP* collection.]

♫ 📻 ♫

Waxin' the '60s: Not to be outdone, KRLA/Los Angeles heated up its corner of the West with its own roster of super-jocks. OK—raise your hand—who remembers the TV game shows, *Gambit*, *High Rollers*, and *Tic-Tac-Dough*? How about the often salacious *Newlywed Game*?

If you've cleared the cobwebs from the corners of your brain—and you young'uns have looked them up online—you know that Wink Martindale hosted the first three popular trivia shows and Bob Eubanks introduced the original game that made newlyweds squirm, possibly causing break-ups before they finished honeymooning.

But the handsome hosts have more in common than dazzling smiles and television good looks. In 1961 Wink and Bob were climbing the broadcasting ladder together, as KRLA's listeners woke up with Wink and went to bed with Bob. Oooooo!

[*Image:* Pictured in air-time order: Wink Martindale, Roy Elwel, Dick Moreland, Jim O'Neill, Sam Riddle, Frosty Harris, Bob Eubanks. KRLA/Los Angeles June 30 to July 7, 1961. *BFYP* collection.]

Hello? Is this the party to whom I'm speaking? We're <u>live</u> at BFYP 84.8-FM, the redheaded station with Rockin' Rochelle taking your requests!

... Shout! Shout! ♪ *But ... don't knock yourself out ...*

Burt Sherwood
Best known at WMCA/New York City

By the end of the 1950s Burt and his blushing bride, Anne, had returned to WMCA/New York after a trippy working honeymoon in Cuba. Nearly caught in Castro's takeover crossfire, they settled down to married life in the Big Apple.

Burt heaved a sigh of relief to be back in the mundane safety of WMCA's Good Guys studio—perhaps not the first, but certainly one of the savviest radio stations to focus on "personalities" and capitalize on their collective popularity.

Still early in the development of radio personalities, some stations' old attitudes preferring "announcers" persisted, according to Burt. "[In 1960] We only had one phone in the studio, and DJs didn't answer it." What?!

[*Image:* WMCA/New York survey August 9, 1957; though Burt slid in a little later, these pioneering DJs were (top/bottom, left/right): Gallagher & O'Brien, Bob Callan, Ernie Stone, Bert Knapp, Alun Williams, Dave Leeds, Murray Kaufman (yep, before the "K"), and Ed Welch. *BFYP* Collection.]

Don't assume however, there was no interaction with listeners. Apparently Burt excelled as an instigator. "The police always said I did [rile up the fans], 'cause they were always yelling at me, tell 'so-and-so we're going to shut down that radio!'"

It amazed Burt that in New York there were "eight million people sleeping under the same moon and none of the radio stations had interaction with their listeners." The smaller markets said Burt, allowed DJs to be much closer to their audiences—more fun for DJ and listeners.

At that time, they weren't even allowed to make public appearances unless it was for charity, like those held at the expansive Brooklyn Catholic High School. My, my, how a few short years changed lives behind the microphone as dawn rose for radio stations that realized the DJs' marketing power of their fans.

Alan Freed came along with a new bounce to the music—the radio world turned upside down and sideways. Alan may or may not have answered the phone, but he had an on-air knack for stirring his listeners into a frenzy. Burt loved his style.

"Alan and I linked up at one point years earlier on a weekend in Cincinnati, so when I got to New York, I looked him up," said Burt. By that time, Alan was spreading his Rock & Roll energy around WMCA's rival, WABC—a short-lived gig, as the payola monster engulfed him. Burt was there ...

He'd been to visit Alan, who came into the room and Burt lamented, "The press was following him. I don't know how the hell they got up the elevators, but they did—the elevators had been sealed."

Hounded by media, Alan took refuge with Burt, "We stood there and talked for about fifteen minutes, and I told him, 'My gosh, what are they doing to you?!' I reminded him how wonderful his career was, and he said, 'I'd trade places with you in half a minute.'"

Alan's downward spiral had begun, recalled Burt. "He was living over a garage at someone's estate in Long Island, with his wife and two kids. Completely a victim of the system."

According to Burt, WMCA selected songs for play by committee. Occasionally they'd allow a DJ to single out a favorite. He recalled a moment in the late 1950s ...

"I picked the Everly Brothers one day and they laughed like hell at me. Nobody had heard of them; neither had I, but we broke the record for them." ("Bye Bye Love" hit #2 on WMCA June 28, 1957.)

We talked a few minutes about the music as it was when he first arrived at WMCA. Burt worked with music director, Alan Lorber, whose record lineup reflected a "mix" of the day with Sinatra and the big bands.

"When we went into Rock & Roll," said Burt, "we scratched our heads about what to play." Like it did for social mores and staid lifestyles, Rock & Roll simply didn't conform to their "old standards." Should they continue with Ol' Blue Eyes and buddies? New music called for a new process.

It didn't take Alan long, however, to come up with their own top 40. "He walked in one night and said, 'Here's your music.' There were forty records lined up to the top of his finger. He said, 'You play 'em one through forty and then start 'em over again.' And that's what we did, all night long."

Are you into the Sixties music? Do you think you recall Alan Lorber's name? You should ... he was a prolific composer and arranger who worked on "Breaking Up is Hard to Do" (Neil Sedaka 1962), "Close to Cathy" (Mike Clifford 1962), and many other of the decade's gems for our listening pleasure. Alan was instrumental in WMCA's Sixties success.

The good ol' days with a flock of jocks

"You don't control too much, as a jock," mused Burt. If you try to control too much, you're not a jock very long." With a nostalgic pause, he said, "I like the fact that I've been there."

"Been there" means making history. Chief announcer, Alun Williams, introduced their first all-night Rock show, which Burt took over when he arrived. Legendary program director Ruth Meyer (first woman to hold the position in New York City radio) brought the "Good Guys" to New York audiences.

Upstart WMCA began a rivalry with WABC that soon forced WMGM (in early 1962) to find a new role in radio. Their battle became so fierce that even high-flying WINS left the fray, forced into talk radio in 1965.

The stations may have been battling ratings, but the DJs most often respected each other and kept the peace. Jock or PD, Burt treated everyone like family. Every radio market was a small world and he was determined to enjoy it.

Guys like Arnie "Woo-Woo" Ginsburg, "... the king of Boston at WMEX—he did well and got out," recalled Burt. "He was a good jock. I wish I'd had his pipes. Whenever we were on the same plane, he was always in first class. Greg Austin, 'Austin in Boston,' was a jock-and-a-half. He decided it just wasn't for him; and Harry Harrison used to be my relief man at WMCA."

Some of them were very close ... at least for the time their transient jobs would allow. While at WMCA, he and Anne lived with their baby in a one-bedroom Manhattan apartment. To escape the city, they rented a little house in Connecticut where they and popular DJs Scott Muni, Barry Gray, and Herb Oscar Anderson, lived within five minutes of them. Every Sunday was a ritual party.

"The money was coming in like I'd never seen before," said Burt. "I took my ol' convertible and went all over Jersey, visiting Texaco stations, which sponsored my shows." But the good times and good friends would soon be a fond memory.

"Herb Oscar is stolen from us (WMCA) and goes to WABC. About two months later, Scott Muni ... boom! He's gone. Well, the next thing I know, I get the call. But the only guy who got caught tryin' to make the switch, was me. And I ended up in the unemployment line. Best thing that ever happened to me."

How he got from there to here ...

Disillusioned as a DJ, and "doing everything in New York to try to stay alive," Burt soon turned back to station management, but ...

"When I got out of there in 1963 I had a nice sabbatical and finally went down to Daytona Beach for about three months and put together a group with a fella named Bob Price." They scouted stations and borrowed from John Lindsay [later, mayor of New York] to buy a little Brattleboro, Vermont station. Burt promised to do everything, *except* go on the air, unless it was an emergency.

They soon picked up two more small stations—all playing Burt's trademark format, of course—and sold them for a profit about three years later. "I managed stations all over the place," said Burt.

His management proficiency took him through 1976 and beyond, reviving or rewinding as needed. WNAC "the Triangle" in New Haven (Connecticut) was memorable, and he brought back a couple of decaying stations in Indiana before heading to Philadelphia's WIBG in its post-Rock & Roll days.

As manager of both WMAQ and WKQX/Chicago, Burt lamented, "No raise in salary, just manager of both. WMAQ was NBC's pride and joy—we really took that thing to the top—Top 40 *Country!*"

True to his word, 1963 in Vermont, marked the last time Burt sat down at the mic as a DJ. About his radio career, Burt shared, "I got lucky, but I knew what I wanted and I hired only people who had more talent than I did."

Today: Years later discussing his career with Anne, she confessed her opinion, "You were a better station manager than a disc jockey."

"I think I was half mad at her," said Burt, "but I think she was right." Their son, Jason, followed him into radio for a time, but behind-the-mic wasn't for him, and he eventually slid over to television. Burt and Anne are enjoying the retired life. [*Image:* Courtesy of Burt, c. 2009; a life to smile about.]

In a streetside window on the world, BFYP-FM watched her struttin' by ... yep, those boots were made for walkin' and Rockin'!

It's now or never, baby, you best surrender ... you might be the **Devil in Disguise!** ♪ But you can't fool me ...

Norm Prescott
1927 ~ 2005
Best known at WBZ/Boston, Massachusetts
(Interview with son, Jeff Prescott)

In the 1950s, Jeff Prescott let us peek into his childhood as he gazed backward, recalling his awe of Norm's DJ days at WBZ-AM/Boston. Norm and his family hobnobbed with celebrities; Nancy Sinatra even mentioned their family's visits to the Prescott home in her book about legendary Ol' Blue Eyes—Frank Sinatra.

But another blue-eyed lady-killer story takes the cake in my kitchen, with a remark from Jeff. "In one of my dad's contests back in about 1961 or '62, he gave away two strands of Elvis Presley's hair."

Excuse me ... *two strands?*! And that excited listeners? "Yep, and it got written up in *Time* magazine," said Jeff. That was then, this is now ... framed, authenticated strands *still* sell on eBay starting at $0.99. Pair with a 1956 TOPPS original card or other special framed memorabilia and expect to pay up to $400.00 or more ... I kid you not!

We tagged along with Jeff a little longer, as he recalled Norm's move to WBZ-TV. I listened in on his eight-year-old mind spinning behind-the-scenes images and VIP treatment. "I did a live commercial with my dad for Dove soap, and they brought in a dove. The birdcage *smelled*.

"I remember my dad asking, 'Well, what do you think of Dove?' And I answered, 'It smells like "dooty"'." He could have scored a precocious spot on Art Linkletter's "Kids Say the Darndest Things" with that line! (Segment of *House Party* TV show.)

As Jeff matured, he ventured around the radio dial to listen to teen fave, WMEX. His love for the microphone was fueled by other radio greats and role models, Jack Gale (Fenway), Arnie "Woo-Woo" Ginsburg, and Larry Glick.

[*Image:* You were really cool if you scored an official WMEX pen. Yes, it's in our *BFYP* Collection. We're cool.]

"I'd get mysteriously sick when WMEX had a contest I thought I could win. I couldn't win too much, 'cause we knew Arnie. He'd let us [a friend or two] come down to the studio and watch him—he was on at night—that was, like, the *coolest* thing!"

Not to mention a few celeb encounters. "We got to meet Ricky Nelson, The 3 Stooges, Pat Boone ... very cool."

Though enjoying fun times at one of the country's oldest radio stations, after the payola fiasco Norm moved solidly into television in 1963. By '65 he and partner, Lou Scheimer, formed Filmation Associates, producing animated and live action programming.

You may "vaguely" remember some of their series titles that glued us to the boob tube during the next twenty years. A smattering of early shows included: *Rod Rocket* (1963), *The New Adventures of Superman* (1966-67), *Aquaman* (1968), *The Hardy Boys* (1969), and *Fat Albert and the Cosby Kids* (1972).

"Don't mention my dad," said Jeff, "without mentioning The Archies," referring to our quintessential Sixties animated teen counterparts in a TV garage band.

Through The Archies, Norm merged his love for both radio and TV, with their not-just-for-kids teen programs, *The Archie Show* (1968) and *The Archie Comedy Hour* (1969). The Archies band even had a Top 10 hit on the radio with "Sugar, Sugar"; a song recorded specifically for the show.

Ah, honey, honey ... the Bubble Gum Pop tune sweetened our summer of 1969.

Norm is even listed in the "acting" credits for seasons one and two of 1973-'74's *Star Trek: The Animated Series*.

Today: Though Norm excelled in radio, TV animation stole his heart. After a bumpy start, Filmation Associates carried him through a satisfying second career. With fifty-three years of marriage to wife, Elaine, and a full lifetime with sons, Jeffrey and Michael, Norm began animating our clouds in entertainment heaven, July 2, 2005.

His dad's radio days left an indelible mark on Jeff, who followed his idol into the biz. We'll tune back in to Jeff Prescott in 1970 (*BFYP* Book 3) ... as he sneaks behind KLA's microphone at the University of California, Los Angeles, radio station. Ah yes, our good ol' rebel days!

♪ 📻 ♪

Waxin' the '60s: Phase II of life in the 1960s emerged with new electric guitar technology, which created sensational sounds that added dimension to our love ballads, and complemented the rise of girl groups.

Multi-track recording was put to use by a youthful, experimenting Les Paul, now considered a pioneer in the solid body electric guitar. And the music industry took off again.

Radio song charts began to experience radical diversity; adding more DJ hype and artwork to their rather plain charts.

The word "radical" suffered an even more profound identity crisis across the next three decades. Through the 1950s its original meaning, as an adjective describing the fundamental nature of something that diverges widely from the norm, slowly evolved to slang for bitchin' or amazing. By the mid-1960s we turned it into a dark and sinister noun.

Translation? Political and musical rebellion. We smoked a little dope and chanted make love not war, as civil unrest became "radical."

[*Image:* 1960 Les Paul Gibson Standard Sunburst guitar.]

We hope you're be-boppin' along, enjoying our hit chart of Rock & Roll DJs ... a BFYP-FM exclusive!

Like a **Rubber Ball** ... ♪ we'll bounce your Top 40 from coast-to-coast.

Rick Snyder >Part 1
Best known at WTRY/Albany, New York

Rick Snyder is New York radio through and through. "I started on the air in Syracuse, New York, at age twenty in 1961, 'practicing' on WOLF, a 'legendary' 250-watt 'flamethrower,'" Rick said, facetiously. I heard the hint of a smile in his voice.

The mini-watt station would have had trouble throwing a feather, but hey, it was a start and that's all Rick needed. First, to get there ...

Love of music most often runs in generations, as with Rick's family. "I was always surrounded by music. My mother played the piano, my aunt sang, and I played the trumpet," said Rick. "But the only music that was constantly available was on the radio."

City stations reverberated through the countryside sparking the adventure in Rick. "I was in Syracuse listening to St. Louis, Cincinnati, Chicago, Philadelphia, Boston ... they all came in at night. I thought to myself, I can do that."

The impressionable eleven-year-old mimicked his favorite disk jockeys and at sixteen, bought a tape recorder and taped his own mock shows. "After a few tapings, I was better than the guys on the radio, and I was having fun!"

One day he rode his bike across town to WOLF and watched Denny Bracken doing his DJ thing. (Another station with a studio window on the world.) Denny invited Rick and his friend into the studio. It didn't take long—watching the DJ say a few words while the engineer did all the work—Rick was hooked.

He mused, "I can remember the words, 'this is the job for me,' going through my brain, at that age."

Eighteen-year-old Rick wangled his way into his first studio at Syracuse University's WAER-FM to broadcast the news. In 1959 FM stations like the one at Syracuse, only appealed to the Beat Generation's cool, Jazz audience. "Unfortunately, the only people who had FM radios were my parents—so *they* could hear me," said Rick.

His perception of FM radio was a shadow industry, with colleges and a few commercial stations buying in; but few in the populace had receivers. DJs' quick wit and other words of wisdom floated largely unheard on the FM airwaves. Undaunted, Rick was "on the air"!

He often listened to the popular, local top 40 stations, WOLF and WNDR, and enjoyed, emulated, and envied, one of their DJs. "I'd heard Peter C. Cavanaugh on the air for a number of years, and one night when I turned on his show—he wasn't on! His substitute said, 'Peter isn't here tonight because he's graduating from high school.'"

Rick was in shock. "*I* was graduating from high school too! I met Peter the next night when I visited him at the station and we've been close friends ever since!"

With his ultimate DJ goal always in mind, Rick wanted as much experience as possible. When Peter C. Cavanaugh landed a gig at WTLB in Utica, Rick headed down there after 11:00p.m. and ran the board for him. "I was pretty good at it!" he exclaimed, as if he thought he wouldn't be. His weekend gigs kept him close to the action and he made more tapes ... and had more fun.

Tommy Saunders*, another DJ acquaintance (who eventually put in thirty-plus years at KYA/San Francisco), suggested Rick check out Boston's Graham Junior College. He enrolled in their eight-month accelerated radio broadcasting course, and Tommy hired him to go on the air at WOLF in August 1961.

(*See the KYA October 22, 1962 music survey in the Tom Donahue story—Tommy's there, too!)

"And then it was *really* fun," said Rick. WOLF used him first, as a weekend jock and news guy, then overnight DJ. After just four months in the all-night show, they gave him the big break to afternoon drive guy!

DJs listen to other DJs. That's how they learn and become inspired. While at WOLF, Rick found one energetic, quick-stepping fella he just couldn't take his ears off. "I sat in a car with the sales manager, listening to Joey Reynolds, recently hired by WNDR, for the afternoon shift. The only negative I could pick out was, 'Geez, he talks too fast.' He was [and is!] *great* on the air." Rick too, would soon get first-hand WNDR experience.

Though WOLF's ratings grew and their listeners loved their little 250-watt station, a new program director spelled dramatic changes and Rick wanted out. His friend, Peter, now at WNDR, came to the rescue.

Also in Syracuse, the 5,000-watt station noticed WOLF's blossoming popularity and tried to nip it in the bud. Competition between the stations was intense. Might as well go with the winner, thought Rick. WNDR hired him in May 1962. Another smart move that put him in good company.

Threesome with a happy ending

"I met Dave Laird at Channel 9 just about the time I went on the air at WNDR," said Rick. "We hit it off and immediately became good friends. One night though, he mentioned the name of a girl he was dating. We were dating the same girl at the same time!"

Opting to save his friendship with Dave, Rick thought to himself, "I should stop seeing Carol right away because it sounds like he's in love with her."

Cupid must have been listening. "Well, I did and he was, and they were married—and Dave and I have remained friends to this day!"

About this time, television and radio began to realize their potential power in working together.

"WNDR took a busload of listeners to meet Dick Clark in Philly on American Bandstand," said Rick. It was a highlight for Rick and the kids, some of whom actually danced on the show.

He wouldn't meet up with Dick again until the Atlantic City, New Jersey, Beatles concert on a sultry August day in 1964, when he was part of Albany, New York's WTRY. What's so special about that?

"I have a picture with The Beatles and DJ Lee Gray—and that picture is on Lee Gray's website—and they cut me out of it! I was standing over Lee's left shoulder, and they just chopped me off!"

A surprise for Rick—Lee Gray's, son, David Darling, generously provided great photos for use in *Blast from Your Past!* including the original image that catches Lee AND Rick—with The Beatles. Rick's peeking over Lee's shoulder while Paul eyes the camera.

But we're getting ahead of ourselves. Before hitting WTRY's airwaves, Rick polished his platter-playing skills while at WNDR in 1962, and sailed on through to WTRX in Flint, Michigan, prior to scoring the gig in 1964 at WTRY. Mid-Sixties at the Albany powerhouse station was a local DJ's dream job.

Rick's WTRY days were special not just for the close association with The Beatles and other big-time celebs. Also a hit was the DJs' camaraderie, which included a WTRY bowling team, when bowling was the rage for every age.

Rick's stories take us down his ten-year DJ career path, meeting The Beatles, Rolling Stones, Roy Orbison, Little Anthony and oh, so many others, along the way. Enjoy more of his wild-n-crazy radio ride in the second half of the 1960s.

[*Image:* Rick and Lee in WTRY Big Sound Survey for December 19, 1964, with Ed Reilly, Don Weeks, and "Rebel" (who looks less like a rebel than anyone!) BFYP Collection.]

Waxin' the '60s: We're cruisin' the drag through the early to mid-Sixties, radio blaring our fave tunes; a car full of West Coast kids heading to the drag strip.

Our top twenty tunes, however, could differ from our Midwest and Eastern peers astronomically. (An oft-used space term of the era.)

Though both coasts watched "Surfer Girl" hang ten, only small stretches of asphalt airwaves boosted the bitchin' car tunes to the top of the charts.

Well I'm not braggin' babe so don't put me down | But I've got the fastest set of wheels in town ...

The Beach Boys spun a doubleheader at #16, on *KFWB/Los Angeles' Fabulous Forty Survey, October 5, 1963. Their bi-coastal favorite, "Surfer Girl," slipped down the chart a tad, while flipside, "Little Deuce Coupe," felt the high. (*Las-Solanas.com/arsa/surveys.)

Go ahead, give 'er a spin! Ask that little gal over in the corner to twirl on down the road with you. Flip on BFYP 84.8-FM, rev up her engine and ... you know I'm talkin' 'bout that little deuce coupe in the used car lot, dontcha?

Hot wheels or not, the B-side song didn't make the cut for Milwaukee's September '63 WRIT listeners, nor other stations east of the Rockies. That didn't stop a rousing rendition of red-light-green-light, across the country.

[*Image:* By October 1963 Milwaukee's WRIT radio fans mused, "Funny How Time Slips Away" (Johnny Tillotson) as it climbed the chart from #17 to #9 in just a week. Quick on its heels, and without Google Maps, apparently they thought they were only "24 Hours From Tulsa" (Gene Pitney), racing it up to #10 from last week's #18. *BFYP* Collection.]

BFYP-FM leads you North ... stopping short of Alaska, we Watusi our way through the cool green wilderness of the Pacific Northwest.

Cold and rainy he is NOT, and on a chilly day he made someone's name smokin' hot! *Louie Louie ...* ♪

Ken Chase
aka Mike Korgan
Best known at KISN/Portland, Oregon

Towards the end of the Fifties, Mike cooled his heels at KLMS/Lincoln, Nebraska, waiting to hear the outcome of an offer from Star Broadcasting. It would mark another life-altering change for newlyweds Mike and Carol. Just not in the way they'd expected.

Mike assumed the "big city" of Omaha was calling him. Carol stayed in the car while Mike moseyed in for what he thought would be a brief, uneventful meeting. He would soon learn that Star Broadcasting also owned another station a tad further away.

Still, he was game for anything and barely skipped a beat to say, "OK, I'll take it," on the offer of KISN in the Pacific Northwest.

Yes, ladies, he accepted the job without consulting his new bride ... "I went back out to the car and said, 'Well, they want to move us to Portland, Oregon.'

"Portland!" Carol was beyond shock. "She hadn't even wanted to move to Omaha," admitted Mike.

Somehow, he would have to convince Carol that Portland was not as far away from Nebraska as Mars; and that the Pacific Northwest's rainwater is good for your skin.

Carol began to protest, said Mike, and mimicked her feminine voice, "'But I don't want to move that far. All my family's here!' Then I told her what they offered to *pay* me, and without missing a beat, she said 'OK.'"

KISN was the powerhouse station in Portland in the Sixties, with over half the radios in the city and surrounding areas tuned to it.

The station's DJs alternately enjoyed and detested the notoriety that came with their jobs. Management was well aware of how to capitalize on their DJs' popularity, which did not involve their respective wives.

"Single" DJs attract more female listeners. So their stipulation on Mike's arrival was that he could not "be" Mike Korgan. He'd have to choose an on-air name, to keep his married life away from fans.

He was at a loss for a name. What attracts girls to a guy? Looks and money. Right, ladies? Remember 1960? With a little creativity, he thought, "Ken" of Ken and Barbie fame, and Chase-Manhattan Bank. Mike Korgan became Ken Chase. Clever!

In major radio markets, DJs "back in the day" were celebrities. A fact that awed Mike when he arrived at the trendy station. Coming from the laid-back Midwest, he recalled his first brush with fame.

"You'd go to a supermarket opening and hundreds of people would show up to see you! The day I came to Portland they had this promotion going for about a month, 'The new animal at the zoo.' We actually set an attendance record at the Portland Zoo."

You realize, of course, who/what the "new animal" was—yep, Mike, aka Ken Chase. "I was in a cage in a gorilla suit. I changed out of the gorilla suit and jumped in a convertible with two pretty girls in bikini swimsuits on the back, and KISN radio written on the side. And my wife has *never* forgiven me!"

KISN's fishbowl studio faced one of the busiest streets in town. "That was a trip all by itself," said Mike. "People would come to the window ... teenage girls ... and hold up notes. They weren't *all* requests for songs. [Wink, wink.] You wouldn't *believe* some of the things they wrote—and it wasn't just their phone number!"

[*Image:* Ken sports the popular flattop hair style (left/middle) gracing KISN's survey May 6, 1962. Cute stick figures! Courtesy of Ken.]

Okay, let's give it to 'em right now!

Mike savors his DJ moments often. "I used to go up [to a spot above the city] and look out over the city and think, wow, over half of these people are listening to my show!"

One 1963 ratings report claimed an 86% audience share for "91-derful KISN, Yours Truly."

It didn't take long for Mike and Carol to settle in; and Mike's interest in radio reached out to making the music he played. Not content to watch the records spin, Mike wanted to produce the vinyl platters.

He was in a good position to meet bands and songwriters with his local teen dance club, "The Chase." Let's see, what's a good song to start with? Something simple ... not too many words, lots of guitar work.

A high school band that Mike also managed wanted to record a popular garage band record. He set up the studio and orchestrated their performance. Mind you, the best equipment was not at hand ... "make do" was the day's mantra.

But how hard could it be to record a song with four choruses consisting mostly of one guy's name?! It's April 1963 and simple songs were "in." Richard Berry wrote it in 1955 and first recorded it in 1957. But it took the fresh-faced kids in The Kingsmen to run it up the charts. Have you figured out the title?

Not everyone agreed with Mike's arrangement ideas for the iconic song, "Louie Louie." "We walked out of the studio [after recording] and they were so upset with me. [One of the guys said] 'That's the worst song I have ever heard in my life. It has a mistake in it.'"

But Mike was adamant. "It's a fit," insisted Mike. "I don't care what you say, it's a fit."

The so-called mistake, however, was the least of the song's problems. Jack Ely's vocals muffled the words—honestly, could *you* understand them? And after the governor banned its play in Indiana for indecent lyrics, the FBI took notice. What was he saying? Was it too lewd and lascivious for our innocent teens? (See me laughing!)

"They talked with everybody who had anything to do with the song," said Mike, "except me—and the guy who sang the song!"

Why was it so garbled and difficult to understand the words? Mike's explanation is for you musicians ... while the rest of us will simply scratch our heads and mutter, uh-huh.

Snatching up coats, placing them strategically, and moving blankets, Mike totally isolated the bass guitar as much as possible in the tiny recording room. Another ah-ha moment and he shoved the boom mic up to the ceiling; under vehement protest from the engineer, he prepared a ribbon mic for the session.

Pointing to the boom mic, "I said, 'Jack, I want you to scream at that thing. The words are not important in this song. It's the bass. I want you to chant into that microphone.' Then I quoted Stan Freburg." He mimicked the venerable composer, singer and author. "The song is about *dancing*, 'If they can't dance to it they won't buy the *rec*-ord! You know that.'" He was so right.

Mike went even more technical on me and discussed "tuning drums." (If you music buffs want to know his take on that—email me.) I think I tuned out until he caught my attention again with an alternative for "mixing it down" to suit the sound to the studio monitors (big speakers), as was common.

Mike went out to his car and grabbed one of the little six-by-nine-inch speakers, "You know, like what went in the back seat of a '57 Chevy," said Mike. He mixed it down on that little speaker. "*This* is what the kids are going to listen to." And the rest is Rock & Roll history.

More controversy surrounded "Louie Louie" as Paul Revere & the Raiders also recorded the song in the same month—in the same studio, with the same engineer—and scored more local fans. But even with its flaws The Kingsmen's version fared better nationally and scored instant fame for every "Louie" in the country.

[*Image:* "Louie Louie" finally hit the #1 spot on WKNR/Detroit's November 21, 1963 Music Guide. *BFYP* Collection.]

When all was said and done, Mike didn't disagree about the perceived mistake, and laughed about it. "If you listen to the song, every band in the *world* [that covers it] repeats the mistake! Thirty years after we recorded it, I got the chance to stand on the sidewalk at the same place where they told me that, and with local cameras rolling and even MTV, I got to say, 'I told you so!'"

Conflicts and cash?

You might be asking yourself about now, isn't a disk jockey producing a record rather a conflict of interest, in the manner of payola? A viable question considering events in the industry at the time.

Says Mike, "When the owner of the station found out I had an interest in a record, oh, he just threw a hissy-fit. 'Oh, you're playola/plugola—you can't' ... blah, blah. Well, OK, so maybe it was a *little* conflict ..."

As we chatted, Mike reflected on the scandal, "I'd been through the payola thing you know, way back then. That was a big issue—I pretty much covered my ass. I didn't take any money, but they'd [record promoters] bring a bottle of Jack Daniels …"

And what of the FBI investigation? After playing the record backwards and forwards and upside down, they dropped the inquiry.

Mike speculates his involvement in the record's production had something to do with their interest to investigate. "But guess what happened?" Mike asked. "When you ban something, it becomes that much more in demand!"

And it's *still* a top request at Boomer bashes! No self-respecting 39 and holding-plus party would be any fun without a loud sing-along of "Louie Louie"!

You better move on …

Mike revels in his KISN days and loves to reminisce with stories of fans and celebs. "About six blocks away from the studio was a kind of bad part of town … the bums hang out, like skid row and occasionally, one of the bums would wander up to the radio station window with a bottle of booze."

One scruffy fella was particularly memorable. "So one afternoon I'm doin' my show and I turn around, and this bum is coming through the studio door into my control room. He says to me [Mike lowered his voice with a slight slur], 'Hi, I'm Roy Orbison.' I said, 'Yeah, and I'm the president of the *U*-nited States. Get outta here!"

You do know what's coming next, right? "I turned around and everybody in the station was standing at the other window watching this. And then I realized, hey … that really *is* Roy Orbison."

Of course, this story and many throughout *BFYP* requires you Boomers to search your memory banks for a time in life when we weren't restricted by locked doors and security scanners. Young'uns will need to trust we're not lyin'.

But even in fiction there is usually truth lurking in the background … here's one more for ya …

"Another day somebody walked through the door, pulled my chair back (it's on wheels) and sat down right in my lap and says, 'Where's the microphone switch, boy?' [Mike mimics a Southern drawl.] I pointed, he turned it on and said, 'Hi folks! I'm Jimmy Dean!'"

Jimmy turned to Mike and demanded, "Why're you playin' this record?!" He reached over and grabbed the record player arm. You know that "whoop" sound a phonograph needle makes as it's whipped across a vinyl record? Agh!

Mike laughed. "And he said, 'Now. Where's "Big John"?* I wanna hear m'record.'" (*Jimmy not only topped the country charts but he charted at #15 with "Big Bad John" on KISN's December 24, 1961 Fabulous Fifty Hit Parade.)

But it wasn't only the stars who shook up the DJs—sometimes it was one of their own …

Crazy is as crazy does.

"It was a crazy station," Mike continued, lost in reverie. "Don Steele had a little too much tequila one night and a whole bunch of us DJs were downtown, and [Mike aped Don's popular intro] 'The *Real* Don Steele!' picked me up *bodily*, and carried me across Broadway!"

He couldn't believe Don's action, "What the hell did you do that for?" Mike exclaimed. Don says, "I think I love you!"

Mike disagreed, "I don't think you do! That guy was somethin'. He would sit in a bar, look around, and girls would be around us, and he'd say, 'I eat pussy.' The girls would giggle ... none of 'em would admit if it embarrassed them."

Now remember folks, this is creeping through 1963. We were only a few years past the Stepford society, when everything sexual was behind closed doors— albeit, not necessarily your own.

Mike worked with Don about six months before California called Don back to the Golden State with gigs at KEWB/San Francisco and Los Angeles' legendary KHJ. Before he left, says Mike, "He bought and sold a bridge a couple of times. Don said, 'That's my bridge.' One day he got out there and stopped traffic. 'You can't come across my bridge,' he told drivers. He was a crazy man!"

Don wasn't the only wild man. "We all were crazy in those days," Mike admitted. "I don't know how we lived through it!"

Making a lane change.

Shortly after "Louie Louie" Mike decided it was time to switch things up and he boogied across town to KGON. He convinced the owner to turn his elevator music station into a Rock & Roll station, giving KISN its first local rival. "We went very hard Rock and picked up not only the teenyboppers, but the Blacks."

Um, "hard Rock"? Heehee ... the Righteous Brothers ... "In those days they 'sounded' Black. I brought them to town, met them at the airport about 1:00 a.m. with my wife," Mike recalled.

Bill Medley and Bobby Hatfield were hungry. But Portland rolled up the sidewalks early in those days. Food in the middle of the night?! "There's a bowling alley open ... and we took them to Amato's Lanes. They really liked the food!"

Although KGON nearly put KISN out of business, Mike still counts his wild 'n' crazy KISN stint as his most memorable moments. He graciously catered to the stars ... Cher was bored and wanted a coloring book ... and he never tired of his fellow DJs' antics ... like Bill Western's marriage to Miss Oregon and three-day stint on a roller coaster.

The listeners were trippy, too. Radio in the good ol' days was local and personal. KISN gave teenagers from the community an opportunity to show off their broadcasting talent. "We chose a gal from each high school, and they were the fashion reporters—and when you got to be one, you got this little pin—a microphone that said KISN on it." What a cool collectible to scoop off eBay!

And what of today's radio? "I can't name one personality on the radio," says Mike. "In those days you had to have pretty much what you gotta have now, to be on television. But even the people on TV don't have *that* kind of personality ..." Mike's take on today's music?

"There's no style. Everybody's got that whiny little falsetto. [Back then] There was a difference between a Ray Charles falsetto and The Platters'—you don't find that divergence anymore."

Today: Although son, Todd, who volunteered his dad's story for *BFYP* is immensely proud of Mike's radio days, Mike didn't stay in radio. He and Carol soon opted to hone their cooking skills, moving out of the broadcast biz. By 1996 the certified executive chefs opened a quaint B&B, and volunteered as caretakers for the Heceta Head Lighthouse in Florence, Oregon. Their daughter ultimately took over their enterprises, leaving Mike and Carol free to travel, take boo-coo photos (above, c. 2009), and write books about their love of food.

It was a long road from Nebraska to Oregon, but Mike never regretted being kicked out of school to date Carol. They celebrated their 50th wedding anniversary in November 2009.

Waxin' the '60s: Did Rock & Roll fuel the racial unrest in mid-twentieth century America? Some would say so—the inequities certainly became more obvious as "race music" rose up the radio station charts.

Artists and disc jockeys fought to give race music its place on the charts. Black artists came into their own with tunes like Mary Wells' 1962 hit, "You Beat Me to the Punch." It became Motown's first nomination for a Grammy in 1963.

With other top tunes like "The One Who Really Loves You" (1963), and her signature song, "My Guy" (1964), Mary became Motown's most consistent hit-maker in their early years.

Rock & Roll runs rampant on BFYP, from Middle America Motown, trippin' West and lookin' East, for something with a wink!

Pssst ... Pssst ... hey, *Come a Little Bit Closer* ... ♪

Sandy Deanne with Jay and the Americans!
Howie Kane and John Reincke (Jay #3)

We wound up the 1950s, with Sandy and fellow Jay and the Americans rising to modest local fame in New York City, as The Harborlites. You might recall asking your main squeeze, "Is That Too Much to Ask?"

Of course, it didn't hurt The Harborlites' growing fame that Sandy and WINS DJ Cousin Brucie dated sisters. With a few member changes they soon followed their 1959 debut hit by morphing into Jay and the Americans and hitting the charts hard with 1962's "She Cried."

At this time the J&A lineup included Sandy Deanne, Kenny Vance, Howie Kane and John/Jay Traynor.

[*Image:* Courtesy of Cousin Brucie, shown with Jay and The Americans c. 1962. *Love* Cousin Brucie's leopard suit! Don't tell anyone, but his dog had one too.]

"Our record company was pushing the flipside, 'Dawning,'" said Sandy. "Nothing happened, so because it hadn't met with much success, we went back in the studio to record more stuff."

The song had been roaming the West Coast charts for a good six months, when a DJ (who remains a mystery at this writing) locked himself in his L.A. radio studio and played "She Cried" nonstop 'til the engineer cried. (Okay, I made up the engineer's reaction, but I bet I'm not far off!)

With that push "She Cried" leapt onto the charts at Sacramento's KXOA March 2, 1962, at #16 and KRLA/L.A.'s March 9-16 chart at #17. By March 31 it broke #1 on San Bernardino's KFXM "Fabulous 59." It slowly rolled from turntable to turntable, across the states.

"It moved from city to city from California through the Midwest," said Sandy. John chimed in, "Dick B [Biondi] was kind of the 'big man' in Chicago (WLS) and one of the guys responsible for making it a pretty big record."

This is the type of disc jockey influence prevalent at a time when they weren't restricted by rules and formats. Artists had direct access to them and vice versa. Records and careers were made over a bottle of wine, dating sisters, and the DJ simply loving the hell out of a song.

"She Cried" debuted on WABC/NY's Silver Dollar Sound Survey at #16 on April 10th. It took more than a month, marking unusually long staying power for the diffident tune, but the soulful song made it all the way to #1 by May 15th.

"By the time it got to New York," said Sandy, "it had fallen from #1 in California. This guy, Fat Daddy in Baltimore, was playing the heck out of the record like the guy in California. He got so excited he told their agent, 'I'm bookin' these guys to play a hop.'"

As he told the story, Sandy spoke faster, with an energy that stripped away the years. "We showed up to sing the song at Fat Daddy's Hop; Fat Daddy was a black DJ on a black station. When we showed up, Fat Daddy's eyes got real wide, 'I thought you guys were a black act!'"

A true professional, Fat Daddy took them in stride and the hop was a hit. Though Jay and the Americans never thought they had the black sound, as Sandy said, "Every act we looked up to was a black act, with the exception of Dion and the Belmonts." The Drifters, Frankie Lyman and the Teenagers were their inspiration.

They were in good company under the wing of power producers Leiber and Stoller, joining the partners who had written an early string of Elvis hits.

Sandy, Howie, and John were a challenge on our conference call to keep straight who was talking. Often we chattered over each other, and more than once they finished each other's sentences. There was no mistaking however, their passion for the music and gratitude to the DJs who helped them mold their lifelong careers in music.

DJ Murray the K jumps on British bandwagon

And it seems everyone has a Murray the K (Kaufman) memory. "He called us his 'rabbit's foot' and was playing all of our stuff," said Sandy, "because we were local (from Brooklyn) and brought a certain following to his live shows.

"I'll never forget when The Beatles came out with their first record. I heard Murray say, 'Listen to these guys! These guys are a joke! They sound like a bad garage band.' He was playing either 'She Loves You' or 'I Want to Hold Your Hand.' Three weeks later, Murray was announcing himself as the 5th Beatle!"

By 1964 Jay and the Americans had recruited a new Jay, aka David Blatt, to replace John Traynor. An a cappella rendition of the unrecorded "Cara Mia" (eventually released in 1965) convinced them Dave was a great fit—Sandy's parents and several neighbors ran over to see who was singing—without a doubt, he had the chops to carry the band forward.

One of Jay and the Americans' most enduring hits, "Come a Little Bit Closer," charmed the radio charts in 1964, but began as an afterthought. According to Sandy their record company said, "'You've got ten minutes—go do what you want.' We recorded that track in about ten minutes flat."

They went about business and forgot about it until Jay heard it on the air. Says Sandy, "He stopped the car, ran to a pay phone—there were no cell phones in those days—and started screaming at United Artists. 'How dare you release this record! It's the worst piece of junk …' The UA rep finally got a word in edgewise and said, 'Well it's really strange that you say that because next week it's #3 with the bullet, in *Cash Box*, and *Billboard*.' Jay said, 'Nevermind!'"

While DJs were obviously instrumental in many musicians' careers, at times they came in handy for other things. Though Cousin Brucie and Sandy dated sisters, it was Jack Spector, one of the WMCA/NYC Good Guys who introduced Sandy to his wife of forty-plus years.

And DJs can be unnervingly spontaneous … fast-forward to around December 2006. Jay and The Americans had just begun playing together again and headed over to Buffalo, ready to interview with legendary DJ Joey Reynolds.

The ol' group had just reformed with original member, Marty Sanders. When they entered the studio, Joey told Marty to go out and get his guitar—he wanted them to play *live*. Yipes! They didn't feel prepared with new Jay #3, but the troopers elicited a "Wow, you guys really sound good!" from Joey.

Today: You can hear Sandy, Marty, Howie and Jay #3 on their website (JayAndTheAmericans.net). "Little Senorita" is a campy, catchy tune and their first record in more than thirty-five years.

They've all had "real jobs" in the interim, and now either retired or balancing time with touring. Like Sandy and wife, Merle, enjoying their Hewlett, New York fashion boutique, when not at home on the New Jersey shore.

Says Sandy, "Older bands *now*, they keep in shape, work out, get sleep, and take vitamins. They used to take [mind-blowing] drugs … now they're taking vitamins and Viagra!"

[*Image:* "Come a Little Bit Closer" debuted at #21 on the KDEO/San Diego Fabulous Forty survey, October 24, 1964. *BFYP* Collection.]

C'mon ... get close-up and personal with Rockin' Rochelle at BFYP-FM. I won't bite ... hard. Just nibblin' on your ear while you listen ...

Oh, baby, you're a fast talkin', slow walkin' kinda guy! Stroll with me down Memory Lane, *Mohair Sam*! ♪

Cousin Bruce Morrow >Part 1

aka "Cousin Brucie"
Best known at WABC/New York City
(Actually, he's "best known" wherever he goes!)

"Hi cousin, what's buzzin'? This is big Cousin Brucie swingin' right along bringin' music into your mad pads and wailin' wheels."*

Hit Parader magazine lead with his quoted patter in their two-page spread on Cousin Brucie in their October 1960* issue. 25¢ got you the hit scoops on your fave music, stations, and DJs!

[*Image:* The editors squeezed in a cameo picture of Bruce on the cover, nibbling on Joni James' shoulder. *BFYP* Collection.]

Wrestling with Bruce's radio gigs timeline, I consulted my fun collection of Rock & Roll memorabilia. Though we didn't have the infinite memory of the Internet back then, but we did love our celebs—thank goodness for endearing and enduring magazines—because what I'd found listed for him on the Internet left out a city or two.

Bruce was indeed still at WINS/New York for a time in 1960, soon moving on to his first of two stints at WABC. However, for a recap of where he was in the late 1950s ...

A scared kid barely wet-behind-the-ears, Bruce cut his DJ eye teeth on a radio stint in Bermuda in 1958, and endeared himself to the islanders. With a few lessons under his belt— personally and professionally—he triumphantly returned to the States hoping to clone the atmosphere of Bermuda community in the Big Apple.

He slid into powerhouse WINS in New York for his next stop on the Rock & Roll Radio circuit.

Bruce arrived to prove his personal power at the 50,000-watt powerhouse station with a fresh perspective and plenty of New York chutzpa. Dramatically defying PD, Mel Leeds, Bruce created and defined his familial personality. Everybody's favorite cousin was a household name to New York listeners by the time Frankie Avalon asked "Why" at the top of the charts in January 1960.

Why? Because they loved him.

Though a hit with listeners at WINS, the seven-year contract he was offered when "Cousin Brucie" was born came up noticeably short, just over two years.

While not unusual for radio, it was disheartening for Bruce, as "he who shall remain nameless" (shhhhh, don't tell anyone I told you it was "Murray the K"), coveted his time slot, and snagged it with industry power, over Bruce's audacious youth.

Even with the sourness it caused between he and Murray Kaufman, Bruce admits, "It probably was the best thing that happened to me. It taught me another object lesson in life and made me move on."

Next up on Bruce's turntable, his first, short stint at WABC. An infectious smile lights up the September 21, 1961 "Swingin' Sound Survey." [*BFYP* Collection.]

Great broadcasting icons split wax-spinning sounds with Bruce: Dan Ingram, Herb Oscar Anderson, Charlie Greer, Fred Hall, Sam Holman, and Scott Muni. What's not to like?

A memorable mini-gig, it wasn't long before Bruce skipped down to Miami for a sunny stint at WINZ, reminiscent of Bermuda.

Pivotal to Bruce's broadcasting success, "I spent a very happy year there. That's when 'Cousin Brucie' *really* started to fly."

WINZ kept him busy! Giving him the star treatment, promotions boasted "New York City's Cousin Brucie coming to Miami!" They played up the family moniker and his listeners invited him into their homes in record numbers.

He boasted fans all the way to Jamaica and the West Indies, who also fell in love with their new cousin. He flew every weekend to Jamaica to appear at stations JBC and RJR for shows.

Still smiling and drying the water from behind his ears, Cousin Brucie soon cut a groove back to New York, where he says, "... the contemporary Cousin Brucie legend really started."

New York wounds healing, satisfaction was his when Hal Leo of New York's WABC asked Bruce to return to their studio core in the Big Apple. He gladly signed on at the WINS nemesis.

The second time around at WABC proved to be a personally "... tough, tough time in my life," said Bruce; also his most professionally successful years. The Clear Channel station held his attention—and thus, their fans'—for eleven "fabulous" years. (About 1963-1974.)

Part of the reason for his longevity was his connection with the artists that he shared with his audience.

When we left Bruce and Sandy Deane (of Jay & The Americans) dating sisters back in the late Fifties, it was just the beginning of Bruce's influence on the artists of the era.

"I knew Jay & The Americans when they were the Harborlites," said Bruce. Their friendship continued into the Sixties, despite Bruce's leopard print suit! (You may have noticed it an image in Sandy's story.)

New Jersey's Palisades Park was a happenin' venue in 1962, until its close in 1971. Playing host to early Motown artists and Rock & Roll bands, Bruce's listeners followed him to the park and helped launch more than a few careers.

Songwriter, Chuck Barris, and singer, Freddy Cannon, repaid the favor with a top ten tribute, "Palisades Park" (1962). The B-side song (to their "June, July and August") found play personifying the summer sounds.

While at WABC, Bruce enjoyed his fans as much as they reveled in their on-air cousin's antics. "I had a huge fan club. A hundred and fifty-thousand card-carrying members. These kids became very much part of my family and every place I went they'd show up ... and we'd party in the street!"

What's in a name?

"Cousin Brucie" is more than a name. Family has always been important to Bruce, and he connects with his fans because he *treats* them like family. Especially the young'uns. Much to the chagrin of one particular school principal.

Bruce's television special at a country club, with numerous Top 40 artists, was too much for the local high school's kids to miss. They left the campus en masse to watch the show!

Their principal called him on the carpet the next day—definitely not a "red carpet"—and said he was suspending the whole school. Though Bruce pleaded with him on the kids' behalf, the taskmaster followed through. Perhaps more for show of authority than true punishment. Seriously, like the kids minded?

Over the years, Bruce has spoken on-air and off, to runaway teens who have escaped from what they feel is an intolerable home life. Just as often, he received calls from parents begging him to "speak" to their child on-air, asking them to return home.

Bruce always took their requests seriously. "I'm very proud of what I've done and what I'm doing," says Bruce.

Throughout 1964 our music scene swirled with a beat becoming more restless and insistent, while wistfulness flowed through its center.

WABC's reach to more than forty states gave Bruce a national audience for unveiling new talent. Often DJs and/or producers recognized a rare opportunity to be "the first" to introduce dynamic artists. "WABC was so big that as soon as they began playing an artist's record, they received national attention. We helped the careers of Elvis, The Drifters, Jerry Lee Lewis, Tommy James, Frankie Lyman & The Teenagers …" Bruce's voice trailed off … and the beat goes on.

[*Image:* WABC Silver Sound Survey, February 16, 1963, with a DJ all-star lineup. Top/bottom, l-r: Herb Oscar Anderson, Charlie Greer, Sam Holman, Dan Ingram, Scott Muni, Bruce (Cousin Brucie) Morrow, Bob Lewis. *BFYP* Collection.]

With a perfect storm of music brewing and threatening to land on our shores, "I introduced The Beatles to New York radio," said Bruce. "That's when we became 'W-A-BEATLES-C.'"

This musical phenomenon created legendary competition between stations with a cloak of secrecy to rival the CIA. The Beatles' high-profile popularity in England preceded them and US stations went into a feeding frenzy.

"They would bring it up (a Beatles record) in an armed car. A security guard handed me an envelope and I wasn't allowed to open and play it until nine o'clock." Bruce soon realized however, that his exclusive plays were being recorded in Midwest states and replayed on their stations, to beat their time restriction.

Catching on to the ploy, he foiled their plans with "Do You Want to Know a Secret" (March 1964). "Every ten seconds I obliterated the record with 'Cousin Brucie! Exclusive! Exclusive! Exclusive! Beatles exclusive!' It stopped the pirating of my music."

A 2014 CNN series on *The Sixties* the "Decade that Shaped America," included an episode of "The British Invasion." Bruce Morrow was the featured DJ at the beginning of this eye-opening segment.

While reliving his career with me, Bruce stopped himself mid-sentence, "My mentor, by the way, was Alan Freed. I used to go up and watch him through the window at WINS. One day, as I pressed my nose to the glass dreaming of doing what he was doing, he tapped on the glass, and called me in. 'Son,'" he said, "'this is a very boring business. Go somewhere else. You're not gonna like it.' And I'm very happy I didn't listen to him."

Catch up with Cousin Brucie again in the late Sixties as we turn the page on his shift at WABC, and declare "Peace out!" on the decade that gave us everyone's favorite cousin.

[*Image:* Alan Freed boosted Rock & Roll to epic fame, along with many budding Radio DJs. Print from original WJW/Cleveland, Ohio, poster c. 1952-1954; eBay.]

Hey, hey, ho, ho, it's Rockin' Rochelle at BFYP up for another spin of the vinyls 'round your radio dial at 84.8-FM!

Hold on tight and go 'round slow *On a Carousel* -el ... ♪

𝓜𝓲𝓽𝓬𝓱 𝓜𝓲𝓬𝓱𝓪𝓮𝓵
aka Ron Terrell, Terrell Metheny
Best known at WOKY/Milwaukee, Wisconsin

"Mitch Michael" may have been behind the mic, but *Terrell* was the driving force behind many a radio station's music format, and guided dozens of popular DJs throughout the 1950s and '60s.

He chortled over the role he and his '50s cronies played in the metamorphosis of staid radio "announcers" into bold Rock & Roll Radio Disc Jockeys.

There were still growing pains from Bubble Gum Pop music to raucous Rock, especially in the Midwest. Terrell's first record hop at WOKY in Milwaukee proved the point.

"I had all the Top 40 records to play. All the good stuff. Some kids came up and said, 'We want to hear a polka. I didn't have any. What the hell's a polka? I went home, bought me some polka songs and from then on, I had polka in my records."

♪ ♫ ♪ ♫ ♪ ♫ ♪

Author Note: As a sixteen-year-old in rural California, our family visited my dad's Minnesota relatives. It became apparent, "country" California was not the same as Midwest country! A Saturday night "barn dance" in 1964 included sashaying in a polka to The Beach Boys' "California Girls"! I never laughed so hard or had so much fun. Fortunately, I knew how to polka, thanks to my dance instructor mom, and small-town upbringing.

♪ ♫ ♪ ♫ ♪ ♫ ♪

While reinventing radio with Rock & Roll, most of the young DJs of the Fifties thought, "I don't want to be a forty-year-old DJ," said Terrell. "But now ..."

Determined to rise above the turntables to management by that "old age," Terrell played the DJ part of dashing Mitch Michael for a while longer, to learn the ropes at WOKY.

But public appearances, record hops, and an embarrassing role as "the world's most eligible bachelor" for a station promo, didn't spin his platters. Eyeing more, it wasn't long before he earned some PD creds at Albany New York's WABY, for six months.

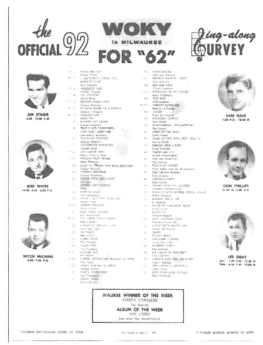

Prior to skipping out of WOKY, however, his camaraderie with another DJ in the early 1960s had its ups and downs, yet lasted a lifetime.

"I'm probably going to tell you the dark side of Lee [Gray] 'cause it makes the bright side so much better.

"Lee was a brilliant guy. Don't know why but he took a liking to me; but I didn't take a liking to him.

"Lee introduced himself and said, 'When I was seven years old, my dad went to work in the oil fields of South America, my mother went to work in the bars of the oil fields of Oklahoma, and I went to hellllll.'" With that inauspicious beginning, they became fast friends.

[*Image:* Both DJs pictured. See Lee Gray's story next. *BFYP* Collection.]

Fun and Friendship head South

Terrell ultimately hooked up with the general manager of WKLO in Louisville and in 1964, took a southeast turn—and a new Program Director was born.

In the meantime, Lee had split WOKY for WIND/Chicago. They kept in touch, and Terrell's friendship became instrumental in Lee's ultimate DJ success.

Over-indulgence was a popular by-product of the Sixties. (Hmmm, did I understate that?) And popular Rock & Roll Radio DJs were particularly susceptible to the vagaries of celebrity. As Lee soon learned.

He wore out his welcome in Chicago in these early days. Westinghouse, WIND's parent company, sent him down to their Alabama station.

Terrell, however, didn't want to see his friend's status and spirit destroyed, so he hired Lee and brought him back up north during his short gig at WABY. Terrell chuckled at the memory, "He was on-air in morning, mid-day, and at night, so he could *not* get into trouble!"

When Terrell left for WKLO he handed the PD reins to Lee, who eventually parlayed his friend's mentoring into program director at the station where, said Terrell, Lee "learned to fly" … Albany, New York's WTRY. But there is much more story in between.

Lee's DJ life from obscurity to a Beatles favorite as told by his son, Royce Lee Darling (with more tales from Terrell) is next … but first …

Remember now, in these days, radio DJs often pulled double duty. Heading over to WKLO, Terrell donned two hats—as the daytime PD—and practicing what he preached as Mitch Michael, nighttime drive jock.

He may have been a happy-go-lucky on-air DJ, but as PD, he ran a tight ship. One 1967 office note from Terrell began, "I am not a fan of memo-writing," but ran on for another couple pages of DJ instructions.

"Going into the news, you must play an up-tempo top 30 vocal. If you tighten up, cut your yak and plan ahead, you will have no trouble."

And about those free radio top 30 or 40 surveys … "Incidentally, we do not print a survey. We do publish, however, the 'Kentuckiana Countdown.' Never refer to *survey*."

So—proof—being a Rock & Roll Radio DJ was not all fun and games.

At WKLO though, a lot of fun people popped up both behind the mic and in front of the streetside studio window.

"We had a showcase window with speakers outside, and one of our fanatical listeners, a guy named Dan, often stood outside watching us. When he wasn't, he won our contests so often that we had to design them to keep him from winning." Whatever happened to Dan?

"He went into radio and uses the name, Dan Mason—now president of CBS [Radio]!" A lifelong radio guy, Dan received the 2014 Worldwide Radio Summit's "Radio Executive of the Year" award.

Once on a nostalgia roll, Terrell was lost in window-watching memories. Diane Sawyer's friends dragged her in front of the window to watch the turntables spin; a couple of strippers from down the street teased him mercilessly.

But even then, a certain danger lurked outside, just beyond their gaze. "We had a triple-pane glass you know, for sound and all," began Terrell in another memory. Fortunately, it was relatively secure for other reasons.

"I was on the air one day and the window shattered! We didn't know it 'til we were cleaning up the glass—somebody shot at me! We found the slug, but had no idea where it came from.

Speculation for the motive in 1965's shooting led to Bill Clark, the Black DJ Terrell had recently hired. "Twice in my life I put Black guys in jobs that had never been held by Black guys before. Not because they were Black, but because they were very, very good. This was before the EEO* stuff and during the MLK* marches." [*Equal Employment Opportunity; Martin Luther King, respectively.]

Though the incident unnerved them, they were definitely not intimidated and Bill continued in his job. But, said Terrell "... we moved him one room back, so the bullets couldn't get him."

I can't think with all that racket!

The music continued to spin for Terrell at WKLO, while admitting he often never heard it. "Listeners were hearing the music—we were workin'! When the song started, we turned it off [the sound] and started cueing up commercials, and stuff, and get ready; right before it'd end, we'd turn it back up and hear the end of it. I did most of my music selecting by early, very antiquated research; also by checking on charts, rather than listening to songs and saying, 'oh, boy, that's a hit.'"

Though he rarely listened to music (something more than one disc jockey admitted), "I had tons of albums. We got a huge number of records every week. I'd come home and have to step over these things to get in the house."

The albums made great giveaways at record hops, says Terrell, "... and one time I went to a flea market and sold thousands of albums for fifty cents apiece—and I still kept several hundred."

Terrell felt the itch to move again, and grabbing Lee Gray, he headed for New York's WMCA in 1968, to finish the decade.

While there, the station began a few tumultuous years of switching formats. "We switched from DJs playing Rock & Roll to half Rock & Roll and half talk," said Terrell. "Some sort of a nightmare that the owner had ... it was such a horrible nightmare."

But it wasn't all bad. His favorite song memory comes from that era. "I got a Gold Record for 'MacArthur Park' [by Jimmy Webb, 1968]. It was awarded for being the last station in America to play 'MacArthur Park,' instead of the first." Why was that so unique? "It was seven minutes and twenty-one seconds long," Terrell exclaimed. "It totally destroyed the flow of the show."

We leave Terrell, aka Mitch Michael and Ronn Terrell, here, as we groove into the later Sixties and early Seventies, when Terrell realized his management and radio ownership dreams.

DJs across the country learned from this music master as he crisscrossed the nation from Texas (KJET and KWIC) to Baton Rouge (WYNK) to Toledo (WSPD AND WLQR) to California (KKBN, KVML, KZSQ) and parts in between.

Today: Retired since 2001, Terrell and wife, Carolyn, made Arkansas home, after a lifetime of radio's nomadic adventures. But is anyone truly retired these days? He keeps his finger on the pulse of radio as it fumbles for its new identity, with the occasional consultancy or interim management gig.

Waxin' the '60s: Remember 1963? No? Too young? Well, let's explore a few notable and newsworthy events in this pivotal year for America and music.

We were be-boppin' to Doo-Wop, jivin' to Rhythm & Blues, and of course, swinging our hips to early Rock & Roll. Maybe we were on a musical high, but '63's restless mood vibrated our music as Surf Rock began to rumble ominously in the engine of a bitchin' *Little Deuce Coupe*.

The year showed signs of trouble from the beginning, with segregation and women's rights, hot topics. Martin Luther King, Jr., declared "I Have a Dream" on the steps of the Lincoln Memorial, during a march on Washington.

And the multi-talented artist, Sam Cooke, found himself "detained" in an attempt to register at a "whites only" Louisiana motel; a distressing display that prompted his 1964 song, "A Change is Gonna Come." "Then I go to my brother | And I say, 'Brother, help me please' | But he winds up knockin' me | Back down on my knees."

About this time, women awakened from their 1950s Stepford lives, to organize readings of Betty Friedan's *The Feminine Mystique*. Friedan exposed women's magazines as publications with men dominating the editorial decisions. News and fiction presented women as June Cleaver-type happy housewives, or assailed them for following a career—Friedan's theory of "feminine mystique."

Add the "conflict" bubbling up in Vietnam and we're on the verge of anarchy. Young men felt a tingling on the back of their necks that often portends personal doom ... it wouldn't be long before we learned a dismal lesson about a "new" type of warfare. The final two months were the worst ... and best ... of 1963— some say, the whole decade—perhaps even, the century.

November 22nd marks the shocking assassination of President John F. Kennedy. He was arguably, one of our best leaders. America mourned, loudly and vividly. It was a time of togetherness experienced in our country that I wish we could have sustained. Alas, only disaster seems to bring us together ... our most recent, September 11, 2001 attack on New York City. And still we cannot get along.

By end of November with spirits at an all-time low, an invasion that had been gaining momentum all year, unleashed its full force on us—the musical kind.

It was perfect timing to lift us up on a high note that penetrated our grief and gave promise to the New Year. Our venerable disc jockeys were only too happy to excite their listeners once again.

Time to pick up a wave at BFYP-FM 84.8 on your dial! Rock & Roll is slip-slidin' around the Beach Boys ... about to wipeout on the Brits' groundswell.

I Want to Hold Your Hand ♪ ... *as we ride the tide to stardom.*

Lee Gray >Part 2

aka Lee Darling
1936 ~ 1996
Best known at WTRY/Albany, New York
(Interview with son, David Darling)

"Lee went from one end of the spectrum to the other," said Lee's longtime pal, Terrell Metheny, "and he was just as committed one way as the other."

Lee finished his military stint behind the mic in Germany, and by 1958 or '59, landed his first civilian radio gig at WKRG/Mobile, Alabama.

As he climbed another rung up the DJ ladder in the early 1960s, Lee met Terrell—known as the affable Mitch Michael—at WOKY in Milwaukee.

Both sporting the chic crewcuts of the day, they also shared a growing passion for radio. With Lee following Terrell's afternoon drive-time shift, their friendship came natural.

"At WOKY," said Lee's son, David, "he was learning as he was going along, working every possible shift he could, trying to perfect his on-air performance."

[*Image:* By June 2, 1962, WOKY's popular DJs included not only Terrell and Lee (two at bottom), but soon to be influential (*BFYP*) DJ, Jim Stagg (top/left), and veteran Sam Hale (top/right); along with Bob White and Don Phillips (middle). *BFYP* Collection.]

Surf Music and Bubble Gum Pop were on a collision course with a strong new beat aimed to turn their world upside down, with a shake, rattle and roll.

Terrell prepared Lee as a well-rounded DJ who would later excel at WIND in Chicago and WTRY/Albany, New York, where he would spend his most famous—and infamous—years.

No one however, can be prepared for the trappings of fame and the rigors of DJ fandom—especially in that heady era.

As Lee learned the ropes, Dick Biondi at WLS/Chicago, warmed up his turntable with an unknown group of "moptops" who surreptitiously landed at the bottom of the "Silver Dollar Survey" on March 8, 1963. It was an inauspicious beginning for the band with the buggy name—albeit misspelled by WLS.

"Please Please Me" by the "Beattles" [sic] didn't appear to please many. Although it crept up to number thirty-five the following week, it dropped off the chart and didn't even make a showing elsewhere in the country.

[*Image:* Courtesy of radio survey eBay buyer/seller extraordinaire, Jack Levin, who graciously sent copies of his 1963 originals, for March 3rd AND 15th, which is *autographed* by Dick Biondi. My brown eyes turned an envy-emerald green.]

The Beatles were on the move, but it wasn't quite time to storm the shores of America—timing is everything, and Lee was not yet in place.

Leaving WOKY, Lee made his way down to Chicago and worked production for powerhouse, WIND. More reporter than DJ, he excelled, but it was a personal strain. They parted ways and soon, he and Terrell met up again. This time, Terrell invited his friend to WTRY.

Lee's WIND experience helped at the popular New York station, soon moving again into the Program Director position. It was November 1963 when Brian Epstein begged him to listen to a new record by The Beatles. Wildly popular in the UK, here, they were still a tiny blip on the radio radar.

Being a DJ and PD at that time, required a musical sixth sense; Lee, said son, David, "... knew they [The Beatles] had something special. He immediately added them to the playlist."

Epstein made the rounds to every radio station that let him in the door, so it's a toss-up as to which "one" was the first to create chaos with "I Want to Hold Your Hand." Lee and WTRY were certainly in contention, but WMCA and WABC (both New York) could have the earliest radio surveys to show for it.

By end of December, The Beatles gained ground, and well, you know what happened in February 1964—popular variety show host, Ed Sullivan, properly introduced us. We succumbed to the charming Fab Four who lead the British Invasion. The London lads have since been an integral part of our musical lives.

Those DJs who gave Epstein's boys a break were granted unprecedented access to The Beatles and Lee took great advantage of his big break.

[*Image:* One of many Lee Gray photos with The Beatles; WTRY rode the popular lads' rising star to top ratings. July 23, 1965; *BFYP* Collection.]

Lee and Albany a hit with The Beatles

1964, '65 and '66 were Lee's heydays at WTRY, as he traveled with The Beatles; and like the handful of his cohorts at various stations, he shared his experiences with eager fans. "You can't imagine what this HUGE Beatles connection did for this little Albany station," said David.

It was radio magic for the whole country, never duplicated. We didn't have Twitter, Facebook, Snapchat, et al, to share notes and up-close experiences, real or imagined. We just had our favorite radio stations and celeb DJs.

"Lee would try to bring the listeners as close to The Beatles as he possibly could," said David. This meant back stage with fellow WTRY DJ, Rick Snyder, in Atlantic City; and spearheading the incredible contest that shuttled two hundred-plus crazed Beatles fans to Shea Stadium's concert on August 15, 1965.

Earlier in the year, one lucky WTRY fan won a dream-come-true trip to London with Lee, to "Meet the Beatles." Teen Beatles fanatic, Jill Kostyniak (Bishop) and her father, accompanied Lee on the flight and David recounted her backstage experience.

[*Image:* Jill even got a WTRY Big Sound Survey cover, July 16, 1965. *BFYP* Collection.]

"When she walked into their dressing room, the first person she wanted to meet was Paul. Seated on the couch just inside the door were Ringo, George and John—she walked right by them. Ringo said, 'She didn't even want to shake me hand. I'll shake me own hand.' Later, she lamented, 'Omigosh, I snubbed Ringo Starr.'"

Always thinking like a PD, after The Beatles left their hotel room, Lee scurried around picking up towels, ashtrays, and other room items to promote on his show. An appearance on *American Bandstand* bestowed the scavenged memorabilia on lucky fans, promoting "the actual ashtray they put their cigarettes out in." David chuckled as he talked, "People went crazy over them."

Lee and The Beatles were WTRY's darlings through 1966. He quickly earned "Beatle Buddy" status which elevated his career for features in teen magazines and more American Bandstand visits. He was on a high.

[*Image:* Courtesy of David; Lee and Dick Clark laugh it up on *American Bandstand*; c. 1965.]

David still receives emails and calls from Lee's fans who say, "'When I would get off school, I'd have my little transistor radio, going down to the record shop, and I'm listening to WTRY.' It's amazing the memories people have."

But life's "nothing is forever" adage applied by 1967 when Lee shuffled radio stations again, skirting the era's perilous edge of Sex, Drugs, and Rock & Roll.

Checking in at Cleveland's WHK was a short-lived break from the chaos for Lee. With familiar urging from Terrell Metheny, now WMCA's program director, he headed back to New York for a while.

As David said though, "He liked being a big fish in a small pond," The *Psychedelic Seventies* soon beckoned and beguiled Lee at WKLO/Louisville, where he met David's mother, Mary.

Lee's story picks up again in those heady Seventies—leather fringe, bell bottoms, and Peace signs—here we come!

Today: David spent precious few years with his dad. Lee's earlier lifestyle took its toll; three months after a successful 1995 heart operation, he suffered a fatal heart attack. Rock & Roll Heaven opened its gates for Lee on March 8, 1996, one week shy of his sixtieth birthday.

Waxin' the '60s: The Beatles led the pack of the British Invasion, soon followed by The Dave Clark Five, The Kinks, and Rock's bad boys, The Rolling Stones (all in 1964).

More boy bands and other talented musicians with charming accents skipped across the pond throughout the '60s. We girls in the US were beyond smitten … try euphoric. [*Image:* From screaming to silently wishin' and hopin' when The Beatles arrived in San Francisco, August 18, 1964.]

[*Image:* The Beatles were inescapable by the mid-'60s. Even Britain's royalty attended the world premiere of *Help!* at the London Pavilion, July 29, 1965. *BFYP* Collection (reproduction magnet).]

We're mixin' it up here at BFYP, 84.8-FM on your radio dial! There's a bright summer moon on the rise ... can you see it in her eyes?

Music lover for the midnight soul sings to **Strangers in the Night** *... ♪*

Alison Steele
aka The Nitebyrd; Ceil Loman
1937 ~ 1995
Best known at WNEW-FM/New York
(Interview with sister, Joyce Loman)

Night owl? Nightjar? No ... Alison was a refreshing song of the nightingale in a flock of nighthawks.

So thought her mostly male legion of listeners on the midnight shift, and restless, chronic insomniacs. Known predominantly for her role in all-night radio shows, Alison played her part to the hilt.

Only a handful of brave and assertive women graced the radio airwaves in the mid-Sixties. Forward-thinking New York station, WNEW-FM, made a statement in 1966 with a lineup of pioneering *all-women* Rock & Roll Radio DJs.

Alison Steele, Rita Sands, Ann Clements, Nell Bassett, Arlene Kieta, Pam McKissick, and Margaret Draper, made Rock radio history. (Though it was done on Jazz station WSDM/Chicago a few years earlier.) Only Alison, Rita, and Nell had any broadcast experience! Talk about gutsy gals.

During their teen years, Alison and sister, Joyce, followed their musical favorites like millions of ardent fans. "It was a ritual *every* Saturday to listen to the Top 40," said Joyce.

Alison also listened to and learned from her radio idols, Martin Block (creator of the *Make Believe Ballroom* show), and well-known BFYP New York DJ, Cousin Brucie.

The Brooklyn native targeted entertainment as her career from her first taste of New York television, at fourteen. The glamorous industry was exciting and mysterious to the impressionable teen, drawing Alison to its bright lights like a moth to a flame.

Alison, nee Ceil Loman, picked up the perfect kid job to get your foot in the entertainment door—running errands for WCBS. Her interest in entertainment at that time was purely teenage excitement.

Shuffling between TV and radio studios during the early to mid-Fifties, the pretty teen attracted the attention of Ted Steele, an experienced disc jockey at WCBS-FM.

Her sister, Joyce, recalls Alison's wistful adoration. Marrying the much older Steele seemed an ideal life to Alison.

Steele programmed his own music list and Alison assisted, learning the radio biz as they mixed and matched personal and professional lives. Eventually marrying, the twenty-year age span ultimately took its toll, and they divorced.

Alison became a single mom to daughter, Heather, when it was less accepted by society, and thrived through it.

Reveling in her independence, by the time WNEW-FM saw her potential, she had spent several years in the industry. Testing the all-girl format at the station didn't last long though, and they flipped to all guys again in October of 1967—with the exception of Alison.

"She was the only girl they wanted to keep," said Joyce. A new Progressive Rock format soon made WNEW-FM an influential station that was emulated across the industry.

After establishing the day shift with Bill "Rosko" Mercer, Jonathan Schwartz, and Scott Muni, Alison "was offered the overnight shift," said Joyce, "obviously, because none of the guys wanted it."

The night air was good for Alison as she spread her late-night wings and flew into the hearts of her listeners. On January 1, 1968, the Nitebyrd took flight.

Ah—you noticed the contrary spelling? Even Wiki refers to Alison with two "L's" and her personality name as the "Nightbird." Right off the top of our interview, Joyce corrected my spellings—and that of practically every source I referenced. "*Alison* spelled it 'Nitebyrd,'" said Joyce, "and her production company was Nitebyrd." So there you have it. All other citations are incorrect and I shall do my part for historical accuracy.

More hysterical than historical, when you work the midnight shift in any industry, you often find the world can be a little wacky and weird. Eternally spooky, the midnight hour can be especially fun when paired with the personalities of Halloween.

As the progressive Rock format invaded WNEW-FM, a peculiar fella preceded Alison's show, spreading his unique, skewered view of the world in the 10:00 p.m. to 2:00 a.m. shift.

Before John Zacherle's WNEW stint, you may remember his rise to freaky fame as a TV horror movie host in Philadelphia and New York City. His penchant for the macabre suitably rooted him in the horror and Halloween niche—especially after Dick Clark tagged him with "The Cool Ghoul" nickname in the late 1950s.

At WNEW, if John spooked his listeners and ruffled their feathers, Alison alleviated their fears and soothed their souls, 'til dawn. He was the perfect lead-in for her, and they became fast friends.

Too attractive to remain behind a radio microphone, Alison was back and forth between radio, television, and live shows throughout the late 1960s. Her fame, however, was in the sultry sound of her voice in the wee hours of the morning on WNEW-FM.

From the opening notes of her show, as she recited poetry in a voice that melted over your ears, backed by the soft strains of Andean flute music, you knew you were listening to the avant-garde sounds of FM radio—and the Nitebyrd. Men wanted her love, and women wanted to be her.

"The flutter of wings, the shadow across the moon, the sounds of the night, as the Nitebyrd spreads her wings and soars above the earth, into another level of comprehension, where we exist only to feel. Come ... fly with me, Alison Steele, the Nitebyrd, at WNEW-FM, until dawn."

Alison's show wasn't all mind-bending music. While she had your attention, she asked serious questions. After the last strains of "Mistaken Identity," (Janis Ian 1968) she oozed out a heady observation. "That's really one of the problems we all have today—to know who we are. Who are you? Do you know who you are and where you're at? It's a big order."

Today: Alison's accolades include the first woman to be awarded *Billboard Magazine's* FM Personality of the Year (1976). Sadly, the lovely Nitebyrd was silenced by cancer much too soon, and soared heavenward in 1995. Alison left an inspiring legacy for women in broadcasting. We'll soar with Alison again as she charms New York's night owls in the *Psychedelic Seventies.*

♪ 📻 ♪

Waxin' the '60s: By the mid to late 1960s, BFYP DJ Kent Burkhart parlayed his radio knowledge and experience into station management and ownership.

Kent knew that hiring the perfect mix of disc jockeys contributed mightily to a station's popularity. But experience told him it wasn't all about the DJs. He also had an ear for listeners' fave stations on the dial, and what songs hit the music charts' high numbers.

This vital, largely cryptic combination of behind-the-scenes data, drove ratings, and station owners forever chased the Golden Ring of ratings.

Think of Claude E. Hooper (and original partner, Montgomery Clark) as the grandfather of Facebook ratings. Matching George Gallup's actions (in early

Gallup Polls), their radio rating system followed the industry's ups and downs. Yes, we "private" citizens have been monitored for many, many decades.

Radio stations rose and fell based on monthly Hooper Ratings throughout the Golden Age of Radio. (Our current form of reference is Nielsen Corporation).

"As a young DJ," said Kent, "you work with a lot of joy and passion, but also with a lot of fear—Hooper Rating fear—if you don't do well in thirty days, you're gone." (And now, ratings of all kinds rule our lives.)

So much of our business and self-worth in this ratings-obsessed society is based on fear of losing our numbers leverage—from popularity to performance, Twitter to credit—we're just a load of numbers.

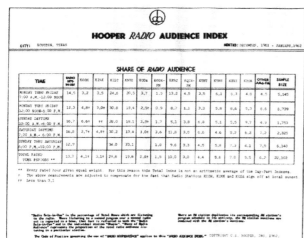

[*Image:* Sample Hooper ratings sheet, Houston, Texas, Dec. '61 – Jan. '62.]

"Not only DJs," continued Kent, "but "Program Directors lived and died by those ratings." They had to—their jobs depended on them.

DJ popularity was (and is, for those few terrestrial stations left, with "live" DJs) a master key in the ratings, so Kent's strategy for his jocks was to advocate "a tight format—don't talk more than a minute at a time, don't talk a lot, let the music be your friend." And Rock On …

Let's switch to the other side of the microphone and see how ratings took a legal turn for one band. Top 40 radio surveys were more than just a list. For bands, their place on the chart could make or break a record. Get on the bad side of a disc jockey or program director, and you could be back playing honky-tonks real quick.

Not getting radio play was bad news …

Breaking news! Call "*Western Union*"!

[*Image:* WCFL/Chicago was hundreds of miles and a whole community culture away from The Five Americans' hometown of Oklahoma City, but Chicagoans loved these guys and pushed "Western Union" to #7, March 30, 1967. Airheads Radio Survey Archive, Las-Solanas.com/arsa/surveys.php, contributed by Gary Pfeifer.]

We're livin' 'it up 'round the dial at BFYP, 84.8-FM. Rockin' Rochelle's in the know with musicians on the go ... go ... going up!

Some would say *I See the Light* ♪ but is it really *Evol Not Love?* ♪

Mike Rabon (Founder) & The Five Americans!
Best known for "Western Union"

As we move into the mid Sixties, British boy bands are everywhere. But Mike Rabon and The Five Americans—John Durrill (keyboardist), Norman Ezell (guitar/harmonica), Jim Grant (bassist), and Jimmy Wright (drummer)—set out to prove the radio dial still had room for some good ol' U.S. of A. boys.

Hailing from Durant, Oklahoma, their budding 1962 incarnation as the Mutineers proved locally fun for a few years, but financially unfruitful. In 1965 on Mike's suggestion, they packed up their instruments and trekked down to Dallas to scare up enough bucks for college tuition.

Did you frequent the Dallas dive, in '65 called Pirate's Nook? You were part of the Mutineer's history-in-the-making early success! There, they caught the attention of local label, Abnak Records. The label's president, John Abdnor, liked their style; with his tutelage and resources he encouraged them to write original songs.

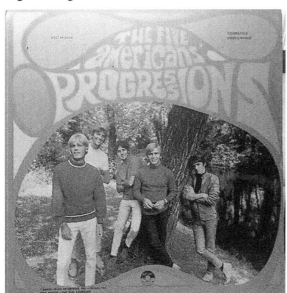

Chatting about radio's part in the popularity and ultimate success of bands at that time, Mike said, "I think the disc jockeys in the Sixties were, um, maybe they were prima donnas. But then so were we. It was a symbiotic kind of relationship [between artists and DJs].

[*Image:* Riding high in 1967 with their album, *Progressions.* BFYP Collection.]

Their lucky break came in a classic opportunity of "who you know, not what you know." The boys scored an appointment with Ken Dowe at KLIF/Dallas. His natural ear for hit songs had caught the attention of station owner and radio pioneer, Gordon McClendon who quickly promoted Ken from DJ to music director.

The Americans played four songs for Ken, which Mike described as "pure garage rock, as rough as rough gets." He recalls Ken's reaction as they nervously played their songs.

"He listened intently but quietly to three of the songs. When we got to the fourth one, he said, 'This song is a hit record.' Ken was able to see past the unprofessional vocals and immature instrumentation and predict 'I See the Light' would be a hit. Ken Dowe at KLIF in Dallas picked our first hit record."

Mike still shakes his head at Ken's prowess with picking songs. "He really liked us and wanted us to have a hit. I thought the song was a throw-away … how he was able to see the potential in that song is beyond me."

Marveling at the mastery, said Mike, "I watched Ken go through the records one day—he got about twenty-five to thirty records per day. He would play the first fifteen seconds of each one and if it didn't have his attention by then, that 45 [rpm record] sailed into the trash can."

Fortunately for The Five Americans, "I See the Light" rose to #18 on Billboard's 1965 chart, thanks to a radio DJ. So Mike likes to remind others that "All artists should be thankful to the DJs." Certainly all 1960s artists—basically the last great decade that DJs actually had a significant say in the music played on their shows.

"We were into attention-getting sounds," said Mike. "So that's why you hear the *dit*-di-*dit*-di-*dit* at the beginning of 'I See the Light' as a different organ sound. We had to have an 'AG' ["attention getter"] to stand out—at least on the first couple of tunes that we wrote." It worked!

If you're looking for their biggest hit, "Western Union," it's a-comin'. But Mike first recalls Memory Lane's radio landscape of the day, and the making of their earlier pop hit, "Evol Not Love."

Back before security guards and locked doors …

"I remember just bein' able to walk into a radio station like WKY in Oklahoma City or WLS in Chicago, see the secretary, and she'd say, 'Yeah, go on back.' I'd see bands sitting in the [radio station's] hallway, playin' just trying to get some attention."

Mike recalls the mighty influence of disc jockeys, "A DJ could make or break your record in a particular market. If you didn't break out in Dallas with Ken Dowe, that was the whole Southwest market, right there. If it didn't break out on KLIF then probably your record would not make it to the Top Forty."

Jimmy Rabbitt was one of Mike and the Americans' favorite KLIF DJs. "He was the first to introduce The Beatles to Dallas," said Mike. An honored career disc jockey, Texas Radio Hall of Famer, Jimmy, is still spinning the platters (so to speak) at KOCI/Newport Beach, California. Rock on!

It wasn't just disc jockeys who helped artists' records along the road to success. Mike points out that even before MTV there were "VJs" (Video Jocks). "In a way, there were plenty of VJs back then, because you had lots of dance shows on. You know, spawned from Dick Clark, which would be the top of the heap, and then you had all these little satellite shows.

"Every place we went—Cleveland, Chicago, Los Angeles—we would do a local TV dance program. And those guys could make or break your record, as well."

And now we come to "Evol Not Love." Mike remembers its rise on the radio with mixed feelings. Since they'd given KLIF the first opportunity to play "I See the Light," they tried to spread the love around Dallas, and their manager gave first dibs on "Evol" to KBOX. "We made such an innocent faux pas," said Mike.

"We were just trying to keep everyone happy. You could make enemies if some sorta protocol wasn't followed, as far as the disc jockeys were concerned," Mike soon learned the Dallas protocol.

"It was *so* important in those days that a particular disc jockey was the *first* one to play the record." He understood it was their job security to have that clout in a market, but still …

Mike insists they didn't withhold "Evol" from KLIF; they might even have received it the next day. It's just that they physically visited KBOX and *gave* it to them. When it comes to competition, first is *first*. KLIF was mad.

What happens when a radio station is snubbed (real or perceived)? "They refused to play 'Evol Not Love,'" said Mike.

[*Image:* Chicago fans found it though, and sent "Evol" all the way to #9, week of May 26, 1966. *BFYP* Collection.]

How did The Five Americans' manager take the news that they didn't even appear on the KLIF chart, let alone acknowledge its top seller status? John Abdnor, the self-made millionaire of Abnak Records, put his money where it counted. "He did the unthinkable," Mike said. "He *sued* KLIF, one of the largest megawatt stations in Texas."

What the astute manager realized was KLIF claimed on their weekly Top 40 Survey that their ratings were "Based on record sales in the metro area."

Really? Their manager challenged KLIF with a check of all the Dallas record stores, learning that "Evol" was THE number one seller in town in mid-1966 (thanks to KBOX).

Although a record may have made it to the top 40 in a market, it was most important that it broke into the top 20 for true success. That couldn't happen without major play on *all* area stations. KLIF's refusal to play "Evol" stunted its growth on the charts.

To be or not to be ... a hit song.

KLIF claimed that "Evol" wasn't good enough to become a hit, making the case a moot point, as far as they were concerned.

"So it actually went to trial," said Mike. "Eventually the case came down to whether or not 'Evol Not Love' could be a hit or not, in the national market. Since it was based on opinion and very subjective, the judge ordered that the record be played to a 'computer' in California to get an independent opinion."

And you didn't even know that computers made a difference in the world as early as 1966, did you? Well, fine. *I* didn't, anyway. I was only interested in classical dance and boys at the time. What did I know about computers?

Fortunately for The Five Americans, a Dallas judge was innovative and as Mike tells it, "The computer was a huge mainframe somewhere in Los Angeles. Our record was played in court over a telephone line to the computer in L.A. and the results gave it a 60% for, and 40% against, 'Evol' becoming a nationwide hit record."

On final determination, KLIF was ordered to change the wording on their Top 40 Survey regarding how they determined the rating. "No money changed hands," said Mike. "Abdnor didn't ask for an award. It was just a spiteful little thing." Was that it and everything was cool again with KLIF?

Afraid not. "They were livid," Mike said. "They never played one of our songs again." And he lamented, "That was sad because 'Evol Not Love' only went to the Top 40 instead of the Top 20, as it should have. Talk about cutting off your nose to spite your face!"

Obviously that didn't stop The Five Americans from achieving top 20 status with future songs, and by April, 1967, they were charting at #7 on WCOL/Columbus, Ohio, with "Western Union."

"Dallas in the Sixties was <u>wild</u>."

Mike laughed in gleeful reverie as he spoke about the decade unabashedly famous for over-indulgences. Celebrities were even more susceptible to all the peer-pressure goodies than the rest of us.

THE BIG 610 BARBER PREPARES HOWARD CLARK FOR A KFRC JET SET TRIP TO PARIS AND LONDON

For them, it was their job to entertain, look cool, and most of all, have fun—or at least, appear to. Some succeeded, content with living in the moment. Others had dreams ...

[*Image:* KFRC/San Francisco rightly declared "Western Union" hitbound on their Big 30 survey, March 1, 1967. *BFYP* Collection.]

Relatively innocent for a little while longer, The Five Americans had put the 1965 college semester on hold as their tunes gained traction on the airwaves.

With "Western Union" they began riding the wild wave. Success proved heady, provocative, and addictive.

"This may sound self-serving," Mike said in his delightful Oklahoma drawl, "but I had a dream to have a hit record. But I think the band just wanted to play, get the girls, and get attention. 'Cause we were twenty years old, ya know." Go ahead ... close your eyes ... remember your life at twenty. Fun, scary, crazy—all three?

With a couple of hits under their belts, The Five Americans took the first step toward a rabbit hole of fun and frolic.

Do you want to know what life was *really* like for popular bands in the Sixties? Yes, of course ... Sex, Drugs, and Rock & Roll ... but with the transparency of the Internet, we've learned there is often a price to pay for all that fame and gilded fortune.

For a true grit peek behind the scenes on stage, Mike's book, *High Strung*, tells it like it was. While an experience he treasures, it wasn't all glitz and glamour. In fact, at times, it was down-right frightening.

"The shower spray mincing my head and shoulders had no immediate effect so I reasoned the only option left was an attempt at complete relaxation. I began to force myself into a sort of amateur state of Zen, staring at the too small letters on the shampoo bottles, letting my eyes drift out of focus, allowing my mind to float. It wasn't hard to do on a full tilt high like this one."

High Strung is a powerful and poignant recollection of how fame affected the youthful musicians of the day—if we believe the news, today is no different.

A niche or a trap?

Was it the spicy trappings of celebrity that brought about The Five Americans' end of the Rock & Roll road? Perhaps partly, but business and the inability to grow with the music they loved, stopped them short of their potential.

Mike and I explored the topic a tad more. I mentioned that it seemed, except for The Beatles, music artists were forced, either by their label or by fan demand, into the niche in which they first began.

"That's so true. The radio stations were clamoring for more communication records like 'Western Union' and some of the high-pitched stuff that we did. It really kinda boxed us in a corner."

Only The Beatles appeared to break that mold by taking control of their talent and producing what they wanted us to hear.

Mike mused, "It used to be said that if the record's good enough, it's gonna be a hit. It doesn't matter who gets to hear it or who doesn't. Somebody somewhere will hear it and it will be a hit—it's so good, it will make its way up. But that's not true anymore. You could have the best record ever written, and it will never be a hit 'cause you can't get it to anybody without going through SO many channels. That has squeezed out a lot of artists."

[*Image:* "Sound of Love" made it to WCFL's Top 20 in June 1967, but none of their later tunes topped "Western Union's" popularity. *BFYP* Collection.]

And does he still receive royalties for their biggies? "I'm just very grateful for the OLDIES stations," said Mike. "In around 1980 I got about $100 every three months for my broadcast royalties. That's for "Western Union," and for *all* the tunes that I wrote. With the proliferation of the Oldies stations, my check now is no comparison. Sometimes, it's $1500-$1600 every quarter."

Many radio DJs of yesteryear are bringing back the historic Rock & Roll tunes on independent Internet radio stations. "I appreciate the DJs," says Mike. "'Western Union' hit the three million play mark in radio airplay—that's the same as playing a 45 [rpm] record back-to-back for ten years straight."

Today: The group splintered in 1969; it took less than five years for Mike Rabon and The Five Americans to create a legacy that will endure as long as Rock and Roll music is played. Where are they now?

Mike Rabon (founder, songwriter, guitarist): Continuing a successful touring career Mike released two well-received albums and briefly joined Texas pop group, Gladstone. But transforming his experiences into lessons learned, he returned to college for a master's degree in school administration and retired as a principal from the Oklahoma school systems. Mike married along the way and now enjoys social networking and writing novels.

John Durrill (keyboardist): John found songwriting lucrative as well, creating "Dark Lady" for Cher and "Misery and Gin" for Merle Haggard. After touring with The Ventures for a while, he relocated and retired in Los Angeles.

Jim Grant (bass guitar, died November 29, 2004): Polishing his considerable graphics skills, Jim ultimately became a founding partner in Dallas Halcyon Associates PR and graphics company; a spin-off of Hill & Knowlton.

Norman Ezell (guitar and harmonica, died May 8, 2010): Returning to school after their breakup, Norman found his calling as a teacher and minister in Northern California.

Jimmy Wright (drummer, died January 30, 2012): Jim migrated to Ohio and honed his camera skills to become a videographer for Breakthrough Ministries.

Waxin' the '60s: Musicians weren't the only ones crossing the pond. [*Image:* 1967 Berkeley hippie newsrag, *Big Beat World Countdown Newspaper.* BFYP Collection.] WFUN/Miami lauded the arrival of new DJ, Jerry Smithwick (top/left), straight from Radio England.

Where there's a will, there's a way. Some Rockin' music wasn't allowed on Britain's staid MOR stations. In 1966 Swinging Radio England, a rebel "pirate" radio ship, anchored four-and-a-half miles off the coast in the North Sea.

Rockin' Rochelle on your groovin' airwaves, kiddies! We're rollin' through our day with simpatico sounds of love and life at BFYP-FM!

Let's play follow-the-leader. Put your ear to the radio and we'll be "**Happy Together**" ♪ ... a family tradition begins.*

Bill Gardner* >Part 2
Best known at KCBQ/San Diego
and WIBG/Philadelphia
*First of three DJ brothers

"The first station I worked for was a *really* interesting station," said Bill. "It was the very, very, very, FIRST Rock & Roll station on FM."

For you young'uns—there was a time, still within memory, when "frequency modulation" broadcasting didn't exist.

Imagine that?! A radio dial full of AM-only stations (amplitude modulation)—no FM, no MP3s and no Sirius radio.

The neophyte frequency first hosted the robust sounds of Classical music. Rock & Roll took a while to jump on the high-fidelity bandwagon. Bill was there in the beginning.

Oh, you're wondering what station we're talking about? Was it in New York? Nashville? Cleveland? Nope. KLZ, an iconic little station in Denver, Colorado, holds the distinction, says Bill. It also lays claim to Colorado's first radio station and still broadcasts in talk radio format. [*Image:* Courtesy of Bill, reveling in his first gig at KLZ/Denver; c. 1965.]

♪ ♫ ♪ ♫ ♪ ♫ ♪

Bill wrote a fiftieth anniversary article for KLZ that published in 5280, Denver's city magazine, *August 2015. Way to go, Bill!*

♪ ♫ ♪ ♫ ♪ ♫ ♪

KLZ futilely tried to compete with Rock & Roll dynamo, KIMN, and needed an angle to capture some of their Hooper ratings. Young Bill made it work!

"At first, none of the record companies would send us their promotional 45s," recalls Bill in his *5280* article, "so we bought the top 25 or so hits. My record collection made up most of the rest of our library."

The little station that could, opened their horizons and flipped the FM switch at four o'clock in the afternoon, August 4, 1965.

[*Image:* Courtesy of Bill, whose happy smile graced a KLZ "Bill"board ad, sandwiched between cars and coffee; c. 1965.]

Bill settled The Beach Boys' new Rock & Roll song, "California Girls," onto the turntable—its catchy opening keyboard intro floated out into the mile-high city's clean, crisp air.

"We became the first full time Rock & Roll station on FM," said Bill. "After us, they tried it in Kansas City, and then New York got one."

It didn't take long for the rest of the industry to catch on to FM's superior sound. KLZ owner, Time-Life Broadcasting, even then, was on the cutting edge of technology; although nearly a decade would pass as we tuned into AM, before FM finally surpassed it on the radio dial.

[*Image:* DJs J. Cloney, Bill (middle), Max Floyd, at KLZ blowin' your mind with FM and that crazy psychedelic background; photo courtesy of Bill.]

FM finally pulled the celebs in ...

"Not a lot of people (celebrities) wanted to come to a little FM station," said Bill, when we talked about his notable interviews. "Occasionally I would get lucky ..."

Though he doesn't recall specific dialogue, Bill remembers a particularly interesting interview with Dean Torrence of the popular Jan & Dean duo. (Think "Surf City" and the somewhat prophetic "Dead Man's Curve.")

"Jan had just gotten into a car wreck (April 12, 1966), so I interviewed just Dean. He said to me at the time that it was one of the most fun interviews he's done. I'd ask him about a song, and he'd say we wrote that because of so-and-so, then we'd roll the song, and come back and talk, and do it again.

We didn't have a lot of commercials so the interview was probably at least an hour long. It's on two of those great big ten-inch reels, Ampex recording tape." And he still has it.

With a couple of years' on-air time under his belt, Bill ultimately headed back home to pick up the mic at his childhood icon, Philly's WIBG. "I worked at WIBG three different times," Bill tells us. "It was owned by three different companies and I think I'm the only one who worked for all three of them!"

He cut his DJ eye teeth on the top-tier station. "At that time [late 1960s]," Bill recalled, "it was owned by Storer Broadcasting and carried a lot of legendary disc jockeys like Joe Niagra and Hy Lit."

But radio jobs are necessarily transient and Bill soon moved down the road to other memorable stations. He scampered around the radio dial in the late '60s, honing his DJ personality. In 1968 he landed at WFIL/Philly for a short stint, and watched the magic of soon-to-be bi-coastal DJ, Dr. Don Rose. Before long, Bill succumbed to wanderlust, trekking over to WHB/Kansas City, Missouri.

For a Philly boy, though, there was nothing like the big city, so the end of 1969 found him again pointed East at Philadelphia's WMMR. Not WIBG, but ...

Entering the *Psychedelic Seventies*, Bill's brothers, Al and Andre, prepare to follow in Bill's DJ footsteps. But they'll need to soar high as Bill takes to the skies with his personal pilot's license. That makes skipping around the country to the best Rock stations easier!

Bill truly makes his mark on the airwaves in the early 1970s when he flies into San Diego. We also hear about KING/Seattle, KDWB/Twin Cities, Minnesota, a memorable lengthy stay at KVIL-FM/Dallas, Texas, and back again to WIBG!

Today: By 1974 when Bill received the *Billboard* Major Market Air Personality of the Year award, he had endeared himself to many fans across the country. Retirement still not an option for the bubbly Bill, he flies to visit family and friends; and as Captain for Grand Canyon Airlines (Las Vegas), enjoys ferrying tourists throughout the scenic Southwest.

We last met for an afternoon of music and memories, at the KCBQ/San Diego 2010 monument dedication. Dozens of broadcast professionals, fans, and friends, gathered for the nostalgic celebration.

Bill and his wife, Michaeletta ("... or as I call her, Mike," says Bill), celebrated their 37th anniversary with a multi-stop flying vacation and a surprise visit from brother, Al. In September 2016, Bill's big smile with "Mike," on board the Queen Mary in Long Beach, California, tells it all! (*Image:* Snagged from Bill's website—BillGardnerOnTheRadio.com—thanks Bill!)

Waxin' the '60s:

Remember When ...

KCBQ/San Diego, December 25, 1965 ...

Christmas Day, with Jack Vincent, newsman Jeff Crane ends his report with, "'... and Merry Christmas, Jack.' [Jack replies] 'And a Merry Christmas to you, Scotty ... I mean ... Jeff.'" Hmmmm, perhaps the eggnogg was a-flowing!

[Reel Radio.com]

♪ ♫ ♪ ♫ ♪ ♫ ♪

WLS/Chicago, December 10, 1967 ...

Ron Riley is on the air and plugged into your radio, "Second biggest climber this week—for some reason—'Snoopy's Xmas.' Snoopy's record we play quite often on Clark Weber's show, as you know. They used to be good ol' buddies—Weber & Snoopy—they used to share a fire hydrant together up in north Evanston!"

[Reel Radio.com]

WLS YEAR END REVIEW
starting December 26th.

Ron Riley   Art Roberts   Jerry Kay
List of the top tunes on back of this survey.

♪

Are you Rockin' with BFYP 84.8-FM in sunny Cal-i-forn-I-A? We're doin' the boogaloo ... c'mon along!

For this platter-spinner, put your hands on your hips and let your backbone slip on your way to the *Land of 1000 Dances*! ♪

Billy Bass
Best known at WIXY/Cleveland, Ohio

Ah yes, growing up in late 1950s Cleveland gave you an edge over budding broadcasters elsewhere—you got to listen to the Moondog on your tinny transistor radio.

Billy reveled in his reverie, "You couldn't go to school [elementary] unless you knew what Alan Freed played yesterday! 'Did you hear the Moondog?' That's all we talked about at recess."

Listening to Billy's excited memories, I envisioned him in the center ring of young'uns on the playground, mimicking Alan's behind-the-mic patter and giving them a peek into his future as a DJ.

If you spent any time at all in Cleveland circa late 1960s and early '70s, no doubt you heard his childhood dreams come true on WIXY or WMMS—both graced with the progressive sounds of Billy Bass.

During this racially confused era (yes, our current era proves we haven't learned much), radio stations liked to maintain mystery about their disc jockeys behind the microphone. Without promotions and station prominence, we often didn't know which DJs were White— think Wolfman Jack—or Black, like Billy.

In my neck of the woods, we didn't care. We connected with them as comrades-in-music, friends, mentors, and six-degrees-of-separation to our hot celebrity musicians. What else mattered?

So in 1964-'65 it was an especially momentous event for F.W. Woolworth, the popular "5 & Dime" store, to include Billy in their management trainee program, which would prove to be his stepping stone to radio. "Even though I was only making $85 per week, I was a very happy guy. This was at a time when many Black people couldn't even sit at their counters."

Billy's stint at Woolworth's was a boon to his struggling young family. But the twenty-two-year-old was motivated and determined. "I went through their four-year program in three years," said Billy.

At their congratulatory event he was introduced as "the best Black assistant manager we've ever had." Billy said, "I looked around the room ... and I'm the ONLY black manager."

Discrimination persisted but Billy was even more persistent. One of his jobs at Woolworth's "and the reason I skated through the training," was to develop the record department.

Back in the day, department stores negotiated directly with the labels, and with a savvy department manager, often presented tunes and artists that were not yet playing on the radio. Independent of the radio, they often were as instrumental in breaking out an artist. Billy recalled ...

"I worked with a rackjobber and brought up the department's sales, which were under $500 per week, to an average $6,000 by the time I left." Nice job!

Underground sound flourished on FM

By 1967, a fortuitous offer from one of the rackjobbers provided an opportunity to work his magic in a music store. Capitalizing on the Summer of Love, "we were ready to serve that ex-Beatnik, pre-Hippie crowd," said Billy. They opened the Music Grotto across from a Cleveland university. "We stocked a lot of folk music, underground music, stuff not yet on the radio."

[*Image:* Billy c. 1968.]

About this time, if a station owner possessed both an AM and FM station in the same market, they were legally obligated to provide only original programming on the FM station.

Pat McCoy, program director for WHK-FM, which had an AM sister station, was "forced" to play "new" music—and said Billy, "I was the guy in town who knew that music."

McCoy offered him a job. Billy balked, because he had no DJ training, but saw it as an opportunity to make more money and have more fun.

It was 1968 and Billy developed a huge following for his alternative music lineup for the six-nine months, on his first DJ job. But the general manager didn't like the program and switched the station to a syndicated oldies format. (Definitely not the "Oldies" we have now!)

It was just the beginning for Billy in the hot Rock Cleveland market. "WIXY 1260," the #1 station in town, began to experiment with new music, and approached him with the all-night slot.

"I was scared to death," said Billy. "They had talent like Chuck Dunaway, Lou "the King" Kirby, Dick "Wilde Childe" Kemp, Bob Shannon, and Jack Armstrong. At WIXY you were the best of the best —and I didn't even know how to run a board! So, imagine WIXY in 1968 taking a chance on a Black DJ on a Top 40 radio station."

Station owner, Norman Wain urged him to join them. Though Billy continued to build his listener base, after several months he questioned Norman about the lack of station promotion for him. "He looked at me as if I'd asked the dumbest question in the world. 'Billy, it's because you're Black!'" he blurted out.

The nicknamed "cultural decade" was mired in counterculture by this time and social unrest was the norm. Wain continued, "Are you crazy? The audience doesn't *know* you're Black. If these people knew you were black, they'd kill you! I'm trying to protect you."

Billy thought the world of Norman, shrugged his shoulders, thinking, if he said it, it must be true ... but must it? Therein lies the problem with many preconceived philosophies. Many are so wrong—at least for some people.

The WIXY Supermen (jocks) basketball team played a celebrity game at Lakewood High School soon after their conversation. "Back in '68," said Billy, "Cleveland was racially divided. There were no Blacks or Jewish people living on the West Side [Lakewood] of the Cuyahoga River, which runs through the center of the city. To this day, many born on the East Side have never been to the West Side."

This of course, didn't stop Billy, a Supermen team player, from heading with the team for a game. "The announcer introduced the DJs," said Billy and ticked off the names, "'Lou King' Kirby, Wilde Childe—and after each one the crowd went 'Yeah!' and he introduced me—'Billy Bass'—and the crowd went, 'YEAAHHHH!' They went crazy! It shocked me, Norman, everybody."

His fans proved, music is the great equalizer.

With a bemused chuckle Billy recalled Norman's response, "'Guess we can show your picture.' The publicity with my picture went out ..."

Billy was silent for a long moment. He knew I was expecting a Happy Ending to this story. Aren't you?

Finally, he said quietly, "... that's when it started ... all the hate calls came in."

Despite those listeners he would never please (then why didn't they switch stations?) Billy continued to build his popularity at WIXY. Were you listening when they allowed him to break format on Sunday nights for an underground music show, "Billy Bass and Friends"?

He helped boost the play of Jimi Hendrix, Cream, and other progressive Rock artists. Nationwide Insurance Company, the owners of WNCR, caught wind of his format and popularity, wooing him away from WIXY.

Ah, but that's a story for another decade ... we'll tune in when the next decade rolls around, to Billy's *Psychedelic Seventies* platter-spinning antics as he coins the phrase, "Cleveland—the Rock & Roll capitol of the world!"

Today: Following a full broadcasting career, Billy was bored in retirement. "What do you do when you're 60, but you still feel like you're 21? I started a second career. Make that a third career." With a belated passion, Billy applied his musical timing to the split-second timing needed to document life as a wedding photographer. [*Image:* Courtesy of Billy. Sporty in 2016.]

Waxin' the '60s: What could be more fun and glamorous in the Swinging Sixties than being a disc jockey?

As we're learning, being a DJ wasn't all it was cracked up to be all of the time, but sometimes, well, spinning the vinyls and chatting with listeners was fun for a day, as KRLA/Los Angeles proves with the Rolling Stones' Brian Jones.

[*Image:* KRLA/Los Angeles BEAT March 10, 1965; on being a Disc Jockey, celeb news, and latest the "Tunedex" Top 30 survey. *BFYP* Collection.]

One guitar riff after another keeps us goin' at BFYP-FM. How's about you? What keeps you goin'? Memories ...

I remember it as if it were *Yester-Me Yester-You Yesterday ...* ♪

Ed Sciaky
1948 ~ 2004
Best known at WDAS & WMMR/Philadelphia
(Interview with wife, Judy Sciaky)

Getting silly in Philly, we let love do the talkin' and music do the walkin' down Memory Lane, with the love of this DJ's life.

Judy Sciaky (pronounced Shockee) cheered the other love of Ed's life—radio. Their common passion for music created an instant bond, and generally personifies radio listeners of the era.

"You thought you were missing something if you weren't listening to the radio," Judy mused. "It was your lifeline to the world. It's what was *happening*."

Indeed, happening was the word of the day for coming of age boomers in radio's golden age, 1960s and '70s. And where better to learn and live radio than in Pennsylvania, one of its cradle states?

Unlike many nomadic, cross-country disc jockeys, Ed spent his entire career growing a legion of lifelong fans and friends in Philadelphia, from WRTI to WMGK, with stops in between at popular stations like WDAS-FM and WMMR (twice), and more.

WRTI at Temple University gave Ed his microphone legs. An avid New York show fan, he hosted "The Bright Lights of Broadway" program. Gaining a following, he soon added the "Broadside" show, a Saturday night folk music program; here, he realized he had a knack for recognizing musical talent.

The Broadcast Pioneers of Philadelphia* site quotes their CEO, and Ed's lifelong friend, Gerry Wilkinson, about a "Broadside" show historical event. Gerry relates Ed's discovery of a special voice of the folk music era.

"A teenager and her mother came down from NYC on the train. Guitar in hand, the young woman sat at the college radio station mic and sang her first (of many) songs that evening, 'Society's Child.' The vocalist was a very young, Janis Ian." (*BroadcastPioneers.com/edsciaky.html)

[*Image:* Ed is just getting started in 1966 at WRTI-FM.]

Ed continued to hone his radio skills through the late 1960s, recording episodes of "The Golden Years of Radio" show at WRTI-FM to air on WXUR and WXUR-FM in Media (Pennsylvania).

His big major market station break came while Ed subbed in another DJ's time slot. He took a listener call from Harry Wolf, a buddy on campus. Wolf urged Ed to talk about current Philadelphia radio.

Discussing several popular stations, he came to WDAS-FM, which in his opinion, needed considerable help to compete with the others. Taking his comment to heart, Wolf phoned his friend, Hy Lit (yes *that* Hy Lit of pioneering radio fame), on-air at WDAS-FM.

Lit wanted to hear Ed's thoughts for himself, so he slapped a long record on the turntable and picked up the phone to call Ed (still taking listener calls on his show). Unbeknownst to Ed, Lit broadcast their conversation live, in essence giving Ed an on-air audition.

Lit's wife, Mim, an obvious fan of the show, called her husband, gushing, "He's really, really good!" By summer 1968 Ed spun the "Soul Sounds" of WDAS-FM.

The heart wants what the heart wants

Graduating in December 1968, Ed basically ignored his degree in math and followed his heart into radio. It also proved to be the path that led him straight to Judy.

"Ed was wearing his former station WRTI 'Broadside' jacket, selling Flyers tickets at the Spectrum arena. We were supposed to have tickets waiting, but they weren't. So I walked up to his window to see how to get tickets, and commented on his jacket."

Ed, on the phone (with buddy, Gerry Wilkinson), put his call on hold to talk with Judy. Nearly half an hour later, Judy had tickets for her whole family, Ed finally returned to Gerry on the phone, and love had blossomed.

Little did Judy know, loving Ed would embed her in many musical adventures. If not em*bed*, at least she would see a succession of tuneful cronies on the couch while they climbed the often fickle ladder of fame.

Long before we women giggled and swooned at the bad-boy image of Bruce Springsteen and his third album, *Born to Run*, Ed and Judy took in a Bruce concert shortly after he released his second effort, *The Wild, the Innocent & the E Street Shuffle* in the early '70s.

Yes, we're a little out of our decade, but it's too good to leave behind and it lays the foundation of Ed's Rockin' radio years to come.

"All I had to do was see him once," said Judy. "Ed was ready to leave after the first set. I said, '*Oh*, let's not.'"

With more personal contact than today's DJs could possibly have with music stars, radio of the era forged many friendships. Introduced through Ed's contacts, Bruce and Ed first met at The Main Point coffeehouse in Bryn Mawr. A lifelong friendship blossomed.

The Sciakys spent hours listening to and talking about music with various budding artists of the late 1960s and '70s—to the point that when skipping through town, the Sciaky sofa became a welcome site for traveling minstrels.

Bruce Springsteen slept on it.

Billy Joel sat on it.

Bonnie Raitt had fun on it.

"It was such an amazing time," Judy recalled. "The music [and radio] scene was such a visceral part of our lives. Not like now, when much of music is just background noise. We *lived* it. Sometimes we hit three concerts in a night!"

Judy reminisced about Ed's love affair with radio. "Ed loved the music and he loved his part in it—the connection to the people—and they loved him.

"We spent hours and hours listening to records. He knew everything about them. Music and radio was beyond a lifestyle—it was our life."

It didn't hurt that Ed's IQ was a little higher than most. "He had an unbelievable memory," said Judy. "He remembered everything—especially about the music—down to every minute detail. Even the matrix number of the record."

Ed's interest in the music is what endeared him to the artists who wrote and sang it. With Ed's help, several artists broadened their audiences in the late 1960s, including a struggling Joni Mitchell.

As Joni traveled the length of the Eastern Seaboard in one gig after another, she took a breather around New York and Philly. Says Judy, "I have an unbelievable recording of an interview with Ed and Joni in a coffee house in the 1960s."

Ed made around $42 a week when he and Judy married in 1969. Though WDAS-FM had bumped Ed's pay up as a wedding present, by 1970 his energetic style took him to work on WMMR, Philly's new and innovative, progressive Rock station.

Coming up, Ed gets comfy in his Rockin' radio home for much of the *Psychedelic Seventies*. Judy shares more celeb stories of whose lives Ed touched, like Jackson Browne, Manfred Mann, Barry Manilow, Annie Haslam of Renaissance, Billy Joel ... and others who sung, sat, and slept on the Sciaky's Magic Sofa ...

Today: A long time diabetic, Ed was on kidney dialysis and his right foot amputated, in 2002. After a wonderful weekend making the rounds of Broadway shows with Judy in 2004, his heart, so full of life, could take no more. Ed was posthumously inducted into the Broadcast Pioneers of Philadelphia Hall of Fame in 2005. [*Image:* Courtesy of Judy.]

Waxin' the '60s: As we tuned out—or with our radios, tuned in—and turned on with the new album music, Psychedelia began to edge into our lives. Most prominently in a futuristic shape that was the perfect companion to a dreamy high. British accountant, Edward Craven-Walker, obviously trying to clear his mind of numbers after work, gave us the soothing lava lamp.

American rights were snagged by Adolph Wertheimer and Hy Spector, turning the Lava Lite Lamp into an iconic product that spans the decades. Yes, I have a modern version—if only I'd known to keep my original. [*Images:* left / 1960s lava lamp; right / "It's Only Rock 'n' Roll" lava lamp, *BFYP* Collection.]

At BFYP-FM we can boogie woogie, twist and shout, and when we stop spinning we'll tell ya what it's all about!

All ya gotta ask is, *What's New Pussycat?* ♪

Best known at WLS/Chicago, Illinois

When we left Ron in the late 1950s (*BFYP* Book 1) he'd just scored his first big-boy dream job at WOKY/Milwaukee, as their all-night jock. Owned by legendary radio family, the Bartells, it segued from staid family programming into pop music in the 1960s and '70s.

Listening to a lively 1960 WOKY aircheck (ReelRadio.com), Ron's words rolled smoothly off his tongue seemingly without a thought to them, "We're havin' a WOKY swingin' fun time [ding, dong sound effect] at the twin chime! Here it is the first week of school—brings back ol' college memories. I was a big shot in the frat house. Yep, in fact, I was the head of it—'Frathead Riley' they used to call me!"

But Ron didn't have long to make his mark there. About a year into his gig, Uncle Sam called.

In an era of military pride, Ron was in the Reserves and tagged to go on active duty "They called it 'the Cold War,'" said Ron.

"WOKY rehired me when I returned two years later, but I was itching for more money in a larger market."

During the early '60s Ron did the DJ shuffle trying to find the footing that would stabilize home life for his new bride and a kiddo on the way. He spent a short three months at KXOK/St. Louis, but hoofed it back north to where he was most comfortable.

Still favoring WOKY, Ron became the vacation fill-in guy for both WOKY and WLS/Chicago. "I did afternoons at WOKY, slept a couple hours and did the all-night show in Chicago." Despite the hour-plus drive between cities, says Ron, "Best thing I ever did."

With great exposure from the two big stations and after a short stint at WHK/Cleveland, WLS PD Gene Taylor called Ron back "home" in 1963. Taylor said, "Hey, I just got rid of that Biondi [Dick of course]. There're only two other people we're considering."

"Once known as the 'Prairie Farmer' station since radio was invented, I think," said Ron, "its new owner, ABC, was turning it into an awesome 'flamethrower' AM Rocker on 890." Its nighttime reach spanned more than half the nation—yep, Ron was excited.

"I just died for three days," Ron said, recalling the agony of waiting. "This was long before cell phones, so a landline phone was never out of my sight."

He was so eager that to this day, Ron remembers the secretary's name who finally called him. "Marlene Branagan phoned and said Gene wants you here next Saturday." I hung up and cried! All that emotion—things had been so unstable for so long in my life. Greatest thing that ever happened to me."

Riding the wave of new Rock & Roll on WLS in May 1963, Ron became one of the station's popular "Swinging Seven" DJs. The ratings soared, and WLS music and personalities soared with them, solidifying the station's place in radio history. [*Image:* August 6, 1965 WLS survey. *BFYP* Collection.]

Of course, while Ron helped create a broadcast legacy in the U.S., four fab guys were gearing up in the U.K. to make world history.

Excitement! Excitement!

Ron recalls Friday, August 20, 1965 like it was yesterday. "It was the first Beatles concert at White Sox Park. Four or five of us from the station attended and it was the most unforgettable experience in my career. We were sitting right next to those guys on the stage, and you could hardly hear the music—it was magnificent!"

The DJs followed the Fab Four to their press conference, and Ron spoke with them, passing along the brief chat, to his fans. Finally, he had outgrown "Smiley Riley" and for his WLS fans, became forevermore, Ron "Ringo" Riley.

WLS owned Chicago's airwaves in the mid-Sixties and Ron rode the waves with it. He worked with other groups to help them gain exposure, including those

like "Chicago" which evolved from a local garage band.

A record heard on WLS meant other stations followed in their musical footsteps.

[*Image:* Ron with Chad & Jeremy, c. 1967, *WLS Personality Album*. *BFYP* Collection.]

Though The Beatles didn't need much help, Ron enjoyed breaking out other British bands, on his

Sunday show, "British Billboard—new songs from England." *Riding along on a carousel, will I catch up to you?* ♪

"I broke The Hollies," said Ron, "and was the first in the country to play "Bus Stop." [1966] Graham Nash and I still email now and then; as do Chad & Jeremy." The latter duo rode in on the early British wave with their May 1964 offering, "Yesterday's Gone."

In addition to his connection with the British Invasion, another stand-out memory of the Sixties for Ron were the vinyl disks he and Clark Weber recorded for the service men and women overseas.* "I still get emails from former listeners—guys who were in Vietnam during the war, asking for copies of those shows." (*ReelRadio.com/rr/index.html#cwrrwls)

Ron chuckled, recalling how the records were recorded. "We got there [at the station] at seven o'clock one morning, just the two of us, and ad-libbed a 'show.' We B.S.'d about stuff and played Rock, and called out to the servicemen we knew would be listening. 'Hey guys, here's a plug for you!' And we'd play a Budweiser commercial. It was kinda corny, but these guys really loved it."

Like many of the pioneering Rock Radio DJs, Ron loves getting close to the fans—especially at the record hops. Granted, they were lucrative and many DJs doubled their salary with those events, but Ron said, "By going out to the schools, we got to be 'real' to the kids. They really idolized us, and associated us with the groups they loved." He mimicked an eager, youthful fan, "Oh God, you saw *Paul*?! You *touched* John Lennon?!"

Ron and buddy DJ, Clark Weber, played up their faux on-air feud at the sock hops around Chicago, rolling out to Indiana, Wisconsin, and Michigan. With Weber a pilot, they were just a hop-skip-and-bumpy flight away.

Although, at one time, their animosity was real. Weber cranked out tunes as the morning guy on WRIT, and Ron rode the night skies at WOKY, vying for ratings. They'd patched up their differences by the time they found themselves working together at WLS; but of course, they couldn't resist continuing the feud on-air, for the sake of ratings.

The mid-Sixties were certainly magical and when Batman's waning fame was revived with the debut of a television series (January 1966), he became everyone's hero once again.

Radio stations across the country devised imaginative Batman-themed contests and shows.

So ... with Ron's WLS popularity at its peak as a Rock Radio superhero, it didn't take much urging for him to don a cape. In an instant he appeared as *Batman*!

[*Image:* Did you belong? Cool members received a pin (c. 1966) and a membership card. *BFYP* Collection.]

Ron took it to a higher level with "Ron Riley's Batman Club," complete with Ron dressed as Batman for fun events. As a member in 1966 Chicago, you were officially in the In Crowd.

But all good things must come to an end, or so the saying goes. "WLS got a new program director in 1968," Ron recalled. "He tightened things up a little and at the time, I think the [*Chicago*] *Tribune* wrote, 'at thirty years old' I was considered to be an aging teenager, probably not suitable to run a teenage show … so they let me go. It was a good long run."

For many pioneering DJs, the 1960s were the glory days of Rock Radio, and Ron is no exception. His fans still appreciate him—note to Ron seen on an Internet forum: "It's the music of my life and the time of my life. Thanks Ron!!!"

Stay tuned … we'll catch up with Ron again in the *Psychedelic Seventies* as he Rocks into WCAO/Baltimore, for a decade-long gig.

Today: "I spent around sixty years in broadcasting and especially loved those glorious Rock music days of the 1960s and '70s," said Ron. With a finger in many media pies, he never truly retired from radio or television. Ron continues to entertain his legion of fans in frequent guest spots and appearances, and counsels media classes, reminding fresh-faced students of ethics in broadcasting.

"To survive, one has to be creative, cooperative, keep contacts, and be ready to take on any meaningful job you're tasked to do." He admits, "It wasn't always easy, but what a great time I've had."

We're keepin' it real, man. BFYP 84.8-FM on your dial, is the howlin' station for all the cooool tunes. Awoooo!

Makin' money. Makin' a living ... but *I Was Made to Love Her* ♪ ...

Have mercy! >Part 2 of 3
aka Robert Weston Smith
1938 ~ 1995
Wolfman Jack Goes Bigtime ...

The early Sixties emerged as a magical time of discovery and innovation for Bob, for radio, and for our evolving society. Surprises were everywhere.

Meeting Lucy "Lou" Elizabeth Lamb threw the confident hipster, Robert Weston Smith, for the proverbial loop. Enjoying life as a chronic dater, "Mr. Suave immediately got real lovesick."

He'd been staying at his sister Joan's, in Alexandria, Virginia, for a while, and dropped all his pseudo girlfriends to pursue the lovely Ms. Lamb. it was time to ask if he could bring Lou home and introduce her to the family.

Bob hoped this would help her see him as more than a guy who "spun records at a black station, hung out with a lot of shady-looking people around town, and dressed like a pimp." Never mind that he *was* a pimp ... "But only part-time." Oh, well that's different. :-)

Lou, whose heritage brags a long line of elite North Carolina bootleggers, found herself attracted to the wild child in Bob (that bad boy attraction, you know). Their mutual love of music made for many new experiences for her—as he grew more smitten.

Together, they discovered master musician Ray Charles, an emerging force in black/white music crossover that already dubbed him "The High Priest of Soul."

While he wooed Lou, Red Guavi, a local grocery store owner, thought a nightclub partnership was a great idea. Interracial and controversial, "The Tub" called a Quonset hut home, and like most of his other side jobs, some of it was legal, some, not so much.

About the same time, Richard Eaton figured he'd sell WYOU while it's at the top of its game. In walks Max Resnick, a Washington D.C. radio man, who forced a switch from the popular format to a "beautiful music" station.

He also nixed the DJs' good times by firing Tex Gathings. That left Bob to decide if he wanted to keep *his* job by ditching his Daddy Jules persona for Resnick's required "Roger Gordon."

No more cool rhythm and blues, folks. "Roger" played Sinatra, Mantovani, and the heavy strings of early pop Nat King Cole—"Music in Good Taste."

Bob hated the transition, and felt worse about his new guise "than I do about the fact I was transporting weed and brokering mattress action on the side."

But if you're anywhere over the hillside of thirty-nine and holding, you know life is a series of wild, weird, sometimes withering, or wonderful, twists of fate.

Without those changes, Bob would not have met Mo Burton. Hired for the "new" WYOU-turned-WTID advertising sales, Bob and Mo danced around each other the first few days until it was clear they were kindred spirits.

As Bob recalled, Mo "was about Danny DeVito's size and shape ... a dyed-in-the-wool New York Jewish liberal, with the accent to match."

It didn't take Mo long to get the lay of the land and stomp into Resnick's office to let him know the new format was never gonna work. He convinced the owner to compromise and Bob was able to format the music "more into the Count Basie realm."

He had to continue as Roger Gordon, but managed to give the guy a little more soul. "... at least I could come out of a record during my drive-time shift saying things like, 'I know that makes you feel good. I know I just touched a button somewhere in someone's soul.'"

Mo taught Bob some of the finer techniques of great sales, which he hoped would also work on Lou in his efforts to create an exclusive relationship. Though he had completely dropped other liaisons, Lou continued to date other guys. She wasn't ready to commit.

From crazy to ingenious

To stretch their ad imaginations, Bob and Mo tuned into "crazy" stations like WLAC/Nashville, with John R. (Richbourg), and XERF in Mexico. Mo, a brilliant money manager, and Bob, the consummate DJ and budding sales guru, listened and learned.

Finally, they felt ready to strike out on their own. Mo found a tiny, failing station to buy in Shreveport, Louisiana, and asked Bob to go with him.

That created a dilemma for the lovesick Bob. Until ... Lou finally succumbed to his charms. He'd wanted her to marry him practically from day one, but before Louisiana became a major factor, fate stepped in with a little, well, *big* ... push.

We all know sex is a powerful presence of life and sometimes it just takes over. In the 1960s that could spell disaster with a capital "B". It led to pregnancy for moralistic Lou, at a time when birth control pills were not yet viable, and she hadn't made up her mind about her suave, but salacious suitor.

While Bob sat behind the microphone, she sat behind the wheel of his car, and drove all over town, listening to him, anguishing over her options. Admittedly corny, he'd dedicate "Call Me" to her (by Chris Montez, hitting the top ten at KYA/San Francisco, March 1966*). She did ... and they'd talk through their dilemma.

"The most important course in my whole life was set the day she put aside all the plans she had for herself and agreed to be my bride. Without Lou in my corner, I would've been a goner long ago."

What mid-twentieth century gal wouldn't have swooned?

♫ ♪ ♫ ♪ ♫ ♪ ♫ ♪

* *Now's as good a time as ever to address an issue you'll find if you read Wolfman's* Have Mercy*! It's obvious and fairly understandable that Wolf became a little confused in the retelling. Names, places and dates may not be as they appear in the rear-view mirror. Discrepancies abound for example, regarding these years. 1) His marriage to Lou—1960, 1961, 1962, or 1966—the year "Call Me" hit the charts?; and 2) when he worked where. Thirty years had already rocked by, even as he wrote it. The fickle ambiguities of memory!*

♫ ♪ ♫ ♪ ♫ ♪ ♫ ♪

So, let's ignore the song reference—though it made for great, sappy sentiment—as the book returns to Christmas, 1961, when Bob and Lou (and baby bump) headed for Shreveport.

They left Virginia with little to show for all of Bob's lucrative sidelines. Lou was just as glad, since most we're marginally legit at best; but Bob felt like he was starting on the bottom rung again. He needed a little stimulating inspiration.

The sun set on their way through Alabama and Bob zeroed in his radio dial on XERF. The high-powered rebel station based at the US/Mexico border, and on the fringe of radio sanity, continued to capture his imagination. [*Image:* vintage post card circa 1960s.]

Broadcasting from a 250,000-watt transmitter in Mexico, the Del Rio, Texas-based station pumped out 19th century style preachers, energetic gospel music, some hillbilly tunes, diet plans, baby chicks and sex-drive boosting pills long before Viagra.

Bob took it all in, subconsciously forming a new plan for freewheeling XERF. But first, Shreveport and married life, was waiting. Oh, and it was *Country* music. More than a few guitar riffs from his rhythm and blues roots.

KCIJ-AM 1050 was no get-rich-quick scheme for Mo and Bob. The 250-watt daylight-only station took a high spot on the dial, and a low spot on the budget balance sheet.

Says Bob, "KCIJ was one of the hardest-working gigs I ever had." On first glance though, Mo knew what to do; the financial wiz said let's go hillbilly all the way.

Catering to the audience who favored "Big Smith" overalls, and thanks to his expanded waistline from Lou's cooking, Bob became "Big Smith with the Records." The guy who loved to sleep in, rose to sign on at sunrise with a mug of coffee as he cracked open the mic.

With a clang of an old cowbell hanging on the wall, listeners heard, "Friends, we're gonna give you a song now by Lester Flatt and Earl Scruggs, called 'I'm Using My Bible for a Road Map.'"

After his shift, Bob hustled ads for the station until dinnertime, hawking "A dollar a holler," on the air. It was hard work, but took only a couple of months for Bob and Mo to see results.

He'd lost his slick Ford Galaxie 500 with most everything else, back in North Carolina. Even with a new baby girl (Joy Renee), Bob was able to work advertising trade-outs for a new Oldsmobile Starfire convertible—and tuck-and-roll zebra skin seats. "No sense in looking just like everybody else," said Bob.

It was at KCIJ that Bob began forging relationships with the "wild preachers" on XERF. Most importantly, he was introduced to how they worked their business—taping shows and paying radio stations to run them. He tucked that information into his DJ/radio management cap; a promising hint to the future.

Daydreaming or visionary?

Though KCIJ was working for him, Bob couldn't stop daydreaming about XERF and noodling over an emerging concept. The core of it broke through in a dream ... from then on out, he couldn't be stopped.

Envisioning a program patterned after the preachers, Bob cultivated a deep-voiced, animalistic character who played his beloved rhythm and blues, and talked you into shelling out your dollars for the next best thing to sliced bread.

Into his character, he infused shades of the hundreds of horror movies he'd watched, with the voice he once used to terrorize his nephews. Rather than frightening though, this magnetic DJ would be cool and hip, like those he had emulated since childhood.

In his dreams, this booming voice belonged to a station and a life that stretched far beyond KCIJ's 250 watts.

By 1963, his son (Tod Weston) rounded out their family, a deal between Mo and another station owner had boosted their revenue, and Lou learned she loved family life more than the solo dreams she'd once harbored. Bob also cheered his son's birth, but ... "the Wolfman was wanting to get born, too."

♪ ♫ ♪ ♫ ♪ ♫ ♪

And just why did he add "Jack"? In hipsters' lingo it had become a catch-all name and greeting, like "dude" for the beach boys. It seemed a natural for Bob—"Dig that fine set of wheels, Jack."

♪ ♫ ♪ ♫ ♪ ♫ ♪

Listening to a demo tape of "The Wolfman Jack Show," Mo hated it—mostly because he sensed his star ad salesman and face of the station guy, slipping away. Lawrence Brandon, Mo's new partner who owned Shreveport's 5,000-watt K-REB 950, loved it.

Bob talked Lawrence into a Mexico trip that would schmooze XERF's management, run by Arturo Gonzales, into the Wolfman show and "maybe do the wamboozie with the girls down there."

Lawrence hopped in the Wolfman's convertible, and they headed for Boys Town, the equivalent of Ciudad Acuña, Mexico's red-light district. Cantinas and brothels courted the military boys and cowboys, alike. Where else to get a room and learn the local gossip about XERF?

The US-Mexico border town in 1963, had not moved much past the days of horses and six-guns. They wondered how much of its rough-and-tumble action they would see, personally.

Upon learning that the route to XERF did not include an actual road, Bob and Lawrence kept their cool through a dubious ride via a sketchy "cab," deep into the desert, to the station's massive transmitter.

Its power not only reached most of the corners of the US, but up close, it forced car headlights on, stopped the hearts of birds unlucky enough to fly close, and made the station personnel just a tad loopy.

XERF's politics and finances were a tangled mess that worked to Bob and Lawrence's advantage. The Mexican government threatened to shut it down for not paying wages and taxes, sending in a receiver—*interventor* in Mexico—known only as Montez, to control its assets.

That of course, only exacerbated the issue, as the guy operated it with all the aplomb of a low-level mobster, which still left the employees without pay. Bob and Lawrence walked into their heated meeting at just the right moment. [*Image:* vintage post card of the Mexico transmitter circa late 1950s.]

With taxes still owing and the workers backed by a union, which sent a representative to Mexico City to strike a deal, Bob financed a takeover to whip XERF out of the hands of the *interventor.* And that was just his strategy in Mexico. Bob's early sales training revved into high gear.

It didn't stop there

For their thousands in cash to make it work, Lawrence would need to rob the Shreveport station's cookie jar—without Mo's OK.

"… pulling off this big maneuver," said Bob, "was going to take some stupid impetuousness, blind luck, and shameless double-crossing. That's where I came in." Armed with "massive amounts of guns and ammunition," and a "hairy-looking 60-millimeter machine gun left over from WWII," they filled burlap bags with sand, topped with barbed wire, and blockaded themselves in the station. Yes, this was a real Western-style takeover.

It was time for Bob to begin his calls to the XERF preachers he'd enticed to advertise on KCIJ in the past year, and let them know there was a new sheriff at XERF. He demanded twice what they'd been comfortably paying, with payment made directly to him, in Del Rio, Texas—out of Mexico's hands.

After refusing to pay and thinking Bob was bluffing about yanking their late-night shows, they all called Montez to complain—that's when the fun began.

First, the usual taped shows preceded a Spanish-language program, and moved on into Paul Kallinger, "your good neighbor along the way," whose popularity spread up to the northern reaches of the US. Next up, the preachers expected their shows as usual …

Bob opened XERF's mic in the preachers' time slot with, "Aaaoooooooo! All *right*, baby. Have mercy! Good golly, Miss Molly! This is the Wolfman Jack Show, baby. We gonna par-ty tonite! We down here in Del Rio Texas, the land of dun-keys."

Behind his nervous rap, played Ernie Freeman's popular blues instrumental from 1955, "Jivin' Around." Though panicky, Bob Smith was in heaven. Without any commercials to cut to, it was just Wolfman, the microphone, and the music …

"Makes me want to get naked every time I hear it, baby. I'm runnin' around naked in the studio right now, beatin' my chest. And I wantcha ta reach over to that radio, darlin', right now, and grab my knobs. Aaa*oooooo*!"

I should say … phew! With that, XERF etched itself in pop culture history as the site of Wolfman Jack's premiere live performance.

After a euphoric night and the next week of raking in the preachers' dollars that got them back on the radio——all still behind the barricade at the station—he contacted Mo at KCIJ. Though Mo had fired him many times over the years, he didn't see the vision the other two had, and blew a gasket about Bob's dipping into the Shreveport funds. For the first time since he hatched his plan, Bob worried for his family.

After payback plus premium interest, Mo came around. Wolfman warmed up the airwaves at midnight after the preachers' programs, and XERF became a driving force for US radio stations to reckon with.

But ... remember those guns and the barbed wire?

They were there for a reason.

Lou had arrived in Del Rio to see for herself, what Bob was up to this time. They decided a reunion tryst should come before a visit to the station. XERF played low in the background. Even the soft volume however, couldn't disguise the eruption of noise that began a staccato rat-a-tat-tat from the radio.

Bob sat up and turned the volume higher, gunshots ringing out over the open mic. Yipes! Leaving Lou in the hotel, he scrambled around town gathering all the illegal guns and ammunition they'd stashed.

With a pocket full of C-notes, he grabbed as many guys as he could buy who weren't too scared, and pushed the pedal on the old station-owned pickup to bounce it atop the sand, out to the transmitter.

Just like John Wayne's westerns, pistoleros sat atop horses, in a semi-circle around the station, guns blazing in the stark, silent desert night. When Wolfman and his ragtag crew hit them with the truck's headlights, the horsemen began to scatter.

Just like the cavalry, Wolfman and friends saved the station defenders who were quickly running out of ammo after the hours-long fight. The fierce-looking machine gun had proven essentially useless—only four rounds out, it jammed.

After all was said and done, two of the horsemen died, and a couple of Wolfman's employees were transported to the hospital for minor wounds. The Federales arrived at dawn, set up their folding furniture and conducted a field hearing. They determined one pistolero was killed by friendly fire from behind, and nothing said about the other.

With some fast talking by the station's only bilingual employee, and the last of their C-notes, the Federales packed up and left.

In the week after, the preachers found Bob and Lawrence more palatable than Montez, and Bob morphed solidly into the Wolfman. But suspecting Montez wasn't done with him, he sent Lou back to Louisiana. None too soon.

Way weary, he had just settled on the hotel bed after a long day, when the phone rang. The desk clerk whispered urgently that Montez was on his way up with gun in hand.

Wolfman grabbed his own revolver, flipped off the lights, and slid under the bed. Simultaneously, the door was kicked open and Wolfman heard bullets from two guns spraying the room.

Yep, just like in the movies, he counted how many rounds Montez fired and when he got to twelve, he shot back and winged Montez enough to send him flying out of the room.

Three days later, as Wolfman's midnight hour approached, one more sniper attempt played out in the desert on his way to the station. Wolfman felt the sting of a bullet crease the tip of his nose; but other than a hairy ride and more bullet holes in the station truck, he eluded the attacker. "Nobody knows what eventually happened to Montez, but those were his last shots."

XERF settled down to its preaching and selling, and life with the Wolfman howling at the mic.

Bob the family man, though, knew he needed to return to the salesman's life at KCIJ. He loved the freedom to operate out of no-man's land, but Lou, already known by many as Wolfwoman, urged him back home.

Out of sight but not out of mind

He left XERF's day-to-day operation to the loyal station employees. Wolfman's taped shows sent from Louisiana, continued building an audience on the station that could reach to the stars.

Mo not only forgave Bob his eccentricities (again), he gave him another failing peanut whistle station in Minneapolis to turn around. Wolfwoman and the kids settled in with him and as they turned the corner into 1965, life was good.

Bringing in many of his lucrative preachers' programs, and a young Jewish guy with a half hour show to reach his community, it didn't take long for Bob and KUXL/Minneapolis to make Mo even happier.

XERF and XEG, another super-station Bob picked up to manage out of Monterrey, Mexico, continued to thrive. Although Wolfman's legion of fans grew by the day, Bob didn't think KUXL—or any US station—was quite ready for him.

As we dip into the late 1960s, restlessness provoked by a "conflict" that acted more like war, and urban racial tensions flaring, found their way into the music of the day. From anti-war tunes to angry guitar riffs, we reacted to it like a caged animal, pacing in impatient frustration.

Bob felt the same twitchy turmoil, as he played nice with the Minneapolis station … all the while, missing the high of live performance. Wolfman on XERF was satisfying … to a point.

We've talked throughout *Blast from Your Past* about so many of the DJs enjoying a special *connection* with their audiences. Wolfman needed to broadcast live. Like the wolf that personified the inner Bob, a slight pacing trembled through him, waiting to connect.

It would soon be time for Bob Smith to thank Mo Burton for the incredible education he received, and strike out on his own.

To create the live connection for Wolfman Jack and finish his trek to the Hollywood Hills sign, Bob Smith needed to meet Mr. Harold S. Schwartz, "king of border radio."

Harold's infamy came as the official American representative for four Mexican border blaster stations: XEG and XERF, the two under Bob's control, and XELO (Laredo) and XERB (Tijuana). Bob had an idea to make even more money as a Mexico-US liaison, and finally release the Wolfman from his tethers.

Bob's brainstorm comes a little later, as he thrust Wolfman Jack into the Southern California spotlight. Winding up his decade of antics in the closing tale of the Swinging Sixties, we'll hint at Bob's move full-swing into the *Psychedelic Seventies*, when we finally met the Wolfman, face-to-face ... so to speak.

Look for Rufus and the next Wolfman Jack break, to end the Sixties.

♪ ♫ ♪ ♫ ♪ ♫ ♪

* It bears repeating that Wolfman Jack's convoluted rise to fame and fortune may never be told in truth. Embellishments, time, and scattered stories take their toll. All of the parts and pieces may still be "out there," but unless they're glued together soon, the real story will fade away with the ghosts of yesteryear's radio airwaves. Wolfman Jack tales in BFYP Book 3: The Psychedelic Seventies, *as told by his longtime friends and DJs, Lonnie Napier and Frank Cotolo, are as factual as we're gonna get.*

♪ ♫ ♪ ♫ ♪ ♫ ♪

Chugga, chugga, BFYP is chuggin' along on your radio dial at 84.8-FM!
*Rock or Country, I learned quite a lot ... **When I Was Young** ... ♪*

Jim Higgs
Best known at WKMI/Kalamazoo, Michigan

Jim is one of few DJs who can honestly say he has come full circle in his career. He now owns the small whistle-stop station in which he first began his lifelong love affair with radio.

It's no wonder Jim has been a popular DJ on the radio for so long—his voice is at once, strong and comfortable, with a hint of mischief. Just how we listeners like 'em.

As a boy in Plainwell, Michigan, Jim fell in love with the magic of radio. "I could go anywhere I wanted to go [listening to radio]." He laid in bed with his little transistor radio tuned to his favorite DJs in New York, or Syd McCoy's all-night jazz show on WCFL/Chicago.

He slipped into a smooth, deep tone, "Hey, hey, old bean, it's the Real McCoy!" But jazz waned as Rock and Roll Radio became broadcasting's new frontier in the late 1950s.

Many of the Sixties DJs grew up emulating a very different sound. "Franklin McCormick, on WGN [Chicago], was another influencer for me. On his all-night Meister Brau* showcase he often read poetry. 'Vagabond's House' took fifteen minutes to read. *When I have a house—as I sometime may—I'll suit my fancy in every way.* (Don Blanding)

"When I started listening [to radio], Top 40 hadn't even started yet. I heard all the great radio dramas: *Lone Ranger, Sergeant Preston of the Yukon* ..."

And Jim loved every word. There was no doubt in his mind what he wanted to do with his life. Not even his high school counselor could talk him out of a career in radio. Not that he didn't try.

His requisite senior class visit to discuss life after school, yielded only negativity as the counselor shuffled through various flyers on hand, meant to inspire. "He came to broadcasting promos," said Jim, "and read with emphasis on key words, '*long* hours, *low* pay, have to *move* all the time.' He tried to talk me out of it."

Jim's parents, owners of a photo developing business, lobbied for Jim to join the family biz. "I'm sure," said Jim, "dad's still waiting for me to grow up and get a *real* job." (Jim's dad was still with him at a spunky eighty-seven years old at the time of this interview.) But following school, he did help the family in the shop for a while.

Thank goodness for friends … the summer of '62, a buddy casually mentioned, "Otsego [WDMC] station is looking for an announcer." Jim laughed, recalling the moment. "I thought about it … for about ten or twenty seconds! Of course I headed over there."

Having read numerous books on radio broadcasting, Jim knew that the starting point generally grew from the records library or sweeping the halls, to gradually work your way up.

First and foremost, an announcer needs a good, strong voice. "I auditioned in a little studio, reading the news. I felt forward, going in and asking for the job as announcer—but I did—and I got it." He chalked it up to good genes.

"My only mic experience before," said Jim, "was school fundraising events on a P.A. system mounted on a car, driving all over the small town, yapping away." (Imagine that now!)

A nervous wreck, with his stomach doing flip-flops, Jim showed up the next afternoon and got through the first hour; then two hours, and discovered, "it wasn't all that bad."

It still wasn't Rock and Roll. "There was a much different attitude in DJs and music," said Jim, "between major markets like WCFL and WGN, and small, local stations like WDMC."

But it was a start …

His first gig was short-lived and Jim found himself back at the family business about May of 1963. Experience is everything—well that and his comfortable on-air timbre. By July he was flush with three simultaneous job offers.

"I accepted one but it was nearly an hour's drive away. When I returned from meeting with them, I'd had another call from a station five miles closer and ten dollars a week more." For Jim, the move to WHTC in Holland, Michigan, was a no-brainer.

"I called the first guy back to tell him I couldn't be there at six the next morning. He was really quite ticked at me—but, oh well!" Nothing personal, just business.

Jim began as the afternoon FM announcer. Terrific, right? Ah—don't forget what year we're in. Only the tip of the FM iceberg was visible in 1963 and WHTC still broadcast "beautiful music." Jim even spent an hour of his show in classical, patterning it after Syd McCoy's formatting.

When he scored a coveted AM slot a few months later, there was still no real Rock and Roll there yet. He emphasized, "This was *Holland … Michigan*. Rock and Roll was a definite no-no. I pushed the envelope every chance I got though, and occasionally slipped through a Chad and Jeremy record."

He really lived dangerously, when he played a Beatles' B-side. "That was about as far as we'd go."

WHTC kept him busy for a few years. Jim honed his radio skills; but dare he dream? He had always coveted WKMI in Kalamazoo, Michigan.

Nestled in a bend of the Kalamazoo River, WKMI was essentially halfway between Detroit and Chicago. Small enough to enjoy the country, yet large enough for its airwaves to reach well beyond the river's edge.

[*Image:* No-frills WKMI music chart, April 7, 1967; Airheads Radio Survey Archive, Las-Solanas.com/arsa/surveys.]

A tad more chic than WHTC, without the sports scores and household call-in recipe shows, WKMI was all about music. Finally ... Jim found an opening niche at WKMI in 1967 and moved up the lower ladder rungs through the end of the decade.

By early Seventies, Jim made program director and nurtured its music to dominate the airwaves.

"In the beginning," said Jim of his thirteen years there, "we played what you might call 'chicken rock.'" They pecked at Rock and Roll's fringe, making a little more headway toward the good stuff, as Jim realized his DJ dream.

"When we played a record, it practically guaranteed sales." By 1973 Jim and WKMI broke some of the greatest music of the era.

We'll catch up with Jim again in the *Psychedelic Seventies*, as he name-drops ... it was a *Peaceful Easy Feeling* ... ♪

Today: Jim gives a whole new meaning to the phrase "home office." He now operates WAKV which up 'til about 1990 had broadcast as WDMC, his Otsego

DJ alma mater. His still-strong voice flows over the airwaves from his home/basement studio, pleasing the locals and keeping the Rock rollin'.

Waxin' the '60s: With all the happenings of mid- to late-Sixties, from movie actor Ronald Reagan's unorthodox rise to California governorship, to escalating Vietnam battles, we looked fervently for benign relief. Anything to remind us that life can be fun.

For some of us, it became a time of change. Not just a different day, month, or year, but a different life, as we welcomed home soldiers ... or not ... graduated from high school or college ... took life to the next level or leveled out. Emotions ran the gamut and so did our music.

Late summer of 1966 proved liberating and more than a little loony. Life in the city was a far cry from the red dirt and rural antics of my country upbringing.

City or Country, "cruising the main" was still a way to connect with our peers. One hot August night ...

Crammed into the front seat of a cute boy's blue, 1960 Chevy convertible, we were bellowing out Car Karaoke long before you young'uns think you invented it. [*Image:* A Barrett-Jackson 2013 classic sale.]

"Remember when you ran away | and I got on my knees ..." the tune, the lyrics, and the sound of "They're Coming to Take Me Away" was just too much to resist for sane people in a seemingly *in*sane world.

The crazy song hit #2 for Napoleon XIV on KFRC/San Francisco's Big 30, with Sam the Sham & the Pharaohs biting on Napoleon's heels at #3 salaciously singing, "Li'l Red Riding Hood." "You're everything a big bad wolf could want ... awooo!" Yep, we were a frustrated society!

BFYP-FM is helpin' you rise 'n' shine! The big ol' sun is playing hide an' seek with a silvery cloud spinning on heaven's turntable ... wake up!

I Saw Her Standing There ... ♪ and mornings were never the same ...

Dave Mason
aka Dave Rosati, Dave Roe
Best known at WSAY & WBBF Rochester, New York and WKTQ Pittsburgh, Pennsylvania

Dave travels through adventures and misadventures making his way 'cross country from New York to San Diego in a lifetime of twistin' an' shoutin' on the radio.

You may have known him as Dave Rosati or Dave Roe in the Sixties. However you knew him, his friendly, comfortable voice made "Dave" your friend.

Some disc jockeys of the era *chose* broadcasting, others fell into it. Their reasons are as varied as Rock's guitar licks—fascinated by the engineering, a gypsy at heart, or looking for a "cushy" job (joke!)—but as with Dave, more often than not, it was the music.

"The first 45 [rpm vinyl] I ever bought—actually mom bought it—was 'Whole Lot of Shakin' Going On' by Jerry Lee Lewis," said Dave. [Hitting the top ten in October 1957.] "I still have it, but the label is obscured and the grooves are shot, 'cause I probably played it on everything from a real phonograph needle, to a nail."

Dave's vinyl record collection is highly prized. However, do you, like Dave (and most of us), lament that you didn't know enough to keep your vinyls pristine?

He doesn't know exactly how many is in his collection of 45s and albums, but he lost two to three hundred alone, in a Nashville flood "way back when." And of what's left, he says, "They have a lot of meaning to me. Maybe not to a lot of other people, but some stuff, had I *not* written on them, or carved my initials, or my girlfriend's name on it ... they would be *worth* something these days."

The painful inflection in his otherwise fluid voice echoed lament for loss, but he treasures a few survivors. Dave ticked them off, "'Got a Match?' by Frank

Gallop [1958]; first song by Paul Revere & the Raiders, 'Like, Long Hair'—it's like Tchaikovsky turned into boogie-woogie [1961]; 'Jamie' by Eddie Holland. It's a one-sided 45 rpm station copy. [October 1961.] One-sided copies are really rare."

At a time when DJs had more clout to play a record without being accused of payola, new songs were often introduced with a 45 to the radio stations with "DJ copy" stamped on the label. If the DJs or program directors liked it, they played it for listeners, creating a local test market.

"DJ copies," said Dave, "especially Beatles' records, are very, very, collectible. Look for those with the group's name misspelled—like two 'Ts' in 'Beattles.' I think their 'Please Please Me' is one.

Dave and I discussed how the Sixties DJs shaped our listening preferences.

It started in the Fifties, before the payola scandal, back when it was the music that mattered.

"One of my big influencers," said Dave, "was Bill 'Hoss' Allen at WLAC/Nashville. The big fifty-thousand-watt blowtorch covered the South at night. Hoss Allen, 'John R' (Richbourg)—played the 'race music'—Hoss would have story after story, after story [about the songs and their artists]. He got into radio because he loved the music."

WLAC electrified their listeners in the late 1950s and early '60s, including Dave, with "The 50,000 Watt Quartet" DJs—Allen, Gene Nobles, John R. and Herman Grizzard. The four staggered their shifts through the 1960s, but were instrumental to bringing early Blues and Gospel artists to mainstream.

"The station reached eighteen Southern stations at night," said Dave. "When Top 40 stations were playing Pat Boone, he [Allen] played Fats Domino's 'Ain't That a Shame.' He made it possible for Black entertainers to break through."

When Rock & Roll arrived on the scene, other music genres began to fade; our parents groused about losing Big Band, Jazz, and Polka radio stations to the youngsters' loud noise.

Fast-forward forty or fifty years, to the 1990s and early 2000s. We Boomers are now crying a river for our beloved Rockin' radio stations! Elvis and even The Beatles are mostly relegated to a few "oldies" terrestrial stations and impersonal Internet streams.

But remember, early Rock & Roll was the creation of rebel youth—that never fades away. Though terrestrial radio isn't pumping the trend, Boomer musicians are still carrying the Rock & Roll torch in recent years that saw Bob Dylan awarded the Nobel Prize for Literature, and a two-weekend nostalgia event in Coachella's backyard that rivaled the annual upstart.

Face it, kiddies, "new" music is still deeply rooted in, and mimicking "our" music. "It is!" exclaimed Dave when I mentioned that thought. "I had to laugh when I heard the popular song 'Clumsy' by Fergie—and the opening licks are straight from a Little Richard song! Yeah, when 1958 meets 2008." [It was certified Platinum in February 2008.]

With the mention of 1958, we dove back into Dave's early years ...

Dave spent a memorable summer of 1961 on Cape Cod where he could tune into WINS/New York and hear the energetic ramblings of "Murray the K" [Kaufman]. "Everybody listened to Murray the K," said Dave. "I wrote him a letter as a kid, asking advice about how to get into the business—and he actually answered!" Meeting Murray the K twenty years later, Dave was still tongue-tied. "He was one of the funniest people in the world."

Another influencer for Dave was WKBW/Buffalo's Joey Reynolds (another *BFYP* DJ). "Joey was one of my idols in high school. I listened to Joey all the time in the mid-Sixties."

Besides Joey and Murray, Dave was impressed by Tim Kelly, a "guy on a little station." The guy on the little station eventually co-founded the venerable Premiere Radio Networks.

Dave's "little station" was WSAY in Rochester, New York, in 1966. He got his feet wet in the industry and after a year or so, ambled out to WLEA/Hornell, about sixty miles away, where you might have known him as Dave Rosati. He really wanted to work for Rochester's WAXC, but the non-compete contract clause was binding.

"So I told WLEA that I got drafted, and went to work in Hornell." Of course, you know what happened next ... Dave received his military physical notice while there—the precursor for the draft. You know, when you put something "out there" ... Karma, baby!

The sprint at WLEA lasted about five months, when he migrated to WENE in Binghamton, New York, owned by radio and television guru, Merv Griffin. "Dave Roe" got in the groove with you as he spun out Gary Puckett's "Lady Willpower" (1968). It's now or never ...

The Army beckoned three months later.

Dave spent the latter part of the Sixties and early Seventies pounding his boots in Vietnam. His return stateside assignment took him to California—and opened his eyes to even more incredible radio experiences.

"Stationed near Salinas, I could hear almost every single radio station in the state. San Diego FMs at night, San Francisco [KFRC], Fresno [KYNO], and thought you know, if I weren't so homesick I'd want to live here."

Though Dave headed back East after his stint in the Army, it didn't interrupt his keen interest in radio—nor his interest in the Pacific Coast.

"A lot of us DJs have similarities, but we get into radio for different reasons. Shotgun Tom [Kelly; another *BFYP* DJ] for example, is really into the nuts and bolts of the creation of the radio product. He talks about jingles, equipment, that kind of stuff."

Dave heard Shotgun as a budding, now-beloved SoCal DJ and paid him a tremendous compliment. "I related to a lot of people over the years —like Shotgun, who is perfect. He impresses me every day. But I'm not that perfect. I get too easily distracted."

"I just got into it because I LOVE the music. I love the songs and have fun playing them." He affected his behind-the-mic voice, "'I got a bunch of songs I want you to hear and I think you'll like them!' Even today I get so deep into the music that I forget I'm on the radio!"

Then again ... what more do you want in a DJ?

We'll catch up with Dave again having fun frenetically spinning the music, in the *Psychedelic Seventies*, at WAXC (yep, he made it), WBBF, and lookin' cute at "The Q" WKTQ in Pittsburgh. Were you there?

Today: Without giving much away, I can tell you Dave did make it back to live in California, with stops at San Diego's biggies like KGB and KOGO. Last heard, Dave's a shiny addition to KXSN, Sunny 98.1, where great Rock & Roll Classics continue to thrive. More radio adventures await him. [*Image:* LA Radio People; LARadio.com/wherem.htm.]

Across the country they're swingin' 'n' swayin' but in sunny Cali we add a little jiggy to it at BFYP 84.8-FM.

But wait ... hey, hey you ... Get Off of My Cloud! ♪

Shotgun Tom Kelly
aka Tom Irwin
Best known at KCBQ/San Diego
and K-EARTH 101/Los Angeles

It isn't a stretch to say Shotgun Tom Kelly, known to friends and family as Tom Irwin, is an inspiration behind today's SoCal classic Rock & Roll Radio.

Sound a little biased? You betcha. I've been Shotgun's fan since the '80s and thrilled to connect with him for a brief bio.

As with so many of the intriguing interviews I've compiled, Tom's story alone, could fill a book. Let's dive into a mini-history behind the iconic DJ, whose many admiring cronies call "Shotz."

BFYP follows young Tom Irwin from 1963 at the venerable KDEO in San Diego, up and down the California coast, working with some of our DJs already mentioned, while turning us all on to some groovy music.

"It's because of mom that I got into radio," admits Tom.

"Tommy" was about ten when he arrived home from school, to find mom listening to KOGO-AM. A San Diego DJ broadcasting from nearby Oscar's Drive-In, hyped some giveaway sports tickets, interviewing listeners on the air. She urged him to get on over to the Lemon Grove hangout (it was a sleepy little community east of San Diego around 1961).

Tom resisted but mom persisted and ultimately, "I got on my bike and went down there." Tom peered through the window of a portable trailer. He was fascinated with the guy in horn-rimmed glasses, fiddling with two record players and a microphone. The disc jockey looked up to see the wide-eyed kid staring through the glass.

Tom lowered his voice with the memory of Frank Thompson, "He opened the mic, 'And we have a young man here who's looking through our mobile window as we broadcast at Oscar's Drive-In. Come in here, young man.'"

Tom stumbled into the trailer as the DJ asked, "What's your name?"

Recalling his pre-teen falsetto voice, Tom said, "My name's Tom."

"Well Tom," Frank picked up, "what we have here are the L.A. T-Birds coming to San Diego at Westgate Park. You have four passes to go!"

"Oh thank you very much," nervous Tom said. Slick for a future DJ, huh? That day made an impact on him, though, beyond the sports tickets. "I went home, built my little radio station with extension speakers and that got me started in the biz."

Tom looked for more places to view DJs in action. At the time, Frank was the easiest, as KOGO's remote disc jockey. His show went out to listeners every day from different locations, easy access for an eager kid on a bike. Tom pedaled out when he could. "Guess I was a pest," he confessed.

It wasn't long before he found another mesmerizing disc jockey to visit, who would become a lifelong friend.

Mentored by Clark Gable of the airwaves

"I had a paper route and used to listen to this guy while I folded my papers. I'd deliver them, with my little transistor radio hanging on my bike, listening to Jack Vincent at KCBQ. (A compelling, *BFYP* 1950s pioneering DJ.)

"When I finished my route," said Tom, "I'd go to the studio, knock on the door and Jack would let me in! I'd actually get to go in and see him!"

Jack was a huge influence on young Tom. Once he graduated to cars, you couldn't keep him away from Jack as he watched him deliver commercials, news, and spin the platters of his favorite songs. Tom even took future wife, Linda, to see Jack.

"She and I used to visit Jack quite often. He had an open-door policy—anybody could walk in—and one night ..." Shotgun's memories flooded back to mind as he told another Jack story.

A rather disheveled guy discovered the unlocked door during Jack's show and asked him what this place was; Jack told him it was a radio station. The guy said, "Oh, okay, I'm outta here." As he took off, Jack noticed the blood dripping from a gunshot wound.

And yet, Tom still wanted to be a DJ.

In fact, he often visited a favorite kids' hangout that was legendary as San Diego's DJ-dreamin' corner—7th & Ash—KCBQ's fishbowl studio.

When possible, radio stations across the country would position their digs on a prominent corner so people could peer in and watch the DJs workin' the turntables. Many a future disc jockey spent their afternoons hanging out, while their idols flipped records.

"It was really neat," said Tom. "I used to stand on that corner for *hours*. They had a mirrored ceiling, so as you looked up to the second floor, you could see the DJ's hands operate the board. I took a picture when I was thirteen years old, with a Brownie camera. And still have it!"

Another *BFYP* DJ, Neil Ross, also hung out on the famed corner; though he and Tom didn't know each other at the time. "He has almost the same stories as I do about 7th & Ash," said Tom. "A lot of radio wannabes would sit there and look up at those guys."

KDEO, another popular weekend hangout for young Tom, provided a pivotal point in the budding DJ's life. "'Sunny' Jim Price, the program director, used to let me in to watch guys like Ray Willis, Robin Scott, and Tom Schaeffer, the news director—he was quite a guy," recalled Tom. KDEO was his behind-the-scenes introduction to radio.

Tom soon talked Jim into hiring him to help the jocks with remote (live) locations—he was the roadie. "Back in those days they actually took the turntables, microphone and the teletype machine out there. I ripped off the news from the teletype machine for the disc jockey and greeted people where they were broadcasting." He started at $1.25 per hour.

Donning his big boy pants

Tom slipped into his "DJ voice." "That was my first job in radio—at '*Radio KAY-Dee-Oh!*'" Tom listened and learned all through his adolescent years, 1963—1965 at KDEO. And it paid off before he even finished high school.

[*Image:* KDEO October 24, 1964; Tom learned from DJs (top/bottom, left/right) Robin Scott, Buzz Baxter, Chuck Daugherty, Hal Pickens, Bobby Barnet, and Larry Boyer. *BFYP* Collection.]

Disc Jockeys who are into the music never listen to just one station, or one type of music. Such is the case with Tom. But back in the early to mid-Sixties, AM was still king, with FM stretching its newborn arms to those looking for something a little different.

"I heard this station from Mexico," said Tom, "it was called 'Rock 95'—this guy, Chuck Johnson was there. He was the program director and general manager, and I heard him on the air, started listening to it. He played soul music." Something about him struck Tom's radio soul.

Continuing his reverie, Tom's deep voice was mesmerizing as he described the scene. They boasted a picture window, too, "down at the corner of Logan Avenue, which is in the African-American community," said Tom. Although it was a "really small station" it caught young Tom's attention. He was still a gofer at KDEO, but auditioned for Chuck who hired him—as a DISC JOCKEY—for XEGM Rock 95.

Yep—not something Tom often admits. "I always leave this out of my interviews," said Tom. But he confessed that his *first* on-air radio job was in a tiny station with one turntable and two tape machines—one to put promos on and another to record shows. And with only shades of Rock crossovers.

"We had to talk in between putting records on. We recorded our shows from that studio and Chuck would truck it over the border and they'd play it back over a Mexican station."

[*Image:* Chuck Johnson played XEGM Rock "95" Soul, October 24, 1966. *BFYP* Collection.]

It was 1966 and Tom was still just a high school kid with big dreams. "I enjoyed myself, but wanted to be at a more *professional* station—I wanted to be *live*."

Facing two years of high school before graduating, he took advantage of vocational work experience and attended school half day, working at stations the other half.

Better to be half-alive than not!

"I quit Rock 95 and went to KPRI-FM—my first *live*, on the air job," said Tom. It still wasn't the Top 40, but he was just getting started. Though small and quirky, he made the most of his first *real* radio gig.

"I remember the year I started there because I recall the big thick albums we played (on A&M Records). They were a *professional* radio station with a big [control] board and two turntables. I actually got to go on-air and play jazz, and Sergio Mendez, Steve & Edie, and the Brazil 66."

KPRI stretched Tom's skills quickly, showing him there's more to radio than music. Besides public service announcements and airing a Sunday morning Catholic mass that emanated from the local St. Joseph's Cathedral, Tom learned how to conduct a fun kids' show.

Sponsored by George's Wonderful World of Cakes, Tom was a natural with kids. "It was the Uncle Tommy show," he said proudly. "I got to do a couple of hours live. One hour playing kids' music; and I would record my mom doing stories as 'Aunt Betty' and play them on the show." This experience served him well later, when he hosted children's television shows in the Seventies.

Though thoroughly excited about learning everything possible while on the job, Tom longed to spin the Top 40 vinyls. "To get a job at the Rock and Roll stations," said Tom, "which were all directional antennas, you had to have a first-class radio license."

Mind you, the radio schools didn't teach you how to be a DJ—but you learned more than you needed to be an engineer. And the big time Rock and Roll stations wanted guys and gals who could be both.

[*Image:* Courtesy of Tom; dedicated to his books at Ogden's, circa 1968.]

Tom chose William B. Ogden Radio Operational Engineering School in Burbank, California, to prepare him for the big gigs. In an intense curriculum, by 1969, he followed graduates like Robert W. Morgan known on both coasts; and popular TV game show host, Bob Eubanks, who began in radio.

Fresh out of school, in a "now what?" moment. "I wanted to be a "boss jock," said Tom, bursting into a jingle. "*Boss Radio ... 136 KGB!* I wanted to work at KGB in the worst way."

Tom soon discovered KPRI jocks weren't on KGB's acquisition radar. "They hired from stations like KACY/Ventura "Boss of the Beach," KYNO/Fresno, KDEO/San Diego, and KMEN/San Bernardino—"*K-MEN, one-twenty-nine ...*" another jingle from Tom. So Tom set out to make a name in Radio.

Managing to keep his real name as he rose in the biz, he loved being just plain ol' "Tom Irwin" through the end of the Sixties. Of course, we know that changed. Next decade's tales share his fun name game story and rise to the top of the DJ ladder, where he stayed, for a lifetime career in radio.

Today: Tom and lovely wife, Linda, spearheaded a 2010 campaign erecting a majestic KCBQ monument for San Diego's beloved Top 40 station. Numerous awards cap his lengthy and venerable career, to include 2013's Hollywood Walk of Fame Star.

[*Image:* Tom with the Walk of Fame star; ShotgunTomKelly.com.]

After several years at K-EARTH/Los Angeles, weekending home in San Diego, Tom retired as their official radio Ambassador in 2015. Of late, he simply enjoys the fruits of retirement and special appearances.

We're playin' the hits at BFYP-FM! As time goes by, no more kiss-is-just-a-kiss tunes, because frankly, my dear, I don't give a damn ...

Let's have **Fun, Fun, Fun** *... ♪ oh no ... daddy took the T-bird away ... and ... no! Not the transistor radio!*

Jack Vincent
1917 ~ 2017
Best known at KCBQ/San Diego, California

Jack is the Daddy-O of the late-night show. "I worked twenty-seven years there, during their 'glory days,'" said Jack, "and on air most of that time (1955-1967)." Jack's tenure at KCBQ is still an unbroken record. (1955-1982)

For thirteen years on the night shift, Jack's soft tones soothed your soul from midnight to six in the morning. As we've heard from a few other DJs, the night shift in a radio station can be verrrry interesting.

Jack didn't broadcast from KCBQ's famed 7th and Ash window studio —like, what's the point—it's dark. Secluded at its transmitter site in Santee, about ten miles east of San Diego, Jack has some great stories to share about our sexy, swingin' Sixties.

He chose radio over construction in the 1950s. Suffering with a work-related back injury, Jack figured being a disc jockey was less dangerous, and landed at KCBQ.

Hired as an engineer, for a behind-the-scenes gig, he accidentally became a reluctant DJ and settled comfortably into KCBQ life.

The Clark Gable of the airwaves enjoyed his fortuitous career and a few perks along the way.

[*Image:* The Big KCB"Q" Survey for December 10, 1961, gave us seven handsome DJs and one dashing ... *duck*?! *BFYP* Collection]

Forgive us as we chat randomly—stories may be a little out of chronological order. Our interview took place when Jack was ninety-one years old. Some dates are a little fuzzy, and I suspect some events happened earlier or later, on the winding path of Memory Lane; but his stories are no less vibrant. We'll just tell 'em as they come ...

"A situation developed when Elvis was in town," began Jack. "San Diego used to have a big skating rink downtown and it was decided to have the Elvis show there. Elvis was to be at the rink by seven o'clock, so the station could broadcast him. "The system [throughout the evening] was to keep hyping Elvis' appearance and make you think he was going to be on 'next'; but next was always some 'Joe Blow' performer. [So *that's* where our network news television stations got the idea!]

"Finally at ten o'clock that night, Elvis went on, and the place just went *wild*. Girls were throwing their panties on stage, and screaming and hollering, and sailors were jackin'-off ..."

I took my eyes off my notepad and looked at Jack with a bit of disbelief at the last part. He smiled impishly and nodded. "I got this story pretty damn straight from the guy who cleaned the floor the next day!"

Jack was a popular remote location disc jockey and spent many shifts at a hoppin' local hangout. "We had a lot of high-class people coming in at Pat's Drive-In," Jack mused. "I'd guide them down to us on El Cajon Boulevard [while they're listening on their car radios]. We had a salesman from Hershey candy, so I'd have boxes of chocolates [to give away], and the beer man would leave a case. I never knew what I was going to end up with the next morning ..." Love those leftovers!

Um, not sure where the beer man came from in a burgers and malts drive-in, and Jack didn't elaborate; but anything was possible in the mid-Sixties. "It was kind of a fun life," said Jack. His gently lined face lit up with a grin. "It never acted like a job. It seemed like I was on vacation all the time."

Vacations in the Sixties, especially in San Diego—much like today—involved summer, alcohol, and skimpy swimsuit-clad bodies, all hours of the day and night. Bikinis became largely accepted in the early 1960s; and well ... often swimsuits were optional.

[*Image:* Clark ... I mean, Jack ... flashes a randy smile as he spins the vinyls at KCBQ, c. 1963. Courtesy of Shotgun Tom Kelly.]

Betwixt and Bewitched in the Midnight Hour

As we sat together on a sofa at Shotgun Tom Kelly's home in SoCal, Jack recalled one of his vacation-at-work nights. He's on the air at KCBQ as usual ...

"I never locked the door," said Jack. "One night a girl knocked on the door and she said, 'Jack, you sound real sexy on the air. I just wanted to see *how* sexy you are.'"

Now remember, this is the guy who could take on Clark Gable in a look-alike contest. Surely, she was smitten.

[*Image:* What do you think of the resemblance in this cameo mashup?]

JACK VINCENT

"She's got a fifth of whiskey and a bottle of chasers in her hand." What could he do but invite her in?

"So I'm playin' the records and I had a tape that I put on sometimes, if I want to take a break about two in the morning. Come two o'clock, I turn around—and I had a divan about like this in my studio—I turn around and there she was, laying without any clothes on."

Yahoo for summer vacation! Ever the gentleman, the firmly married disc jockey politely invited her to leave.

During his tenure at KCBQ, Jack's taste in music ran the gamut from Big Band Era through Elvis, The Beatles, and what he termed "the New York bunch."

Though he favored the music of the 1930s, from his youth—something we all do—Rock and Roll had enough tunes that he liked, to make his job enjoyable.

"Early on we played a song with big band sound, like 'Poor People of Paris,'" said Jack. The American instrumental version of the French song topped radio charts in 1956. It's reported to be the last #1 chart hit before Elvis's "Heartbreak Hotel" broke hearts and chart records.

Jack's radio engineering school training served him well on both ends of his long career. As life does, his role at KCBQ changed around 1967, and he finished his "vacation" with them through 1982, as an engineer.

In tribute to Jack's passing five days earlier, Shotgun Tom posted on Facebook, "When I was a kid Jack used to let me watch him on the air, reading the news and playing the hits on KCBQ." February 3, 2017.

Highly respected in the broadcasting industry, Jack's name joined other iconic DJs carved into the granite of the KCBQ "Top 40" monument, dedicated at the old transmitter site, in 2010.

Today: Jack shared a few more final words: "In 1982 management decided to drop the union, letting all the union men go. I was one ... I was sixty-five years old, so it worked out perfect. I retired. Now I don't do anything ... just sit back and have fun." He did that—complete with cigar, wine, and pool cue in hand, until eleven months shy of his 100th birthday.

He also had high praise for his best friend and once-coworker, Shotgun Tom Kelly. "Shotgun is the last of the good disc jockeys." Takes one to know one!

[*Image:* Jack Vincent, left, Shotgun Tom Kelly, right, celebrating Jack's 90th birthday in "Tonight Show" style, 2007. Courtesy of Shotgun Tom.]

Waxin' the '60s: The Beatles led the British Invasion, but more than that they brought R&B back to the US and made it OK to enjoy "black music."

At WOKY/Milwaukee, week ending March 21, 1964, The Beatles hogged four* of the top five rungs on the chart. The Dave Clark Five managed to squeeze in "Glad All Over" at #4. [*BFYP* Collection.]

*In order, #1, #2, #3 & #5: "Twist and Shout," "She Loves You," "Please, Please Me," and "I Want to Hold Your Hand."

The Beatles weren't quite finished with the chart as we scan lower to spot "Can't Buy Me Love" at #35, and climbing.

In charming contrast, an ad for the "world wide premiere" of surfing movie, *Muscle Beach Party,* "introducing 'Little Stevie Wonder,'" splashed across the survey's flip side.

We're on pins and needles in the California sun, as time swirls around the vinyls at BFYP, your cooool station.

And here, I thought you'd always *Stand By Me* ... ♪

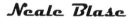

Best known at "too many to mention"

Neale admits to a wanderlust nature. And though we know by now a Gypsy routine comes with the disc jockey territory, in a four-decade Rock & Roll Radio DJ career, "I was hired forty times and fired twenty-two," says Neale. That's a little excessive even for the ladder-climbing media industry.

A self-described "Gypsy Renegade," Neale begins his wild-and-crazy Rock jock odyssey in 1963, and racks up thirty-two radio stations through 1979. He admits that much of the angst which resulted in his departures was his doing.

"I was developing a love for traveling and that evolved into an addiction. After a while, radio became my drug of choice." How did he get hooked? Well ...

In 1960s Sacramento, California, most everyone listened to KXOA's Top 40. Of course, it was the DJs who made it popular, like Tony King (Pete Gross), who later became the voice of the Seattle Seahawks, and the inimitable Don Imus, who used KXOA as a stepping stone on his way to New York City.

In 1961 car makers were beginning to round off the fad tailfins, charging an average of $2,850 for one of their gleaming beauties. Elvis, Roy Orbison, and Chubby Checker topped the charts. DJ Les Thompson slipped their vinyls onto the turntable at KXOA, as he connected with his listeners.

[*Image:* March 2, 1962, finds Les Thompson a KXOA "Ace" with Dale Ware, Jerry Gordon, Gerr O'Neill, and Rick Martel. *BFYP* Collection.]

Neale cruised the Sacramento drag (K Street—now a pedestrian-only walk), just a couple of years before I did. He spotted an ex-girlfriend one night, and she invited him to meet her new fella (boy have things changed), who just happened to be the DJ they were listening to—yep, Les Thompson. With nothing else to do, Neale tagged along.

Watching Les at "work" and fascinated by the "seen not heard" aspect of the job (Neale had a bit of aversion to crowds), he fell in love with radio (in spite of an introduction by his ex-girl's guy).

"There's no cure for that" said Neale. "All you can do is treat the symptoms."

Like Shotgun Tom and Neil Ross, he started out with a dose of education at William B. Ogden Radio Operational Engineering School. He was in good company, taking classes with Jay Stevens (aka Steve Jay), another budding popular DJ who made his mark at KGB/San Diego and KFRC/San Francisco.

The school offered placement assistance and by January of 1963, Neale began his lifelong love affair at KNGL in Paradise, California.

"They only hired me because of my first-class license," said Neale. Hey, whatever gets you in the door, right? And another weathered cliché, you must start somewhere, so Neale's somewhere was reading the weather report and station ID each hour.

1963 sets the pattern of Neale's romp through stations. It took him only a week to realize this was nowhere near his dream job.

Leaving Paradise for parts unknown

So swinging north to country tunes at KPON in Anderson, California, seemed like a great idea at the time. Neale and Lee MacKenzie, a buddy from radio school, shared an apartment in nearby Redding to cut costs. After all, although the pay was low, as Neale said, "It wasn't about the money at that point. It was about traveling and being on the radio—and of course—the girls."

Neale's first big on-air break, he took full advantage of it. Even in a good gig though, the muse of his wanderlust philosophy was already being formed. "If you're bad, you're gone ... and if you're good, you're gone! Because as soon as you can, you go after a better gig." It was only good "for now."

Since the manager/owner rarely listened to his station, Neale assumed he could stretch the format a tad to match his style, without any flak. Unfortunately, taking advantage resulted in another short stay.

Making a demo tape (aircheck) for the future, which soon became his present, Neale do-si-doed over to Top 40 station, KMYC in nearby Marysville.

At first blush, KMYC looked to be his ideal Rockin' station, but his first on-air shift was a sign it wouldn't quite fit his budding renegade personality.

"The manager wanted to dictate every word for me to say!" Neale said with indignation. His tenure lasted one very long, hour. Yes, hour— not day or week—one hour.

Quickly learning that small stations "told you what to do, what to say, with cue cards. I realized early on," said Neale, "I wasn't going to be able to follow that lead." From that point on Neale's love for travel fueled his addiction to radio, quickly creating a life of ... *Radio on the Run*.

It isn't possible to explore all thirty-two of Neale's mostly short-lived escapades that excite our timeline through the Sixties and Seventies—besides, he did just that and more in 2013, with his book, *Radio on the Run: Confessions & Exploits of One of the Last Renegade Rock Jocks*. (Available on Amazon.)

So here we are, it's still 1963 with yet another station to cover. Skipping over to neighboring Yuba City, Neale hooked up with KUBA, station #4, to finish the year with a couple of months of fill-in shifts.

By early 1964, The Beatles had arrived, changing music, radio, and lives. Neale watched the invasion at his parents' home for a couple of months, resting from the previous restless year.

His mom, who experienced radio as a child singer-musician, was compassionate about Neale's career choice. Dad had a little difficulty understanding how and why he couldn't stay in one job; and his four brothers were split on his decision. All were supportive, but two were a tad skeptical about his future in radio.

The events of the day ... President John F. Kennedy's assassination, The British Invasion, and the Vietnam War ... shaped Neale's personal and behind-the-mic attitudes about America's role in the world. DJs of the decade were in a unique position to form opinions, share them, and emphasize them with music.

Youth and optimism about his world and his career, carried him forward ... to the sparkling beauty of the Sierra Nevada mountains and Lake Tahoe. KTHO, a MOR station, played the standards: Frank Sinatra, Tony Bennett and the big name Big Bands.

Neale admits in his book, however, "By this time in my career, to me a station 'format' was more like a recommendation." Oh yeah, he was still stretching those formats, while stretching the patience of station management.

A daytime only station, KTHO broadcast from sunrise to sunset—so besides Neale, there was only one other DJ. Jim Fitzgerald doubled as the chief engineer and morning jock. Together, they brought beautiful music to the stunning and serene setting of the sparkling lake's listeners.

♪ ♪♫ ♪ ♫ ♪ ♫ ♪

While Neale's deep DJ voice captivated listeners in Tahoe's Stateline, yours truly attended high school seventy-five miles west, down the hill; I can attest to the dearth of Rock music in our neck of the country woods. No offense, Neale, but we tuned into KXOA, the station further west in your home town of Sacramento. Funny how often we nearly met in the Sixties—I also lived in Anderson for a time—and our paths finally crossed through memories, so many years later.

♪ ♪♫ ♪ ♫ ♪ ♫ ♪

Itching to get back to Rock music

Neale now neared his average three months at a station. Even morning jock, Jim, agreed it was time to introduce their listeners—particularly the girls—to Rock & Roll. He was happy to let Neale stick his neck out to alter the format—even encouraged it—and as the only other DJ, made himself unavailable to the owner for Neale's last day.

Neale opened the mic and treated fans to his "all new and improved Rock format" for a final six-hour shift. And promptly fired himself.

He finished his stay in Lake Tahoe with fill-in shifts at KOWL which took him to the summer of '64.

Traveling through my little country town that lined the only highway back to Sacramento, Neale landed at his folks' home for another rest. Rest? Uncle Sam had other plans for him.

His number was up and the draft with a stint in Vietnam seemed inevitable. Neale sought and found a way to satisfy both his desire to honor his views on the travesty of war, while fulfilling his military duty.

Choosing to enlist before he was drafted, Neale followed the playbook of a friend and implemented a strategy that took him through the Marine Corps (for which he has great respect) and a stint in the Air Force, all in a year-and-a-half; finishing with an honorable discharge.

After the military discipline, it was time to get back into his freestyle DJ life. He resumed "duty" at KCEY/Merced late 1965, for—you guessed it—a short soirée.

1966 proved to be even more skill-honing and job-hopping, as Neale skipped through five California stations in *one* year.

[*Image:* Courtesy of Neale; spinning the platters at KJOY/Stockton, c. 1966.]

Were you listening to Neale? If you blinked, you may have missed him at KYOS/Merced (a "real" Rock station); KFIV/Modesto; KSTN/Stockton; KJOY/Stockton—he loved their fishbowl studio window which graces the cover of his book—and is where he met lifelong friend, Tim Sommer. Neale slid to a halt back home at KROY/Sacramento.

By 1967's Summer of Love, Neale found himself at station #13, KKIS/Pittsburgh, California. A bedroom community of the San Francisco Bay Area, it flourished with flower children and hippies who ruled the Haight-Ashbury neighborhood. Think Love-Not-War on the radio airwaves.

"It was time for me to move on," said Neale, "not to just another station in just another town, but one that became instrumental in my plan to get to the 'bigs.' Though I went through stations pretty much in a hurry, I had one goal in mind—to make it to L.A. I made it in ten years, but I made it to a major market in just five years."

We were "Groovin'" to the Young Rascals and we'd "Shake a Tail Feather" with James and Bobby Purify. But in San Francisco that summer, it was the "concert on the mountain top" that defined the West Coast attitude.

Spinning through the Summer of Love, Neale spun the vinyls at KKIS/Walnut Creek, California, reaching a large audience with the small station. It had a good signal that reached deep into San Francisco. If listeners were traveling the dial, they'd find it.

KKIS also looked good on his resume, as it piggybacked on the San Fran stations' fame, which soon took him across the blue waters of the Pacific to paradise. But first, a quick Christmas 1967 rest-up with fill-ins back home on KXOA to finish up the year. All that makin' love not war was tiring.

KKUA in Honolulu welcomed Neale with open arms for the afternoon gig in '68, as he prepared for another "vacation" island style. The first major market station of his career—in Hawaii—what could be better?

E Komo Mai (Welcome!)

"It was seven hours after leaving San Francisco when I peered out the plane window to gaze at the most beautiful sunset I had ever seen," said Neale. Our winter is their plentiful summer and the Hawaiian Islands were in full bloom.

At station #15, Neale's first surprise came in a double dose of program directors. Two bosses. Hmmm, this could be a bad omen.

"As it turns out," Neale mused, "Dual PDs actually functioned well for the jocks. So my stay—about six months this time—was one very long beach party."

As a "Haole"—a term for Whites on the islands (yes, there is discrimination against Whites), local girls would have nothing to do with he and his roommate (KKUA newsman), J. Robert Clark. So their dating game was the tourist girls and, said Neale, "It was like being a used car salesman hustling for a sale, every day." Surely they managed.

It wasn't the difficulty in dating that sent Neale back to the mainland, however. Six months in paradise gave him island fever. After a couple of all-night fill-in shifts at KPOI (#16), he headed for Seattle to visit his brother. Deplaning, he learned the sad news of Robert F. Kennedy's assassination (June 5, 1968).

Startled by this event and mesmerized, as we all were, by the days that followed, Neale headed back to Sacramento to visit his family. He sent airchecks out and with a recommendation from Jan Basham, a record promoter in Los Angeles, he soon headed for #17 on his *Radio on the Run* tour of America.

From the balmy palm fronds of refreshing Hawaii, Neale found himself under the dusty palms of KRUX/Phoenix, Arizona. But this gig in the Valley of the Sun threatened to be a mirage. They were "expecting" a full-time slot to open up soon; in the meantime, Neale settled for fill-in shifts. But soon …

One of the evening DJs up and quit—and there was Neale with a full-time slot in a big market. He mentally added a notch to his resume.

[*Image:* Neale traded sea breezes for lots of sand to join the KRUXTERS. August 9, 1968 shows "Classical Gas" (Mason Williams) strumming along at #1; eBay.]

With the end of the Sixties gearing up for the *Psychedelic Seventies*, Neale thoroughly enjoyed the DJ persona with all the perks (girls) and plenty of good desert weed. And I don't mean tumbleweeds. Breathe in … ahhhhhh.

A few great months under his belt didn't erase the writing on the wall as KRUX's ratings slip due to format changes. He knew it was time to boogie.

Neale's ultimate plan to work in the Los Angeles market needed a few more boosts of airwave energy, which landed him at station #18, in Oklahoma City. KOMA was a 50,000-watt blowtorch Rocker with loads of clout. Yeehaw!

Not only was there a huge audience, but with that kind of stretch its signal reached far West of the Mississippi River and all the way to New Jersey. Specifically, Fort Dix, just outside of Trenton.

Now, we know Neale wasn't thrilled with the Vietnam War. Unfortunately, a Fort Dix Armed Forces Radio liaison wasn't aware of that and called Neale while he was on the air one night, asking if he'd like to go "live" with them for three hours—broadcasting his show to Vietnam.

He might have accidentally forgotten to tell the guy about his military past and politics. No self-respecting disc jockey would turn down that kind of exposure!

Of course, Neale passed along dedications and individual messages from his listeners to their loved ones in the war. Along with music and messages, though, he subtly included his personal political observations and opinions, intricately tied into the tunes.

"Here's a song for Private Bob Smith from his wife in Montana … she's hoping that you'll be home soon, safe and sound … and by the way, Bob, we all want you guys home soon, *because you shouldn't even be there*. So for all of you guys over there … listen *very* closely to the lyrics of this song."

KOMA listeners heard Buffalo Springfield warn, "There's a man with a gun over there ..." Although "For What It's Worth" became a war-protest song, Stephen Stills wrote the popular tune about the Sunset Strip riots of November 1966.

Aware of his opportunity as a DJ to comment on news of the day, Neale said, "I can't tell you how many times we would talk over the intro of a song and express our views in a very compatible tone of voice, with the tempo of the song. Never underestimate the power of subtlety."

It's that time again

Neale took it in stride when the station soon suggested it was time for him to move on. "I had no problem with that," said Neale. "Figured I'd 'fail up'—cut myself loose and head to a bigger market. I was ready for another Rock & Roll ride." On to Atlanta and the longest gig of his career.

WQXI (#19, if you're counting along) may not have had the reach of KOMA, but many talented disc jockeys made their way through great careers with a stop at WQXI. Dr. Don Rose sat a spell in the late 1960s, and Jerry Blum's on-air antics inspired episodes of *WKRP in Cincinnati*.

Though WQXI was Neale's longest gig, his tenure wasn't without angst. The music director and he differed on their choice of music for his shift. Sylvia Clark insisted he play songs like Tommy Roe's "Jam Up and Jelly Tight." Too much bubble gum for Neale.

Rarely settling for a simple protest, he said, "One night, every song I played for an hour, I introduced as a Tommy Roe song—but *not one was* Tommy Roe. That drove her over the edge."

By the end of 1969, and still feeling a little homesick after the 1968 death of his grandfather, it was time for Neale to head on down the road again. Opting for a long, slow trip back across the states, rather than his usual cross-country speed race, he took in the sights of the Painted Desert under a fiery setting sun, and stood gaping over the edge of the Grand Canyon.

Neale ended the decade with a staccato of San Jose stations, staying close to home. KOME, KSJO, and KLIV became gigs #20, 21 and 22, respectively.

He landed at KLIV long enough to finish the decade before turning the page with another trip east, to open the book on the '70s.

Making friends came easy to the affable Neale, with several in his romp through stations becoming lifelong buds. KLIV offered up a couple more in program director, Rick Carroll and famed radio personality, Dave Sholin.

Crisscrossing America more than a couple times, Neale tripped through experiences and insights most of us will never know ... unless you spent the Sixties and Seventies with a doobie in one hand and a microphone in the other.

This fast-talking disc jockey connected readily with his listeners; Neale's deep voice is easy to get lost in, which drew them to him. We'll see where he kisses the mic (and the girls) next decade, as Neale trips through ten more stations, on his way to a lifetime record forty!

Today: Moving away from radio, Neale funded the writing of his biography in the glitz and glamour of Hollywood, as author, designer, and feature film cast and crew driver. Now fully retired, life is good.

[*Image:* 2009 courtesy of Neale; reflecting in amazement, his on-the-run DJ career.]

[*Image:* Neale's biography, *Radio on the Run* is available on Amazon. To his astonishment and pleasure, it was included in the Rock & Roll Hall of Fame, Collection 2016, Library and Archives section. Nice accolade!]

Tough to pick a beat in the waning years of the 1960s. But BFYP 84.8-FM is on your side as Father Time boogies on down the road.

Gimme some *Love Potion #9*. I can wait ... *Time is on My Side* ... ♪

Rick Snyder >Part 2
Best known at WTRY/Albany, New York

By now Rick is Rockin' out and spinning the platters at popular WTRY/Albany, New York. He's hitting strikes on the DJ bowling team with Lee Gray (another *BFYP* jock), and grabbing those laid-back listeners who just can't get to sleep between 7:00 p.m. and 1:00 a.m. "Hey Rick, will you play the Rolling Stones one more tiiiiiime?"

As many "Richards" are, Rick grew up as "Dick" and that's the name he began with in radio. But you know how these radio managers are—when he hit WTRY, they wanted to change his name to "Rick Shaw."

"I thought it was kinda corny," said Rick. "I didn't like it." WTRY pointed out though, "Look, we can't have any 'Dicks' on the radio here." So they settled the case with "Rick" Snyder and Rick says, "I'm kinda used to it now."

[*Image:* WTRY's Big Sound Survey for August 27, 1965, featured photos of the August 15 record breaking Shea Stadium concert. Of course, The Beatles owned the #1 spot with a doubleheader of "Help" and "I'm Down." *BFYP* Collection.]

Not your "dick" type of DJ story ...

One of Rick's WTRY fans, Frank C., was blind. He won a ticket, along with six busloads of other lucky listeners, for the Shea Stadium Beatles concert in 1965. Soon after Frank won the ticket, his mom called Rick.

"Frank likes you and thinks you're a great guy. Could you let him hang on your arm, going in and out of the bus and concert? You know, could you watch him?" Now, Rick would have other duties as a DJ, but he didn't hesitate.

"Sure!" he assured her. "Frank was a pleasure to be around," said Rick, of his young friend. "Smart and a great guy. Once we were settled in our seats, I described the concert to him in his ear."

Several years later, WTRY hosted a reunion and Frank and his wife (she is also blind) attended. "It was good to meet up with them," Rick said.

Encounters with legendary artists was another perk of working at WTRY. Obviously New York was a hotbed of the fabulous—among them was the late, great Roy Orbison. Rick met him at another 1965 concert.

They spoke briefly before the performance and Rick asked if he would sing his first hit record, "Ooby Dooby" (a minor success with the Teen Kings). Rick was a bit deflated when Orbison said, "Sorry, we don't do that song anymore."

Ah well. Rick watched the show from back stage, still a plus. As the show began to wind down with Orbison's strong, superb baritone notes hanging in the air, the singer leaned into his microphone and said, "We're gonna do something we haven't done in a long time. One of the DJs asked for it."

Rick was like a little kid at Christmas. "They played it!" he exclaimed.

1965 was a big year for big British bands at WTRY. Since they were just a Stones'-throw away ...

After a Canadian concert tour, the Rolling Stones were heading for New York and their second appearance on the Ed Sullivan show. "WTRY's promotion department tracked them down," recalled Rick, "and found out they were traveling right thru Albany. We invited them to stop over and do a couple of shows for us."

The Stones were still on the early side of stardom, which after the negotiations, worked in the station's favor. Said Rick, "They agreed to do *two* shows in Albany's Palace Theatre for the grand sum of $2,500.00! We were ecstatic and the tickets sold out for both shows in less than an hour."

Fans packed into the theatre and didn't even care that The Stones were a tad scruffy. They rocked the Palace, introducing "I Can't Get No Satisfaction." April 29, 1965—were *you* there?!

[*Image:* Courtesy of Rick; with the bad boys of Brit bands, The Rolling Stones, c. 1965.]

Still excited, "We got an advance copy of the record and we believe that WTRY was the first station in America to play that iconic song," said Rick.

Holy Toledo Batman!

However, as the saying goes, all good things must come to an end. In late 1967, Rick moved on from "The Great 98" to WTTO/Toledo, Ohio, perched on the top floor of the Commodore Perry building.

It was a short gig though, and soon he and wife, Mary Jo, headed back East to Portland, Maine, to form an innovative husband-wife morning team.

"At WLOB we had—let me stand up for a moment." (He took a deep breath.) "We had out*standing* ratings." Rick chuckled.

Though women disc jockeys were still a rare commodity, "Mary Jo proved to be a natural," said Rick. "The Snyder and Snyder Show was a success from day one and consistently scored ratings in the low 40s!"

Once again, new station ownership meant planning budget cuts. Paying two morning DJs was not in their plans. "We went off the air in the end of 1971," said Rick, "but even today, we have people who remember us on WLOB."

Rick spent a short year in advertising sales for WGAN-TV, a Portland television station that "wasn't as much fun as radio." By 1973, TV sales burnout sent Rick to WJBQ in Portland. Hired as the station's sales manager, Rick was quickly promoted to General Manager.

This was a move that positively suited him, as he reigned the station for nine years. It's now become a family tradition, with his son also spending time on the air there.

Although we've taken "Rick the DJ" into the *Psychedelic Seventies* while we're still Rockin' the Sixties, we don't do management. <grin> So we're going to leave him here, as he calls the shots instead of shooting the turntable.

Rick inspired other disc jockeys during his jock days, like New York City's Bob Shannon, who, "as a mere boy," used to visit Rick at the Syracuse stations in the Sixties; and Boston's young Dale Dorman.

And Rick recalls his hero-memorable DJs, "I worked with best friend, Wally Brine (thirty-year Boston air personality); Joey Reynolds [BFYP DJ] "on the air since dirt was invented"; Marv Albert (legendary sports guy); Jay Clark (big market program director); and James K. Davis (big market air talent and program director, and still in the business running stations).

"My on-air hero and idol," said Rick, is Dan Ingram from WABC. Without a doubt, the best top 40 DJ of all time." Just a quick recap of radio with Rick!

A little musing about the DJs' role in the industry: "On my first overnight job we had a playlist of thirty-one songs and two extras, for the whole shift. I could play almost all of them in one hour!"

Rick continued his reminisces, "That was back when we had conversations with our DJs, and they had time to express 'personality.' We did the news and sports, and I begged the PD to let me play oldies through the night." He reveled in the 1950's Doo-Wop tunes.

Rick's DJ pet peeve, "The guys who used to rhyme things just to fill space with their own voice, used to annoy me."

Formats and the radio dial became more crowded as we moved into the 1970s—not only with more artists and advertising, but the explosion of FM popularity, as the industry grew.

DJs, said Rick, were required to adhere to an "economy of words. We had eight seconds to talk, and it better be about the music. If you couldn't pull it off, you were gone."

Today: Retired from full time radio work, Rick stays active in the business as a radio show producer in West Palm Beach, Florida. His many years behind the mic were rewarded in September 2016, with his election into the Maine Association of Broadcasters Hall of Fame [*image*]. An honor he cherishes.

We're back with BFYP Rockin' 'round California's sunny dial at 84.8-FM, boppin' to the beat as we swing ya-all into the Southland!

Marty's headin' to *El Paso* ♪ and Connie croons *You're Gonna Miss Me* ♪ while the Duke of Louisville spins them on their heads.

Bill Bailey
1930 ~ 2012
Best known at WKLO and WAKY/Louisville, Kentucky

In his early DJ days, Bill spun some rural charm with a little bit Country and a little bit Rock & Roll—whatever struck his fancy.

As we talked, I recalled a couple of his airchecks I'd listened to before the interview. His once gravelly voice may have softened a tad over time, but he still had a knack for the absurd that catches you off guard.

Our interview took place in 2008 while he enchanted his co-residents and caregivers at Kentucky's Friendship Manor. His old-world graciousness and converse penchant for mischief, still evident.

A 1967 article at the pinnacle of Bill's WKLO/Louisville success quoted him, "I'm the poor man's version of Jack E. Leonard. When you first hear me on the air, you hate my guts. You think I'm a wiseacre. But I'm not, really."

It was this homespun honesty that endeared Bill to a legion of fans whenever he ambled behind the mic. And it could be the softer, creative side of Bill that carried over the airwaves. An accomplished artist, Bill's love for drawing and painting colored his peaceful attitude throughout life.

Like many disc jockeys Bill drifted around the dial, honing his skills at whistle-stop stations in the late 1950s, stopping probably the longest in Twin Falls, Idaho. The station's call letters long-ago forgotten, Bill focused on family.

It's unclear where he spun the platters in the early 1960s, but Bill said he nearly quit radio about that time. Dealing with the aftermath of the payola scandal, levied strict limitations on DJs' rhetoric. Though never at a loss for words, he didn't take well to scripted formats.

Bill hung on until it appeared in the mid-Sixties, things were loosening up a bit. About this time, he slid into the "Bill Bailey" name (from his Dutch-heritage birth name, Bill Boahn) somewhere in Houston, Texas. I'm suspecting he was coerced into it as a station-held personality name and decided to keep it when he skipped over to Kentucky for some real fun.

Unlike some DJs of the era, Bill didn't take as well to the nomad life and was a little nervous heading into the Top 40 Rock station after a long spell of Country. Maybe that's why he kept "Bill Bailey" around—it was comfortable.

Rockin' the Country

As WKLO's morning man in 1965, the affable Bill landed in Louisville just in time for the British Invasion. While other high energy DJs were rattling bells and tooting whistle effects, Bill said, "I just talk, and I don't sound like I'm sitting on a block of ice."

[*Image:* Bill's flying high at WKLO November 12, 1965. The Airheads Radio Survey Archive; Lee Tucker, contributor.]

Bill soon ruled the airwaves at WKLO and Louisville became home. It's seemingly impossible to know when he was crowned the "Duke of Louisville," rumored to be by Governor Wendell Ford. It was likely at the height of Bill's WKLO days, when then-Lieutenant Governor Ford (1967-1971), listened to him, on his way to the historic Kentucky mansion.

Enjoying all the perks of a popular Rock & Roll Radio DJ in the mid-Sixties, Bill attributed his popularity to a proclivity for saying over the air what many in his audience would like to say aloud, but wouldn't.

Making people laugh came easily to Bill and often he made himself the butt of his jokes. Cashing in on his huge success at WKLO, Bill decided to scoot up north and see if he could duplicate it.

By the end of the decade, his fame had spread and a couple of scouts for way-up-north, WLS/Chicago, made him an offer he couldn't refuse. A bio for Bill on WAKY/Louisville (where he spent the '70s and '80s) quoted WLS-AM/Chicago's program director at the time, John Rook. Bill's salary was "the biggest we've ever offered a new man."

[*Image:* Bill is front and center in an all-star DJ lineup at WLS, November 3, 1969; surrounded by Art Roberts, Larry Lujack, Jerry Kay, Kris Stevens and Chuck Buell. *BFYP* Collection.]

Landing with much fanfare, he couldn't help himself ... only a few days into his WLS gig (1969), Bill cautioned his listeners, "When the wife gets into town, the first thing she's gonna do, is invite ya over for dinner. Look, this is a warning ... I'll tell ya right now, don't accept! ... Every time she serves a meal, I'm stretched out on the couch, and she yells, 'Come an' get it, or I'll throw it to the hogs!' She wouldn't dare. If she threw it to the hogs, they'd throw it back!"

Rolling in dough or not, it wasn't enough to keep Bill in the frozen north. "I gave them their rating—that's all they wanted—said my goodbyes and came back to Louisville. That's when I went to work for WAKY." The Duke was back.

Let's delve into a little station history here—and an aside about Bill's legacy. Spoiler! Bill did finally head to WAKY "the Big 79," around 1971 and decided it felt good. The Duke of Louisville was a comfortable voice on your WAKY morning drive for ten years.

Though this is the Sixties decade and we pause most stories as a DJ plunges into the early Seventies, Bill spent the whole next decade happily sedate—well, as sedate as Bill could be—at WAKY. So we'll leave him to it and complete his behind-the-mic tales, here.

From here to eternity ...

WAKY/Louisville became home for Bill where the Duke made a host of fans and hawked Chevrolet Vegas and Plymouth Dusters. He left in 1981, bounced around a bit again, before retiring from radio in 1994, while kissing the mic at WVLK in Lexington, Kentucky.

Terrell Metheny, DJ (Mitch Michael) and ultimately esteemed program director/station manager, chuckled, recalling his introduction to Bill in 1986. "I was looking for somebody [to hire] and heard his voice. He was talking—and talking, talking, talking, talking! I contacted him and said, Bill, I want you to tell those stories—I want you to spin those yarns, just the way you have been telling them—only I don't want you to do them all at one time. Never talk more than thirty seconds at a time, but spin the yarn ..."

Bill took his advice, though it didn't quite work out at first, the way Terrell imagined. "He finally got the hang of it, but he would be talking and spinning a yarn, and thirty seconds would go by—he'd start a record—right in the middle of a word! ... He was the greatest morning DJ ever."

While we chatted, Bill often rambled in distracted memories. That was okay. We enjoyed the playback of his DJ days. A few wanderings from the Duke:

[*Image:* WAKY'S Big 30 for May 19, 1971 had a "Never Ending Song of Love" for Bill (Bonnie & Delaney at #1). The Airheads Radio Survey Archive; Lee Tucker, contributor.]

"There's a new WAKY in town, on the FM dial and they run little clips of mine on the air, about four times a day. Of course, I don't get *paid* for 'em; but the truth of the matter is, they're a bunch of friends, so I don't worry about that."

Radio and fans: "One of the most enjoyable things for me, when people come up to the radio station to watch us work. [WKLO had a showcase window, with outside speakers.] I invited 'em to come into the studio so I could talk to 'em on the air."

Radio and family: "And I'd have my daughters come in quite often—they were just six, seven, eight years old—none went into radio." He is immensely proud of his daughters. "One is a police officer, married to a millionaire, one is a very successful beauty operator, and one works for UPS."

Radio and marriage: "My best days on the radio was in the Seventies [WAKY]. All of the Seventies—right on up to '81. I had a good time, 'cause I always had a good life. I should be ashamed of that, but I'm not. Married three times—did I say three? Make it four! Oh, my last one was unbelievable—I'm trying hard to forget that one."

Missing the old days: "Radio today is not very interesting and it isn't any fun. And if you're not having a good time, people who are listening to you are not going to have a good time ... that is a FACT, and I've proved that."

On the strict regimen of formatted radio: Bill said, "Well, it was formatted for some, but not for me. I never could follow the format. I went to Chicago [WLS] and made a few enemies up there. I did the job for 'em, don't get me wrong, but I made a few enemies, 'cause I simply don't follow formats. Anyway, I had a great time."

Today: Since 2012, Bill Boahn "The Duke of Louisville" Bailey, has been spinning yarns with our friends in Rock & Roll Heaven. His final gig was a lengthy stay with some fine folks at Friendship Manor (Pewee Valley, Kentucky), a truly friendly, assisted living home. They loved helping Bill continue to connect with his many fans. Visit Bill's tribute page at 79waky.com/billbailey.htm; and hear his deep, husky voice, never without glib chat, at ReelRadio.com.

Waxin' the '60s: There are moments in life when you simply want to make time stand still. While usually caused by a happy event—during a 1960s concert or music festival did you, like me, mentally pause the scene around you to savor its flavor a little longer?

Music can affect us like few other sensory experiences. It evokes emotion—the most powerful of human behavior. Every generation has its moments of, "Wow. This is truly a special time in my life ... in the *world.*" Was this yours?

Many of the disc jockeys I interviewed felt this way; realizing that our music melded with, mirrored, and emphasized the emotions of their listeners.

Other DJs connected with the stream of musicians and singers who vocalized our moods and captured our hearts …

[*Image:* Top of a KFRC/San Francisco Big 610 survey, March 21, 1968. The Beatles ruled the decade. Sadly, there is no artist's attribution for this exquisite piece of art. *BFYP* Collection.]

We're Rockin' the night away at your friendly BFYP radio studio! Come ... dance with us for a while ...

Devoid of The Beatles, *How Does That Grab You, Darlin'* ... ♪

Jim Stagg
aka Johnny Gray
1935 ~ 2007
Best known at WCFL/Chicago, Illinois
(Interview with wife, Valene Staggs)

It's true. May 26, 1966 there wasn't a Beatles song to be had on the Top 20 chart for WCFL/Chicago. Ol' Blue Eyes' daughter, Nancy,* asked "How Does That Grab You," charting at #15.

Turns out, it was just a breather for the Beatles, while they geared up for their third—and final—US tour, August 1966. John Lennon had recently proclaimed they are "more popular than Jesus now." When he slid that off-hand remark into a British news interview, he meant it in context with the waning Christianity in the UK and with his recent exploration of all religions.

But then as now, the media worked us Yanks into a frenzy and before you knew it, your neighbors were burning the Beatles' vinyls. (Oh, the pollution!)

Although the politicized publicity sealed the fate on future Beatles concerts, it didn't deter Jim Stagg from joining them on their final tour.

But first, how did Jim get there?

After his initial rise in the late 1950s, we find Jim struggling with the alarm clock by January 1960, in his big break at WIBG/Philadelphia. They put up with his tardiness for about a month, then told him to have sweet dreams somewhere else. Thankfully, his home town station still loved him. WYDE/Birmingham, Alabama, took him back while he recovered from his career misstep.

By August though, the undaunted DJ with the distinctive voice, attracted attention from the West. KYA/San Francisco made him an offer he didn't refuse. He even allowed them to drop a "G" from his name—whether intentional or a misspelling, it stuck.

Are you cruisin' down the Memory Lane morning drive with him? "I'm Jim Stag ... rolling you out on the soft side, my friend ..."

In good company with DJs Tom Donahue, Bob Mitchell, and Tony Tremayne, among other great voices, they and the California weather weren't enough to keep him happy. Jim's first couple of survey appearances with a question mark photo, stoked fans' curiosity, though it was only because the station didn't have his picture yet.

Jim's classic good looks kept him on the KYA surveys for about a year. Heading into fall of 1961, Jim trekked East again, picking up a cool program director position at WOKY/Milwaukee.

[*Image:* KYA Official Swingin' 60, September 5, 1960. *BFYP* Collection.]

WOKY was another year-long music spinner where Jim honed his skills and made friends of his listeners. As newscaster Raymond E. Spencer declared, "Here's our *man* in Milwaukee, Jim Stag, with hit music."**

Coming off the ode to "Caterina" by the unmistakable Perry Como, Jim welcomed his listeners, "A good, good mornin' to ya ... I'll be here 'til ten to make sure you get up and at 'em ..." (**ReelRadio.com, May 1, 1962.)

Skipping over to KYW/Cleveland mid-year 1962, Jim finally found a place he could settle in at—though he may have been influenced by a lovely young lady.

KYW and Cleveland fans treated Jim like a celebrity, with a stupendous promo on his arrival in the city that would eventually become host to the Rock and Roll Hall of Fame. (RockHall.com)

Jim, however, saw none of the enthusiastic admirers, once he spotted Valene, a recent beauty contest winner, whose prizes included a fun stint interning in KYW's promotional department. As I listened to her fond memories, I thought, this proves Kismet is real ...

"I picked him up at the airport on a warm June day in 1962. Jim disembarked to a crowd of fans waiting to greet him, but he walked right up to me—because I had the KYW sign—and said, 'Hey Babycakes, ya wanna get married?!'"

Valene paused in her memories. "We were married in November," she said wistfully. "He was the most down-to-earth, wonderful individual, but he had to play the persona of a carefree disc jockey." Their whirlwind courtship lasted a week short of forty-five years.

That first week, lucky listeners grabbed up tickets to meet Jim on board a Lake Erie tour boat. "He did very well in Cleveland," said Valene. "He took it to #1, along with [DJs] Ken Draper, Jerry Bishop, Jim Runyan, and the others. It was a fun station."

I'll say ... who wouldn't call breaking out new records and interviewing The Supremes' star, Diana Ross, fun?! Following their on-air chat, Jim urged Diana to introduce the next song—hers of course. A great thrill for up-and-comer, Ross, and her fans.

He liked to research and interview the artists, featuring most of the major music stars of the '60s throughout his radio career.

A prolific name-dropper, but no tippy-toes in interviews

"Jim became known as the person to get an interview with," said Valene. He chatted up the Rolling Stones, Neil Diamond, Frank Sinatra, Ray Charles, The Monkees … just to name-drop a few. "I have nine hundred reel-to-reel tapes of Jim and others from that period. They're just as clear as the day they were recorded," she added wistfully.

KYW solidified Jim's radio stint in history when they sent him and a listener to England for a return flight to accompany none other than newly minted celebs, The Beatles. "George and John took a particular liking to Jim," recalled Valene.

"The other DJs would ask mundane questions [i.e., 'What do you like for breakfast?'], and Jim would come along with a question like, 'Do you know the psychological needs of these teenagers that make them go so crazy?' John especially, *loved* those kinds of questions."

Three years was a long time at one station for Jim—for a lot of restless DJs, actually. By May of 1965 KYW's bright lights dimmed, as grumblings and rumblings caused a major rift between staff and management.

Following Jim's lead, "Practically the whole station went to Chicago," said Valene. "Owned by the AFofLCIO* union, WCFL was still giving farm reports." [*Pre-merger moniker of the American Federation of Labor and Congress of Industrial Organizations and Labor unions in the United States, making it the AFL-CIO in 1955.]

No more corn and wheat news at WCFL after Jim and the gang arrived. "They changed the whole format," Valene recalled, "and went head-to-head with WLS." As you might recall, WLS was in its glory days in 1965. Rumored to be the first radio station to list the Beatles on a survey (March 8, 1963), WCFL was about to steal its Rock and Roll thunder.

Yes, finally, Jim was in his glory at WCFL. He continued to pal around with the Beatles and Chicago loved him even more than Cleveland. The station and the DJ fed off each other for some of the best radio of the era.

An August 1967 aircheck finds Jim comparing British and American radio surveys with popular duo, Peter and Gordon ("A World Without Love," and "Lady Godiva," two of many more hits). His reputation for delving into the depths of Rock and Roll, rather than ask frivolous anecdotal questions, had preceded him. Mike O'Neal introduced, "Stagg Talks to the Stars," in his deep, resonant voice …

Stepping boldly into the interview, "If you look at the English top thirty, you'll find that ten or maybe even fifteen of those songs are done by American artists. And Peter and Gordon are still trying to figure out why." He baited the duo ...

One of the British pop artists admitted, "Even the English hits—most of them are written by Americans." The interview concluded without a concise answer as to why.

"Here's *Ringo*, baby," Jim announced the next song up on the turntable. The Beatles' "Yellow Submarine," is said to be Ringo's most popular lead vocals song. It was still climbing at WCFL, hitting #6 on their October 6, 1966 music chart, with Peter and Gordon's "Lady Godiva" (their last hit in Britain) making its premier on the chart.

"He called his interview segments, 'Stairway to the Stars,'" Valene recalled, "and his 'Stagg's Starbeat' segment was written up in teen magazines." Jim's "Stagg Hit Line" also became a WCFL survey fan favorite, transitioning to a weekly column in the Sunday editions of the *Chicago Sun-Times*.

[*Image:* "The Stagg Hit Line" was a hit, with The Beatles on WCFL survey, October 6, 1966. One day along the way, WCFL restored the missing "g" in Jim's name. *BFYP* Collection.]

The early 1970s were pivotal years for Jim's radio focus, and music in general. FM stations played more mainstream and Jim segued his fan power into politics.

His influence as Chicago chairman of Let Us Vote (LUV), along with Joey Bishop and other top celebrities, were influential in the 1971 ratification of the Twenty-Sixth Amendment to the US Constitution, allowing eighteen-year-olds to vote.

The January 26, 1970 WCFL survey represents Jim's waning days at the station. By late spring, he was chatting away on Miami's WQAM talk radio.

Although Jim's DJ career ended in 1975, music would remain a huge part of who he was, as he opened his first music store, "Record City." It ultimately spawned a popular chain with several locations in Illinois and Florida; the last of which closed in 2005.

Today: Valene occasionally pulls out one of her reel-to-reel tapes, threads it onto the machine, and listens to the smooth sounds of Jim's strong, resonant voice. [*Image:* 2006, Courtesy of Valene.] It refreshes her memories of a man who stole her heart with his first words, and his fans' undeniable affection with his show's trademark last line, "Music is my business. I hope my business was your pleasure."

Waxin' the '60s: Sexy, silly or stately, did your fave DJ have a "personality" name?

Fun fans, like my cousin, Ron, vowed allegiance as an "officially commissioned 1st lieutenant" in "Emperor [Gene] Nelson's "Royal Commandos."

At San Francisco's KYA The Emperor was joined by normal-named, Ed Hider, Mike Cleary, Johnny Holliday, Tony Bigg, Tommy Saunders, and Sean O'Callaghan.

[*Images:* Right, KYA's Top 30 survey March 12, 1966. "The Ballad of the Green Beret" by Sgt. Barry Sandler, held the top spot for a second week. Below, the back of the Emperor's royal card.

Yes, we had so much more fun in 1966 than kids are allowed today.

Are you listening? I say, San Diego, ARE YOU LISTENING?! We're knockin' heads and playin' the hits all day for you at BFYP 84.8-FM ...

The vinyl grooves were spinnin' into a **Whole Lotta Love**'! ♪

Rich "Brother" Robbin >Part 2
Best known at KCBQ/San Diego, California

When he arrived in San Diego Rich finally found his DJ stride, as he stepped into his own personality, and out from behind the mimicking shadow of the Real Don Steele.

With the ocean breeze, Rich refreshed his DJ shtick, and treasured his later friendship with the Real Don Steele. "A sensational human being. Brilliant and lovable, and a great big son-of-a-bitch, too," he said with much respect.

"Everything was basically unremarkable," said Rich of his DJ life, "until I got to KGB/San Diego in 1969. Buzz Bennett taught me about programming and taught me how to have that kind of energy, but only *totally* in my own person—not a Real Don Steele clone."

[*Image:* Caricature of Rich Brother Robbin by the illustrious DJ, Bobby "Van Goon" Ocean. KGB Boss 30 survey, October 15, 1969. *BFYP* Collection.]

Rich's perpetual party style made listening to him upbeat and fun. KGB's rogue reputation prospered in spite of Buzz's admonition to the DJs, "Stay off the phones. If you're sitting there during the records trying to hustle pussy, you're not thinking about what you're doing."

I'm sure that was an effective warning to the mid-twenties DJs, in mid-summer San Diego, with thoughts of chatting up beach bunnies in teeny bikinis. Right.

"KGB became so powerful," said Rich, "because we were reflecting the people. A new song came out—it had to be good and in the top fifteen, or we didn't play it. [But] We'd play four or five songs an hour that were up to two or three years old."

If listeners requested older songs, they'd still play them, on a regular basis. It was just one of their inside tricks to beat the competition—namely, KCBQ. But it wasn't their only trick.

"We sped the tunes up a little for a while. If you do it exactly right," Rich explained, "it doesn't make them sound fast—it makes your competitor sound *slooowww*. But—we didn't have variable speed turntables – we just painted whiteout on the capstand (motor) of the turntable, to make them go faster ..."

Aha. *Now* we know why our home turntables were frustratingly sluggish!

When Rich joined the station, at the urging of Bill Drake (largely credited with infusing the Boss Radio format), KGB led the success of the hyper format in Southern California. He fit right in, and rode its success to the top of the charts.

There was nothing sluggish about Rock and Roll Radio in the late Sixties. Since 1967's Summer of Love, creative minds worked overtime on the music and airwaves, often with a little help from our friends.

Album Oriented Rock hits the San Diego airwaves

Swirling through a psychedelic counterculture of style and sound in San Francisco, a restless rebelliousness crept into radio, as DJs Tom Donahue and Larry Miller transformed an ethnic station (KMPX) into Album Oriented Rock (AOR). It was just the beginning.

At KMPX Donahue slipped the 33-1/3 rpm album of Jefferson Airplane's *Surrealistic Pillow* onto the turntable (before "Starship" soared into space). "Somebody to Love" and "White Rabbit" transitioned from the AOR playlists to mainstream radio and we officially slid down the rabbit hole to mind-awakening music.

Characterized by obscure and longer cuts by innovative artists, AOR began its climb up the listener ladder with FM radio. Still Rockin' strong in 1968, KGB's "'Boss 30' Records" days were numbered.

[*Image:* We started seeing the conflict as pop tune "Venus" (Shocking Blue) and hard-rocking "Whole Lotta Love'" (Led Zeppelin) share the #1 spotlight on KGB's December 30, 1969 survey. *BFYP* Collection.]

1969 saw radio twitching with a seven-year itch, prepping for another format shakeup. Always seeking an edge over the competition, by the early 1970s, Rich Brother Robbin and friends at KGB, began the transition that would serve the San Diego area well, as the new radio format swept across the nation.

Early into the *Psychedelic Seventies*, KGB fired "Boss Radio" and hired Ron Jacobs to finish its transformation. Says Rich, "KHJ [L.A.] would have never been the success it was without him as program director," and Rich saw that brilliance again, at KGB. Not as a DJ for KGB, but for its competitor, KCBQ.

Rich Brother Robbin helped propel legendary Top 40 station, KCBQ, into its glory days, arriving for a whirlwind gig in 1971, and returning more than a couple times over the next twenty years.

A career DJ, Rich flourished in the Seventies. Popping between San Diego and Los Angeles, his addictive, high-energy, fast-rapping patter kept his fans tuning in wherever he sat behind the mic.

[*Image:* Rich enjoys retirement (since 2014), but we hear he still dabbles in radio when the urge and offer occurs.

Today: Rich Brother Robbin is an enduring welcome sight in the San Diego and Los Angeles radio scene. He keeps a finger on the virtual turntable with his Oldies music streaming site at RichbroRobbin.com.

Go—and *Enjoy the Moment ... Again.*

We're gonna Rock, Rock, Rock, all night long at BFYP-FM. Well, at least until Oscar calls his name. Roll out the red carpet, fellas!

Could you, would you, should you ... ♪ *Gimme Shelter*, my friend?

Neil Ross
Best known at KCBQ/San Diego, California

"A program director once said, 'If you can say two clever things an hour, you'll be a star.' I thought, oh, my God, he's right! The trick is not to try so hard. Get your two good things in and keep the rest lean and clean." Neil Ross listened to his mentors and indeed, became a star. It all began ...

KCBQ/San Diego's fishbowl studio was the window into the soul of Rockin' radio for many a budding disc jockey.

"Shotgun Tom Kelly's story is very similar to mine," said Neil, "though he's a few years younger. But we basically had the same experience of delivering newspapers in the early morning hours with a little transistor radio in our shirt pockets, listening to Jack [Vincent] on the all-night show."

With another memory and a hearty chuckle, Neil continued, "We made the pilgrimage down to 7th & Ash, and stood in the street, looking up at this guy trying to figure out how he did what he did, and just wishing like *hell* we could get up there and *do* that job."

Wishin' and hopin' doesn't make it happen, so on graduating without enough backing for college, he scouted around for a broadcast school. In the early 1960s that was not an easy feat. Though there was one close by in Los Angeles, its two-year curriculum wasn't too appetizing for a DJ wannabe in a hurry.

But KSDO broadcaster and neighbor, Otto Miller, clued Neil into the RCA Institute in New York that could get him airwaves ready in six months—and away he went.

"I passed the course and took a job delivering a car across the country to get me back home ..." which made it as far as Salt Lake City. While he was stranded for a couple of weeks, Neil made good use of his time and ... "more for practice than looking for a job, I went around interviewing with stations."

The young Neil must have made a good impression. He'd been home a couple months, making the rounds of SoCal stations, when KMUR/Murray, Utah, called with an offer. He thought, why not? It became his first real DJ job.

The Salt Lake City suburb's top forty station served as a starting point with a whopping 250-watt broadcast that peaked at 1,000 daytime watts. Okay, not exactly a powerhouse station, but hey, you gotta start somewhere.

Neil, and The Chiffons' "He's So Fine," debuted in 1963 to give the pre-Beatles top forty charts a whirl. It was a valuable year as he not only earned his DJ chops but also learned he wasn't yet learned enough. "While in Salt Lake City I discovered that a first-class license was very necessary."

In small to medium markets, which were most DJs' stepping stones to the big time, a first-class license opened more doors because a DJ could double as an engineer to run the directional transmitter.

"In big cities," said Neil, "it wasn't an issue, because they had engineers on staff. I sent out tapes and resumes [to bigger stations on the West Coast] but kept hearing, 'We love your work, but ...' After three or four times of that I decided I needed a license."

Back to the coast he went, to enroll in the same Burbank, California, school that counts Shotgun Tom Kelly and so many others among its alumni—the William B. Ogden Radio Operational School. (ModestoRadioMuseum.org)

Hey buddy, have ya got a dime?

"I was practically destitute when I got out of the Ogden school," Neil admitted. "I had to grab the first job I could, which put me in Lewiston, Idaho." KRLC was not the best place to hone his new skills, given its rural setting across the Snake River from Clarkston, Washington. "I got out of there as quickly as I could," said Neil.

Picture this: 1964, a fresh-faced, nineteen-year-old kid sitting with the tumbleweeds in rural Idaho, eager to explore his new career, wherever it may take him. Back home to the West Coast? Adventurous Southwest? The big city lights of New York? Oh, you're not thinking exotic enough! Aloha ...

"Sitting in the KRLC studios," said Neil, "I got a call from Honolulu. The guy offered me $150 per month *less* than I was making in Idaho—I kid you not! I said to him 'Gee, we must have a bad connection, it sounds like you said $300 per month.'" Neil paused, nudging his nostalgic thoughts to the surface, "And they wouldn't pay for the move. I told the guy, 'God, I don't think I can *do* this.'" Ah, but sometimes, it isn't about the money ...

Neil continued down Memory Lane, "The guy came back with the greatest answer in the world. 'We have studios overlooking the pool at the Waikiki Biltmore Hotel.' I said, 'I'll see you in two weeks!'"

The unspoiled Hawaii of the mid-Sixties was, as Neil put it, "not the kind of place where everybody and his nephew had been." Yet. It was just beginning its climb up the tourist-trap ladder, after Elvis's *Blue Hawaii* (1961) movie featured its sexy side.

Capping the Sixties, when Detective Captain Steve McGarrett ordered, "Book 'em, Danno!" in the 1968 original *Hawaii Five-O* TV series, our 50th state's popularity glittered like the panoramic view of Diamond Head (Lē' ahi).

Neil ambled around three or four stations during his five years on the islands. He spent a year first, at KORL and three years at KGMB—a MOR (middle of the road) music station.

His island memories floated to the background for a moment, to talk about the music that drove his DJ ambitions ...

"I was seduced by Rock and Roll. I never liked music when I was a kid. It was all that horrible early '50s stuff; you know—Patti Page, 'How Much is that Doggie in the Window?'—dopey love songs, and none of it meant anything to me. I found it terribly boring.

"One afternoon visiting a friend, they had a radio on in the kitchen [didn't everyone then?!], and I heard "Tutti Frutti" by Little Richard, and I absolutely fell on the floor! This is wonderful! *This* is what I've been waiting to hear my whole life. Somebody finally got it right." [Neil was able to meet Little Richard later in his DJ life and relate that childhood epiphany.]

Transfixed by Rock and Roll, Neil reveled in Elvis and Buddy Holly ... "and *then*," said Neil, "like the guy said in the song*, the music kinda died. Elvis went in the Army, Buddy Holly got killed, and Little Richard became a preacher. All of a sudden, the music wasn't that great anymore. [*"American Pie," Don McLean, 1971.]

By the time he reached KGMB, "I had no emotional involvement with the music at all," Neil said, speaking of Frank Sinatra and cronies. "It was just a job."

Neil scouted around the islands looking for something more suitable, or at least with more current music. He settled in at KKUA for another year before fate sailed him home.

[*Image:* Courtesy of Neil; mugging for the camera with Sinatra's baby blues watching, KKUA/Honolulu, 1968.]

But first, some of the decade's greatest music celebs lit a musical fire under the impressionable young disc jockey. Neil was in the right place at the right time ...

"While at KKUA, we brought The Doors to Honolulu and I got to spend a couple of hours back stage with them—I was just in heaven," said Neil. "I also met Credence Clearwater Revival—KKUA was one of the first stations to even play their album—it was their first gig as Credence, outside of the [San Francisco] Bay Area."

Kindred spirits ...

Neil naturally gravitated toward another San Diego DJ, Jim Talley, aka Jimmy Mack, who listed a gig at KCBQ on his resume. Neil said when Jimmy first arrived at KKUA, "We talked about who was working at KCBQ and about getting back there one day ... and life went on."

Despite Hawaii's many charms the DJs talked often about the next career step. "One day, Jimmy walked in and said, 'Well, I got the job back at KCBQ. I'm leaving.' He offered to take a tape [the standard DJ's resume] with him and give it to the program director." He did, and a few months later, Gary Allyn called Neil with a job offer. He was homeward bound.

Neil wound up the decade at KCBQ. Originally hired for production work, it wasn't long before someone quit and his boyhood dream came true—HE was the KCBQ disc jockey.

Though he missed the fishbowl window experience by a year—KCBQ moved its studio to Santee in 1968—it still held the significance of accomplishment.

K-West of the Mississippi
C-Columbia
B-Broadcasting
Q-Quality

And for Neil, music began to show promise again. "The Album Rock stuff started to come out, and I *loved* that! Although never one of the FM underground guys, I was very much in sympathy with them and loved a lot of that music. Most of them were just hippies that drifted into radio ... it was an incredibly fertile time for Rock and Roll music. Nothing before, like it."

[*Image:* Artist sketch (K. Koiser) graced KCBQ's Hit List cover October 3, 1969. *BFYP* Collection.]

"I tell my daughter, the difference between 1960 and 1969, is as if a hundred years had gone by ..."

Most of us who came of age as teens or young adults during that decade, likely echo Neil's profound words. The music, the politics, society—it all changed drastically in those ten short years.

And it was just the beginning.

As much as he enjoyed the thrill of KCBQ, even his idyllic boyhood radio station soon became another notch on his DJ belt. "I kind of bounced around for a couple years," said Neil. But it will remain one of his fondest memories. We met at the 2010 KCBQ monument dedication. There was an unmistakable camaraderie that day between all of the disc jockeys who honored the station's role in their lives.

We'll follow Neil into the *Psychedelic Seventies* as he questions choices on many levels. He struggles with his fading radio love affair, through a string of short station gigs in the late 1970s. Change is in the air for Neil—it was a good thing.

Today: Eventually, it was off the radio and into the studio for Neil, as he continues a very successful voice over career. But he treasures the memories of radio that honed his golden voice.

[*Image:* Courtesy of Neil, c. 2003; taking a break.]

More today than yesterday, let's live for tomorrow! BFYP-FM ... inspiration for your inner Rock & Roll muse!

At the end of the day, it's the music we *Cherish* ... ♪

Warren Garling

aka Jesse James; Chris Warren (current)
Best known at WSNY/Albany, New York

There are just some people who know from early childhood, what they want to be "when they grow up." Sigh. As a (really) late bloomer, I've always envied those who were inspired early.

Warren visited his first radio station at the tender age of eleven. Eyes wide and voice high, he came home and declared, "Mom, Dad, I don't want to be Roy Rogers anymore. I want to be a Radio DJ!"

Most parents would have been horrified. To their credit in an era when traditional careers were vogue, Warren's parents never wavered in their encouragement. [Likely thrilled they wouldn't have to buy an expensive horse.]

"I have to credit, too," said Warren, "my junior high guidance counselor. He listened and understood my passion for it. In ninth grade, he told me about a local radio station's intern program—you know, a glorified go-fer program!"

Warren recalled the usual go-fer stuff at WSNY/Albany, New York—making/fetching coffee and such—but he was learning the broadcasting business from the inside.

The MOR [Middle of the Road] "beautiful music" station sent its instrumentals out over a 1000-watt daytime and 250-watt nighttime system. "My folks couldn't even hear it, about twenty miles away," said Warren.

During this time, he continued listening to his favorite stations and making DJ contacts where he could. In 1968, Bob Dearborn—Mark Allen, on-air—grabbed Warren's attention on WPTR. "I'd call him almost every evening to talk about radio. Sometimes I'd 'win' a 45 [record] or album."

Years later, he stumbled on Bob in an Internet forum, and sent an email of thanks for helping him all those years ago. "He responded," said Warren, "and said he didn't remember Warren specifically, but recalls encouraging anyone who wanted to do this [DJ] for a living, 'because I was having so much fun!'"

At WSNY, in addition to serving at the DJs' beck and call, Warren began learning the radio broadcasting ropes.

"I didn't record commercials, but got to take tape-recorded commercials and put them onto cartridges for playing on the air. I cut stories out of the newspapers, and fed them to the DJs for reading on-air."

Go-fer wouldn't leave his hole

His internship lasted through the school year and when summer hit, the other interns dutifully stopped showing up. Not Warren. His mother dropped him off every Friday afternoon, as usual.

A little early teen brashness colored his voice again, as he told me, "I just didn't stop going. Nobody told me not to, so I just started hanging around with some of the disc jockeys."

[*Image:* Courtesy of Warren; Warren might be pondering his next move in 1967, "Let me think about this DJ stuff for a minute."]

What a great gig for an opportunistic kid! Ah, but nothing lasts forever ...

"I'm thinking, at only fifteen years old, that I'm 'in' here ya know, but suddenly by the end of summer, or a little later," Warren recalled, "the station changed formats and went to a top 40 format. And ... that's when they told me to stop coming in."

Obviously a smart chap, Warren maintained his connection to the DJs. He did what the rest of us did—phoned them! "I'd call them and tell them how serious I was about getting into this industry, and eventually, one day ... I remember like it was yesterday," said Warren. "It was the last day of my junior year of high school and I'm babysitting my cousins at their house. The phone rings and it's the disc jockey that I'd been keeping most in touch with at WSNY—the evening guy."

Warren's voice was as excited in the retelling of his story as he probably was when he told all his young friends. Lost in the memory, he said, "The DJ asked, 'What are you doing this weekend?' And I shot back, 'Why?' He said, 'Would you like to work midnight to six Friday night and midnight to seven on Saturday?'"

The DJ had to leave town for the weekend and cajoled his boss into using Warren as a replacement DJ, promising to be responsible for training him enough for the two-shift gig.

Warren laughed. "My cousins had to pick me up off the floor!" Of course, he jumped at the chance, but it wasn't going to be easy—his older girlfriend's graduation festivities were also planned for that weekend.

"So I worked from 7:00 p.m. on Friday 'til 6:00 a.m. in the morning," said Warren. "I went home to sleep for about two hours, escorted her to graduation, went home, slept another two hours, attended her graduation party, went home and slept another couple of hours, and back to the radio station again!"

Phew! Made me tired just listening to his animated memory. Ah, the energy of youth! "It proved to me," the wizened Warren said, "It isn't *what* ya know, it's *who* ya know!"

Come Monday morning, he received a call from the program director. "'I listened to you. You're pretty good. Would you like to come in and do the three to seven afternoon drive for the rest of the summer?'" Warren said to him, "How much do I have to pay ya?"

Of course, they paid him, but Warren chuckled, recalling, "Either he or I should have been arrested for child labor violations. I worked seven-day weeks that whole summer."

Ending the decade of surrealistic happenings

1969—what a summer it was—for all of us. Warren "came of age" on air, as many historical events like the moon landing (July 21) and Woodstock (August 15-18), played out in the summer heat.

Never mind that he couldn't watch Neil Armstrong take his celebrated first step on the moon, live—radio stations didn't have TVs in their studios back then—he was smitten. If he hadn't been in love with radio already, says Warren, "I certainly was by the end of that summer and there was nothing else I was going to do with my life."

Warren broke into New York's radio market with some of the best DJs, when real names were obscured, and fake personas made it fun, silly, and scintillating.

"You had the 'Lively Ones' at WTRY," said Warren, "then there were the 'Good Guys' at WPTR, and suddenly this upstart thousand-watt station—WSNY—is going to be 'Home of the Young Americans.'"

He's long forgotten the real names of his DJ mentors, "Paul Revere," "George Washington," and "Tom Jefferson." And though weekend DJs are notoriously overlooked in radio stations' profiles and promos, Warren did get a cool name.

[*Image:* WSNY August 3, 1969, proudly listing the "Young Americans." Airheads Radio Survey Archive; Geno Rice, contributor.]

"I came in as 'Jesse James,'" said Warren, "because I was just a kid. And, they already had a Jesse James jingle."

For a couple of summers, Jesse ruled the weekend airwaves at "Tomorrow's Radio Today WSNY/1240," proud of its American heritage, with its surveys in "Bodoni type, popular in the 18th Century."

Was it a prophetic coincidence that our futuristic moon landing and WSNY's #1 song on its "20 Top Singles" for that hot August week was "In the Year 2525"? If one-hit wonder pop duo Zager and Evans thought it was a reflection of the technology at *that* juncture, what must they think now?!

"*Everything you think, do and say | Is in the pill you took today ...*"

Warren finished the decade and greeted the dawn of the *Psychedelic Seventies* at WSNY, reveling in the Rock & Roll of things ... and then he became a Country boy! He signed off Rock & Roll to enjoy the twangy side of life.

Still in Albany, Warren couldn't believe he ended up at WGNA. "I can't stand Country music! ... I hear about a new FM station and thought, maybe I could talk them into a new [Rock] format I'd been thinking about." This is why you should always ask questions of a prospective employer ... and he didn't *listen* to the station on-air first.

"I get there and don't find out until after they hired me—they'd decided it would be Country music." But hey, it was a powerhouse station heard in five states. So he stayed ... for twelve years. Yeehaw!

Today: You may have heard Warren in recent years as "Chris Warren" spinning the—well, pushing the buttons—weekends at WTRY/Albany, New York, the old "Great 98." (Now an iHeart Media station.)

That leaves him time to host various podcasts and apply his dulcet tones in commercial voice over work for the likes of McGraw-Hill Publishing and Papa John's Pizza.

Just in case he gets bored, "I'm an instructor/producer for voice acting students at Voice Coaches in Albany, New York, where I'm also Director of Marketing." And he tries to keep up with six-year-old granddaughter, Fia Marie, on her weekly visits. [*Image:* 2007, courtesy of Warren; still an energetic kid.]

Well, Rock & Roll Radio listeners, hear the rumble of the underground airwaves? Set your dial to BFYP 84.8-FM for a musical revolution ...

Big Daddy's knockin' on the door, **Break On Through (to the Other Side)** ... ♪

𝒯𝑜𝑚 𝒟𝑜𝑛𝑎𝒽𝑢𝑒 >𝒫𝑎𝑟𝑡 2
aka Thomas Coman; "Big Daddy"
1928 ~ 1975
Best known at KMPX & KYA/San Francisco, California
(Interview with wife, Raechel Donahue)

Yep, times they were a-changin' on the open range of 1960s radio. It wouldn't take an army to begin a revolution ... just a maverick jock or two. Tom "Big Daddy" Donahue fit the description in a big way.

"I think it was 1966," said Raechel Donahue, "we went to I think, the Longshoreman's Hall—a big hippy ball, down by the Haight [San Francisco's infamous Haight & Ashbury streets]. We got out of the car and looked around; there were all these people with buckskin fringe and feathers in their hair, and wild-'n'-crazy hats, and you know, you see one or two of them [usually] but there were *thousands* of them. Maybe I'm exaggerating; maybe hundreds."

Raechel took a deep breath and continued her memories in her husky timbre, "Tom looked at me and said, 'It's as if someone just lifted a giant flat rock! And we crawled out from underneath.' We're looking around, goin' 'Hey man, hey ... I know you.'"

San Francisco, 1967—right from the get-go it was gonna be a crazy year. Actor Ronald Reagan settled into Sacramento's mansion as governor of California; wild child band, The Doors, released their self-titled debut album; and Golden Gate Park hosted the Human Be-In. [*Image:* eBay.]

Many musicians rebelled against authority and war through their music, decidedly not popular on the AM station turntables. But they resonated with fans who could find them, and FM innovators capitalized on the open market.

Slowly, more new FM stations began to creep onto the radio dial. Smart management catered to listeners who quested for unique music, and DJs who ignored the Top 40 rules. Reveling in its freedom to snub the radio establishment, AOR (Album-Oriented Rock) flourished.

About this time, Tom's business ventures prospered and he became less enamored with AM radio and Top 40. "Tom was sick of bubble gum music – *Sugar, sugar, honey, honey** ..." A late '60s example, Raechel mimicked the lightweight song in her 2002 *Rock Jocks* documentary. [*Archies 1969]

A fan of local experimental musicians, The Doors, the Grateful Dead, Quicksilver Messenger Service, and other trendsetters of the era, Tom's frustration matched theirs. As the AM stations snubbed their music, he Rocked out at home, searching for a groovy alternative to the staid Top 40 format.

Tom wasn't the only one whose attitude changed with the music ... countering a downward spiral of collective depression, hippies ushered in a year of Flower Power and "Make Love, Not War" events—the Human Be-In kicked off the year and led into a steamy Summer of Love. The Donahues would be right in the thick of it.

A find-a-need-and-fill-it kinda guy, Tom began poking around the San Francisco Bay Area looking for a radio station he could make his own.

Early in 1967 Tom found another like-minded DJ in Larry Miller, spinning an oasis of "folk rock" in a sea of foreign-language daytime programming. He "did his own thing" from midnight to 6:00 a.m. on San Francisco's KMPX.

Tom persuaded the station owners to let him replace the daytime shows as their contracts expired, to feature album-oriented rock and local musicians.

[*Image:* 1967 KMPX signed poster print by famed Rock Artists, Stanley Mouse of Mouse Studios, and Alton Kelley. *BFYP* Collection.]

AOR and a staff of chicks

Big Daddy began April 7, 1967 by preceding Larry's show, his mellifluous voice booming with a new radio sound in the San Francisco Bay Area.

With barely a thought of leading a radio revolution, Tom also hired Raechel (nee Hamilton) and charged her with creating a staff of "chick engineers."

"He decided we should hire women because he felt women performed better at technical jobs ... and he thought they'd be more inclined to work hard and not be jealous of the DJ and want to take his job."

By June 10th finally getting some Top 40 recognition, The Doors were lighting up KFRC's "Big 30" chart. The station hosted Fantasy Fair & Magic Mountain Music Festival at the top of Mt. Tamalpais, north of San Francisco.

The rustic amphitheater *rocked* with what's considered one of the first-ever large-scale music festivals. Preceding the more professionally advertised Monterey Pop Festival, it set the stage for major outdoor Rock events.

san francisco

ED MITCHELL - 9 Till Noon On The BIG 610

In an ethereal, idyllic environment, the venue offered visceral vibes of Flower Power and top album tunes *not* on the Top 40, that slid off your mind with the light haze that wafted through the trees.

I wanted the short* "Light My Fire" to go on forever. We swayed as one, entranced with its hypnotic beat. The Doors song sat at #2 on the KFRC Big 30 chart May 17, 1967. The following week, it floated to #1. [*Image: BFYP* Collection.]

*The album version is a heavenly seven minutes of musical mayhem ... that day, I'm sure it was even longer ... and yet, still not long enough.

We might never have tripped out on the raucous sounds of the late 1960s in all its psychedelic glory, if not for Tom Donahue and freeform radio.

Raechel recalled their interaction with many of the decade's rising musical stars: "We had a nightclub called Mother's. All these groups played there. Tom and I had The Dead on our record label, and as the emergency crew. Tom is the one who got Warner Brothers to *see* The Grateful Dead, and negotiated for them a 12% contract, when all the rest of the world was getting 3%. They played the club for free."

Raechel's story, station rules, FM's rise ... and the beat goes on ...

Oh yeah, at BFYP-FM one pill makes you small, and the ones at Mother's are so large they don't fit in the radio at all ...

Go ask Alice why she's singing to the ... White Rabbit ... ♪

Raechel Donahue
Best known at KMPX & KSAN/San Francisco, California

KMPX kick-started careers for several memorable DJs, like Dusty Street*, one of radio's pioneering women broadcasters, and Howard Hesseman, quintessential road-weary DJ in TV's *WKRP in Cincinnati* (1978-82). (*DustyStreet.net)

But for one woman, it wasn't only the music, rebel format, and kick-ass era that claimed her attention. She found a kindred spirit in the man who hired her to help him with his music label, Autumn Records.

What he didn't know is the lovely Raechel Hamilton, a San Francisco State student, wasn't the twenty-two-year-old he thought, but an ambitious seventeen-year-old who graduated high school early. Nor was she about to tell him ... and soon it didn't matter.

[*Image:* Electric moment for Tom and Raechel. BayAreaRadio.org]

Tom Donahue saw a spark in the randy Raechel that he couldn't ignore. Discovering they had more in common than radio and music, Raechel became Mrs. Donahue (they married in 1969) and just like a pair of Tom's thoroughbreds ... they were off to the races!

"I actually never wanted to be a DJ," said Raechel. I really preferred production." But Tom wore her down and soon she was on the air. Did Raechel have an edge over other pioneering women DJs? Absolutely ...

"When I first started in the business I asked every famous disc jockey I knew to give me one piece of advice," said Raechel. "B. Mitchell Reed, Gary Owens—I asked guys I listened to, growing up. Because of Tom's age difference [they were twenty-four years apart] I was able to know them all."

A California girl, Raechel listened intently to the DJs who kept stations like KYA, KEWB (San Francisco) and KFWB (Los Angeles) at the top of the radio ratings.

"I patterned myself after them, rather than what the going style was for women. I learned to play with the big kids," said Raechel.

For a few short years, freeform radio jocks and the FM stations reveled in their music rebellion. Spreading the word in a whole new way of connecting with the listeners, Raechel and Tom transformed KMPX into a revolutionary model for more FM stations.

Spreading the love

Early in 1968 the Donahues were asked by station owners to work their magic at KPPC/Pasadena [Los Angeles]. At both stations, says Raechel, "I trained the disc jockeys. I taught them how to use breathing techniques, and taught them the music." The dynamic duo of radio kept both stations humming.

[*Image:* 1968 unsigned KMPX poster. eBay.]

Unique to FM stations, was the DJs' ability to play a format that followed an artist's thought process in the production of an album. Raechel taught the DJs how to work with an album's theme, or meld songs from several artists. "At that particular time it was really fun to be able to create the show when you could weave a musical topic and tell the story."

She lamented, "But now it's more formulaic Top 40, which is what FM was created to replace. Same old thing, just different songs."

Discussing the then-and-now issues, Raechel mused, "I think it required a lot more musical knowledge back in the day, when you were trying to play a record and read the music mood of the audience. Their mood, along with the political mood of the time ... even the temperature of the day for heaven's sake ... decided what you were going to play next. Sometimes you'd use up the last four bars [of the song playing] until you thought of the perfect record."

Warming up to her memories, Raechel continued with tales of yesteryear. "Certainly the technical knowledge then was just as hard as it is now, but it was a different animal."

Raechel painted a picture of a disc jockey's job in the late 1960s. "You weren't just pushing buttons; it wasn't all automated. You had to learn how to thread a tape machine in seconds; you had to learn how to put a record on the turntable and put the needle on it without ever looking at it. You had to be able to talk on the phone and pull your copy out of a book and read it."

She continued without taking a breath, "You had to be able to make your commercial *interesting*, and get your record ready at the same time. *That's* the reason I think women are especially good at this—it's the ultimate multi-tasking!"

[*Image:* from *Rock Jocks: The FM Revolution 1967-2001*; public television special by Carolyn Travis; Travisty.tv.]

This was the perfect opening to ask Raechel about the pioneering women of KMPX. "Dusty Street was my first [woman] hire. She totally lied. She said she already knew how to do everything. After the interview she went out and got a book at Radio Shack—not the chain we have now —it was a little store for ship-to-shore radio people. That's what a 'radio shack' is on a boat."

You do what you gotta do ...

Raechel let loose a low, throaty chuckle as she continued Dusty's story. "She went down and got the full engineer's manual and started studying up on it and just bullied her way through it, bless her heart. She's the only one in the initial round who I know was very successful."

One woman was a standout for her slicing and dicing prowess, but not in the kitchen. She cooked up a storm in the editing room. "There was this *fabulous* woman named Katie Johnson, who was a whiz with a razor blade."

Marveling at the woman's skills, Raechel said Katie once sliced the Beatles' song, 'Norwegian Wood' into a set of lyrics that subtly but hilariously skewed the words and confused their listeners.

She twisted it up, sent it down the white rabbit's hole and put it on the air! Raechel laughed and said, "We'd have the audience come up and say, 'I think I'm losing my mind!' She taught us all a lot about editing and about creating these intricate stories with little snippets of this and little snippets of that."

Raechel and Tom, along with their like-minded staff of hippie DJs and engineers, kept KMPX and KPPC at the top of the radio ratings in 1968. Not everyone, though, was makin' love and definitely not bringing power to the people. Station management began messing with the status quo, which made the natives restless.

"They had started coming up with '*rules*,'" Raechel recalled. "You know, like wearing ties and no open-toed shoes." That did away with the Birkenstocks!

"The rules were endless. Then it was getting to, 'my wife didn't like this song, or that one' and this was even before we had the Black Panthers* on the air, LinDee, come on! Cut us some slack!" [*Referring to their next gig in the '70s when they *really* let their hair down.]

By March of 1968, the eclectic band of DJs and staff made the owners face the music for raking in a lot of money, while they barely saw $60-$125 per week. After all, it was the era of protests.

Did owner, Leon Crosby, *know* who he hired? Rules were not an option in FM radio—and certainly not for the Donahues.

Methinks ye protest too much

In true communal style, they organized and walked out. "We even had our own letterhead," said Raechel. "The Amalgamated American International FM

Workers of the World, Ltd." Phew! That's a mouthful. It's a wonder there was room on the page to write their demands! But they squeezed some in …

Raechel laughed at their audacity. "We asked for stuff like, the Summer Solstice off with pay, the ability to wear costumes on Halloween, or if and when we wished, plus double pay for the day." Reasonable, right?

"The Great Hippie Strike," as it's known in the industry, became more profound than anyone originally imagined. It waged on from March 18th until May 21st … with more than a little partying on the picket lines.

Crosby hired replacement announcers and staff, while Tom and Raechel were joined outside on the picket line by the Grateful Dead, Jefferson Airplane, along with other local bands, and members of the Rolling Stones. Their allegiance was obviously with the folks who chose to play their music, when the AM stations wouldn't.

After several weeks of head-butting without resolution, Tom and the KMPX owner parted ways.

Not one to be idle while on the picket line, Tom struck a deal with another station that was ready to switch formats. Owned by Multimedia, former KLFR 94.9 flipped from classical to freeform Rock —bet some of its listeners flipped out! The result created icon station, KSAN (FM) "The Jive 95." (Jive95.com)

Raechel and Tom moved in, and morphed it into their kinda music; and most of the former KMPX staff moved in with them. Just like the station-duo of KMPX/KPPC, they overhauled KSAN and its Los Angeles counterpart, KMET.

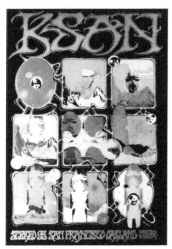

"This is KSAN in San Francisco. Sometimes we do it *fast* … sometimes we do it *slow* … but we *al-*ways *do* it!" (From upcoming: *KSAN Jive 95: the Movie*, KSANJive95TheMovie.com.)

"I had a sharp wit and a barbed tongue," Raechel readily admitted, "and I'm not afraid to use either one of them. I just went at it in a different way."

Apparently it worked. "The newsman at KSAN would say, '*Women* … grrrrr …' the whole time I was there. But when he left the station he said, 'I just want to say, you're … you're a really good jock. *For a girl.* You're a really good jock.'" He had to throw that in …

[*Image:* Through the '70s, KSAN, like other progressive San Francisco stations, utilized vibrant local artists, Kelley & Mouse, c. 1976; eBay.]

KSAN thrived and as Tom's laid-back voice was often heard to say, "You can see, we're gonna be doin' a LOT of boogie'n'."

But Raechel asserted there was more to it than good vibes and great parties. "It was a good place for kids to be able to listen and go, 'Hey, my parents aren't crazy! There's others just like them!'"

KSAN's legend really takes off in the early 1970s, mirroring and fueling society's moods and psychedelia. Was Raechel kidding us with the Black Panthers comment? Absolutely not. KSAN became *everybody's* go-to station.

Those however, are stories for another time … another book … the *Psychedelic Seventies*. Oh, but they're good ones. Just ask Raechel …

"That would be the first of many times when you'd get a knock on the door, and with this heavy sigh … 'Hi. We're from the FBI. We're here again. Love your station.'"

Today: Raechel still considers her years with Tom the highlight of her life. They were short but colorful. Tom's big heart reached capacity when it gave way while at the top of their game at KSAN, on April 28, 1975. In 1996 he received a much-deserved induction into the Rock and Roll Hall of Fame.

Raechel truly left her heart in San Francisco and slipped down to L.A.'s KMET on a permanent basis, where she wowed new listeners with her fun, salacious style. You can still catch the versatile Raechel as a contributor on eHow.com and at her website, RaechelDonahue.com.

[*Image:* Sweet pic from Raechel's website, with permission.]

When it comes to New Yahkers, there's no one finer than your cousin in the diner. He's tuned to BFYP 84.8-FM on your radio dial!

Do you love your family and relish your cousin? Grab that Coney Dog before he has a *Psychotic Reaction*! ♪

Cousin Bruce Morrow >Part 2

aka "Cousin Brucie"
Best known at WABC/New York City
(Actually, he's "best known" wherever he goes!)

Go ahead—get chummy—just call him Cousin Brucie. Everybody does.

Bruce's family of fans grew in the early 1960s as he bounced briefly between WABC/New York, WINZ/Miami, and truly exploded when he returned to WABC in 1963. We talked about his legion of listeners and the warmth in Bruce's voice was unmistakable.

"Radio is the most intimate and probably the closest you can get to the human experience," said Bruce. He shared his family life with his fans, and they with him.

[*Image:* A couple of WABC's pinback promotions. *BFYP* Collection.]

Due to this connection, Bruce abhors the term, "disc jockey" and never allows anyone to introduce him as such. "A disc jockey," said Bruce, "is just someone who used to go in to the studio to tell time and weather, and read the [pre-scripted] cards. I felt I was more than that. I'm a friend to my audience."

Call him "broadcaster," "radio personality," or even late for dinner, but don't call him a DJ!

The mid- to late-1960s Top 40 radio stations ruled the competitive major markets, where it was one big contest of one-up-man-ship. Who can give away the most money, or in the silliest manner? Which of course, translated into the highest radio ratings.

Many of the biggest contests and activities involved the Beatles and "W-A-BEATLES-C" didn't hold back. Beatles look-alike contests and poster art contests were held at WABC, and copied at stations across the country.

DJs Jack Vincent and Shadoe Jackson spun the vinyls during "Beatle Fever" at KCBQ/San Diego. Their March 1964 survey sheets featured a different Beatle photo and bio each week.

They were so popular, it was done again, in May. This time, KCBQ ran a Sketch-the-Beatles contest. Talented listeners' art of each Beatle was published in surveys. Stunning.

[*Image:* WABC 1965, *Cousin Brucie Meets Mother Goosie.* Cute. Many of the Top 40 stations of the day promoted with fun and crazy LPs so you were never without your fave DJ! (eBay)]

But no contest could rival the arrival of Bruce and wife, Susan's, first child, April 4, 1964.

Oh baby, you're just what the DJ ordered!

Bruce had hyped his son's birth—he ordered a boy—to his WABC family of listeners throughout Susan's pregnancy, as he admitted in his book, *Cousin Brucie – My Life in Rock 'n' Roll Radio* (1987). "I'd touted the arrival of this kid as if it were the Second Coming, the Dodgers returning to Brooklyn, and New Year's Eve rolled into one."

It wasn't meant to be a radio event, but what was a guy supposed to do back then, when they weren't allowed in the delivery room? He was upstaged and bored. Finally, chucking the out-of-date magazines in the waiting room, Bruce called the station.

Buddy broadcaster, Dan Ingram, thought the "Nervous Nellie" Bruce would fold under pressure when he flipped the mic on as they talked. But it was just what the radio pro needed for distraction—and to feed his need for return to center stage.

I'm always amazed at how much the wives go along with some zany ideas of our wild-and-crazy radio guys. Bruce not only put his doctor on the air to personally announce the arrival of his son—yes, he got his wish—but somehow sweet-talked his wife into …

"I want the listeners to know that Susan and I already have a name picked out. My son is going to be named Dana Jon—D.J." By this time, the fans felt like his son was their son, and with the announcement, came thirty thousand well-wishes in cards, gifts, and letters.

Hmmm, this from the guy who doesn't like to be called a DJ! Adorable.

By Nov 1966, Cousin Brucie seemed to be a permanent part of the WABC family and enjoyed his familial popularity to the hilt. He would regale his listeners until 1974 when they followed him to a short gig at WNBC/New York, where a fumble for words became his most favorite on-air moment.

"It was kinda weird. We always do live shows and fortunately, I very rarely get tongue-tied," said Bruce. [That and dead air are the bane of announcers.]

"... And nobody was coming up that night [to be in the studio with him]. But I'm doing my show live, the door opens and I looked up. In walked Bob Hope and Jackie Gleason! My jaw drops down and I was tongue-tied in the middle of a commercial! I've met a lot of big stars, but these two ... you're talkin' *huge*!" Both funnymen were top TV variety show hosts for most of the '60s.

When Bruce finally regained his composure and finished the commercial, he learned they were doing a show in Central Park the next day and they wanted him to teach them how to be a DJ.

"I put them on the air, they did commercials, they played records, and they were great." And they rewarded Bruce for his gracious impromptu teaching.

"At the end of the session, which lasted about an hour, Bob Hope said to me, 'We'd like you to come down tomorrow morning; we want you to be the announcer who opens the show for us.'"

Bruce has had many stars drop in on him over the years, but that one was special. "You name it; they've been in the studio. Elvis walking in, I have a million Beatles stories ..."

Stepping out from behind the mic

Memorable but short, Bruce left WNBC to step up as co-owner of several radio stations for nearly a decade.

[*Image:* Were you an early 1970s Cousin Brucie "Womble" at WNBC? (eBay)]

Bruce Morrow (Meyerowitz) was destined for stardom, as Cousin Brucie industry recognition proves: Radio Hall of Fame (1988), the National Association of Broadcasters Hall of Fame (2001), and the National Broadcasters Hall of Fame (2008).

Among his "awards" Bruce appreciated close relationships with Elvis, Paul Anka, Neil Sedaka, and other music giants he helped promote.

What does Bruce think of current radio? "I'm very proud of my industry. Terrestrial radio is having growing pains; I think program directors and broadcasters have to redefine their role. Of course, satellite radio has captured the imagination of just about everyone—it's reaching more people with a variety of programming, and gives the audience what they need."

That doesn't mean he thinks satellite is any better than terrestrial. "Involvement is probably the #1 missing link in terrestrial and all radio —it's still extremely important to get involved with your community and audience."

Bruce lived through the Golden Years of Rock & Roll Radio as fast as he talks, punctuated by tunes and jingles of the day.

Memories of Coca Cola radio ads that practically vied for the #1 spot on radio surveys, can be heard in fun airchecks at ReelRadio.com. Listen as Cousin Brucie rattles through the "WABC Coca Cola Hour" faster than an auctioneer running out of time.

"Hey, it's eighteen minutes now before eleven o'clock. At eleven o'clock, I don't know what he's gonna be wearin' tonight, Chuck Leonard's, gonna be on again—that nut ... his face is painted, he's got the chandelier hangin' and his overhead boom mic, all set to go. ... Imagine being paid for being a namedropper ... that's what's happening here at W-A-Bomb-C, everybody ..." (Reel Radio, WABC September 7, 1965, the Coca Cola Hour.)

Today: Bruce married second wife, Jodie, in 1975, for his longest gig to date. Though he enjoyed station ownership, he missed his family of listeners, and slid behind the mic again at WCBS-FM/New York in 1982. Bruce's longevity and popularity were proven when featured in the classic 1987 movie, *Dirty Dancing*, opening the film as the DJ on your car radio. Changing with the times, he migrated to Sirius Satellite Radio in 2005 and remains a favorite cousin. Somehow, he found time to author two more books; this time, of his favorite musical genres, *Doo Wop: The Music, the Times, the Era* (2007) and *Rock & Roll ...And the Beat Goes On* (2009); both available on Amazon.

At BFYP-FM we enjoy a chuckle ... when do you know "politically correct" is a joke? When everything you say is politically IN-correct! Cue the cowbell.

Take a wild ride on his *Spinning Wheel* ... ♪

Don Rose
aka "Dr. Don" Rose, or simply "DDR"
1934 ~ 2005
Best known at KFRC/San Francisco, California
(Interview with son, Jay Rosenberg)

Since Kent Burkhart gave him a mention in the mid-Sixties, now's as good a time as any to insert another few lines about the rising star of the indomitable Dr. Don Rose.

His legendary KFRC days began in the early 1970s, as do most of his son, Jay's, fond memories. But he needs to get there; so let's explore the '60s migration of Donald Duane Rosenberg.

Unfortunately, that isn't an easy task. Not much is verifiably documented about the early days of "Dr. Don," as he was affectionately known. Since Jay was decades away from making an appearance in the Rosenberg family, we filled in the gaps with a few online bios from the memories of others. (BayAreaRadio.org/audio/kfrc/dr-don-rose.shtml)

Noted in the 1950s (*BFYP* Book 1), Don's interest in radio began early, as it did for many aspiring DJs, by reporting school news. Young Don sat behind the mic for local radio station, KODY/North Platte, Nebraska.

His broadcasting interest took off in earnest at the University of Nebraska around the mid-1950s. According to radio archivist, BroadcastPioneers.com, Don spent his spare time between classes, in the campus radio station, KNUS.

He wondered if he were the only one who discovered that KNUS spelled backwards reads SUNK. It was certainly not an ominous omen for the affable Don, however.

"DDR"—Doctor Don Rose— earned his street creds in the late Fifties and set out to heal his listener's ills with humor. Cornball comedy doesn't work for everyone. For Don, his huge audiences proved there were many who enjoyed this quirky brand of broadcasting.

Pure DDR: "We were supposed to have the human fly* on our program today, unfortunately, he's in the hospital—his wife swatted him!" (*Of course, he's referring to *Playboy* magazine's 1957 short story; later, 1958 and 1986 movies.)

Apparently, it says a lot about the personality of his most avid listeners, that Don excelled as the morning man, coveted by stations across the nation as their wake-up guy. Seriously, who can sleep through a boisterous ...

"Welcome to the yawn of a new day!" Cue the cowbell.

Having skated through a myriad of stations in the heartland, Don finally hit the big time at "Quixie in Dixie," WQXI, Atlanta, Georgia.

It was the mid-Sixties, as we excitedly watched our government's race for space. Don played their Top 30 and recent hits like Marvin Gaye and Kim Weston's, "It Takes Two" (1966). But he just couldn't leave it alone ...

"It takes two—my favorite number! That's what it's all about, friends. That's the nitty gritty. And of course, to simplify things, the fastest way to get a man on the moon, is to put a woman there first, right?!"

[*Image:* DDR topping the February 5-12, 1968 WQXI Top 30 survey lineup, with Stu Collins, Bob Todd, Jim Jeffries, Kris Stevens, Gary Granger, Joe Kelly and Rockin' Ray Robin. *BFYP* Collection.]

Remember Robin, always look both ways before crossing the street

Don left WQXI for Philadelphia's WFIL in 1968, around the time Jay first recalls the popular DJ in front of large crowds and big station promos. Sometimes he brought the fun home.

"I was playing out in front of our house and he came driving up in the Batmobile," recalled Jay. "My dad, superhero! It stayed parked in front of our house for a couple of days." Hmmm, how to become the most popular kid in the neighborhood?

"This is Dr. Don, laughin' and scratchin' ..." If you laughed once with him, you were hooked. Jay thinks his oft-used, unique two-punchline delivery reeled them in. "There'd be one very recognizable line everyone knew and kids would chuckle along with it, followed by one with a 'deeper' meaning."

Like all comic relief, sometimes it works and sometimes it doesn't. Jay said, "Those who 'got it'—got it—and the ones who didn't, wouldn't be offended." Just in case you didn't get it, you could laugh with the ever-present cowbell or long, low moo of ol' Bessie herself.

Jay mused, "There's really an art to that—to do it successfully on a daily basis. I didn't realize how complex he really was until a few years before he died. We spent a lot of time together and he had all these theories I didn't even know he had." Fascinated by his dad and radio, Jay prefers the engineering end of things, where he still excels today.

Dr. Don Rose hit his stride in the 1960s and proved his staying power through more than forty years of radio music and mayhem. Need proof? This line hit the airwaves in 1967 while at WQXI, and applies as much today ...

"Dr. Don Rose reminding you, with man's ability to think and reason and compute, we can now pinpoint most of our current problems. Trouble is, we can't solve 'em."

He ended the 1960s and spun into the early '70s, spinning the "Boss 30" at WFIL. Dr. Don had a few more years to tickle the funny bone of Philly fans before his muse whispered, "Go West young man."

[*Image:* Dr. Don always a fan favorite on WFIL Boss 30, October 5, 1970. (eBay)]

Coming around in the Seventies, Dr. Don needed a doctor.

Arriving in California in the fall of 1973, we never heard the pain behind his on-air smile. A botched heart surgery compromised one knee, and he endured the next three decades in pain—but we listeners never heard him complain, except in the form of a joke.

Today: Dr. Don grabbed his cowbell and headed for Rock & Roll Heaven, March 30, 2005. We'll explore DDR's antics during the tumultuous '70s as he sprints cross-country to KFRC. With country style charm, he won the hearts of urban San Francisco Bay Area audiences, and endeared himself to another whole coast of fans.

BFYP 84.8-FM on your screamin' radio dial came of age and kicked ass in the underground radio of the 1960s. Hot damn! Let's Rock!

By decade's end, Rock no longer played for *Only the Lonely* ... ♪

William F. Williams
Best known at KMEN/San Bernardino, California and KPPC-FM/Los Angeles

Timing is everything. An oft-repeated ethereal phrase that can mean everything or nothing.

William learned early in his career how coincidence works, with chance encounters boosting him up the broadcasting ladder, beginning with KAFY/Bakersfield in 1958.

[*Image*: KAFY's Fabulous 55, October 25-31, 1958 was topped with "Tom Dooley" (Kingston Trio). Airheads Radio Survey Archive; Dale Schwamborn, contributor.]

By 1959, William had swaggered his way through central and northern California, leaving legions of fans in his wake. Weary of KAFY, the primarily California DJ scooted over to KBIS/Bakersfield for a short run.

Another moment of auspicious timing landed him at KDAY/Los Angeles by 1960, with a DJ of legend and lore. Hanging out in the glamorous bar of the Knickerbocker Hotel, he waited for the rest of his life to begin. And getting *paid* to wait!

Destiny led him here, playing a waiting game with payola-maligned, Alan Freed—one DJ on his way up—the other on his way down.

Freed arrived in Los Angeles to escape unending vilification in the Eastern radio markets, hoping to revive his beloved radio career. Waiting for the FCC to okay KDAY's new, longer hours likely didn't help his state of mind. Inaction never does. The radio station owner's strategy was to keep his big "star" DJs under wraps until their new Rock format was in place. Surprise! Life rarely happens quite as planned.

"They put us on the air for a couple hours every once in a while, but were told not to 'do your thing yet,'" said William. "We did that for a while." Mostly, they hung out in the bar. Weeks turned into months.

While the DJs waited, KDAY's general sales manager grabbed life by the hand and took over KUDU—a Ventura (California) station. "The minute he got the job," William recalled, "he wanted me to be program director."

The guy's argument made sense to William. "This place [KDAY] is in turmoil. They're never going to get this format off." But William still wanted to work with Freed, and begged off, "Nah, they're paying me pretty well to sit in a bar." A couple months later, said William, "None of us had been on the air but a few hours here and there, so this guy [also named Williams—no relation] came back down and said ...

Here's the deal ...

Since KUDU's new manager knew how much William was paid to loaf around ($550 per month), he took the ol' bull by the horns. "I'll pay you a thousand dollars a month, *plus* a new car, all your groceries, a place to live— brand new condo—you pick out the furniture you want, and you'll have no expenses."

William couldn't sit still with a deal like that dangling in front of him. "So, I took him up on it! I went from Bakersfield, to Los Angeles, to Ventura, in the first eighteen months of my radio career."

[*Image:* Elvis topped KUDU's Pepsi Hit List, August 21, 1960. "It's Now or Never" ... for William, too. Airheads Radio Survey Archive; Gary Pfeifer, contributor.]

As often happens in radio, KUDU soon became a notch on his DJ belt, and William began dancing the "radio hop," from station to station. "Things just kinda got nuts for the next couple of years. After a few months at KUDU he skipped over to Vegas.

"I did the morning drive in Vegas. Hated the town, didn't like the station." He paused and thought about his last comment. "Well, it was okay." I smiled knowingly—c'mon, it's *Vegas*, baby, there had to be *something* fun about it!

Life got a little foggy around then as he floated around the airwaves, and ended up in Oceanside, California. And we're not even into 1961 yet. Still not feeling "at home," he fidgeted in Oceanside.

Backtracking a bit, he thought about his Air Force stint before radio. He'd joined at seventeen; too young for pilot training, but spent four years as radio operator in the back of the plane and loved the flying.

Before leaving, he'd been accepted to Air Cadet school, but left anyway; he checked with them and the rigmarole to navigator school would have taken too long for the fast-moving DJ.

William scooted over to the Marines [we have all the armed forces represented in SoCal!] and asked, "Need any pilots? Where do I sign."

Alas, not that simple. He'd just missed the age limit for flight training. Undaunted, he wrote to the US Marine Corps commander and pleaded his pent-up desire to fly. William figured it was a dead-end try. Another surprise! He received a telegram four days later telling him to report to Los Alamedas Naval Air Station for testing, and if he passed they'd waive the age limit.

Test passed and orders received, William figured broadcasting was a short-lived career. "I hung up my headphones and headed for Pensacola (Florida).

So readers—do you think his radio days are *really* over? Hmmm ... haven't we already established that life doesn't work that way?

"I didn't realize when I left home that my wife was pregnant with our second child. I found out in pilot training. Since they don't pay much, and I'd already served my military obligation, I had to bail."

Though an unpredictable career, there is always another radio gig around the next corner. "I got my old job back at KBIS," said William. "I was there as program director for a year, made the station #1 again, and got fired ... on Sunday ... my day off."

As we talked, we hopscotched through radio's good and bad traits. "I don't know any of my DJ acquaintances whose first three, four, five years in the biz weren't like that. I mean, you're just a gypsy. You either quit because of some insanity, or you're fired, sometimes your fault, or sometimes they change management. It's just a nightmare."

And yet ... they stick with it. Is radio broadcasting an addiction? If so, William was hooked.

He ran into Ray Morgan, another Don Martin School graduate, about ready to trek through California to scout radio stations for a job. William joined him—first stop, connecting with a new audience in the central area of California, at KMAK/Fresno.

Well, that's the station they stopped at, anyway. Turns out fate had placed that timing thing square in William's lap again.

"Ray and I walked in with our tapes and asked to speak to Ron Jacobs, the program director." Jacobs (who passed away March 8, 2016) would make his mark in radio in a big way throughout the Sixties, as an icon at KHJ/Los Angeles during its Boss Radio heyday, and as a co-creator of the American Top 40.

Erik the Red?

"He had this really red hair and red beard," said William, describing the Jacobs force of nature, "and a belly that was walking about a foot in front of him down the hall, in a shirt two sizes too small, pulled open in front. He's real abrupt, 'Whaddya want?!'"

When they explained their mission to work, Jacobs turned to William first and asked about his experience, and said, "Yeah, I heard of you. You're hired. But not here."

Turns out Jacobs was in on the format for a new station, and when William said he'd work nights, he landed at the innovative KMEN in San Bernardino.

[*Image:* Fresh-faced DJ line-up on KMEN's Weekly Record Buyer's Guide for August 17, 1962, top-bottom/l-r, Chuck Clemans, Donn Tyler, Dean Webber, Bill Watson, Brian Lord, George Babcock, William F. Williams, with weekend jocks, Jim Markham and Gary Price. *BFYP* Collection.]

His buddy Ray, wasn't so lucky, but Jacobs told him to keep in touch.

It didn't take long for William to shake things up at KMEN. He moved from the all-night shift to the noon-to-three gig, and when the DJ shuffle came up one guy short, William recommended Ron for the nine-to-midnight show.

"We held those slots for the next three years," said William.

Getting the new station off the ground and past KFXM, the dominant area station, would take more than blood, sweat, and tears. It would also require foot sores, a hospital stay, and new shoes.

KMEN had only been on-air since March of 1962 and by William's late summer arrival, they needed something to lift them higher in the ratings. Someone's bright idea was a "First Annual KMEN San Bernardino Walk Back-and-Forth."

The brutal route between San Bernardino and Riverside is about the length of a marathon (twenty-six miles), but the semi-desert area is known for its hundred-degree summer days. And the DJs were amateur walkathon participants. Getting the picture?

Radio ratings are addictive, however. William and friends wanted their station to be #1 in their fans' hearts—and in the ratings numbers—which hopefully, will spill over into a raise in their paychecks. Oh, did I mention it was also a competition between DJs?

When they started at noon on a Friday, only a handful of fans cheered them off. By the time they hit Riverside and turned around, of the seven DJs who pushed off, just William and morning man, Chuck Clemans, were still standing (never mind walking).

Along the way they did remotes to urge their fans to join them, some keeping the DJs company through the night.

William recalled the doctor's examination at a critical point. "I've just examined William F. Williams' feet. He has third degree burns on ninety-percent of the surface of his feet and I don't know if I can permit ... but he's insisting that he's going on."

You think that's bad? Another doctor said of Clemens, "Well, I just examined Chuck Clemens and he's hallucinating. I don't know how much longer I can allow this to go on."

"We were finally stopped by medical personnel on Sunday night about eleven," said William. The California Highway Patrol estimated thirty thousand people walked with them. Though he was slightly ahead of Chuck, the station declared the DJs' competition a tie. William was okay with that.

[*Image:* A little cut-'n'-paste visual help on the August 17, 1962 survey, as we did the "Loco-Motion" (#1) with Little Eva. *BFYP* Collection.]

"I was in the hospital for four days at the end. We'd timed this promotion to take place just before the new ratings book came out. I had a fifty-two percent share [of listeners], and we blew KFXM completely out of the water. We were #1 for the next three years."

William and KMEN rolled through the mid-Sixties, if not always in perfect harmony, at least in perfect Rock & Roll sync. His stories for just those three or four years are fodder for a full book—which may be in the works for one of us. There are simply too many for this compilation tome.

Imagine bringing the Rolling Stones to the West Coast, billing the as "... the world's most beautiful disk jockeys present the ugliest Rock and Roll band—the Rolling Stones in concert at Swing Auditorium." Harsh, but it worked!

Or piloting a stunning night ride in a beautiful hot air balloon that inspired a Jimmy Webb tune. William coined the title, Jimmy wrote the Grammy winning song, and "Up, Up and Away," took us soaring with them. (Recorded in 1966 by The 5th Dimension; released the following year.)

"Shortly after," said William, I left KMEN. Loved the station; best I ever worked at and a great ride, but I was just tired of it."

He didn't go far. Though he headed to San Francisco's popular KYA, they weren't in the market for a DJ. He started the drive home, and picked up KLIV in San Jose (part of the large San Francisco market) on the radio. They were a sloppy, no-energy station.

He called the station owner/manager and said, "I don't want to hurt your feelings, but your station sounds really bad." The owner smartly asked William what he'd do to change it, and he became their new program director and morning drive guy.

Nepotism works!

He hired his friend, Ray Morgan, again, along with Brian Lord, KMEN's music director, and, "Within ninety days we went from dead last to #1 in the market."

William liked to find new, or "fixer-upper" stations; he'd do his thing, and hit the streets again. While KLIV was pumping strong, he received a call from Roger Christian "one of those perfect radio voices" at KFWB/Los Angeles. He had a new station going on-air with progressive Rock. "Do you want to fly down and talk about a job?"

William chuckled. "That's like asking me if I want a taco and a margarita!" He hot-footed it down to KBLA for another fun, short stint.

Throughout 1966 and '67, Rock & Roll jammed around another corner. Radio was a little slow to catch on. The new music Rocked the clubs and on the streets, but it took FM stations and progressive DJs like Tom Donahue to finally bring it to mainstream airwaves.

[*Image:* William was in great company at KBLA. The May 30, 1966 jock lineup went like this, top-bottom/l-r, Harry Newman, Vic Gee, William F. Williams, Harvey Miller, Roger Christian, Dave Diamond and Bob Dayton. Airheads Radio Survey Archive, Lee Tucker, contributor.]

"I was seeing an awakening of what became known as 'Sixties Music,'" William recalled. "Oh yeah, I definitely want to be in on this! I want to play the long version of 'The End' by The Doors, which you're not going to hear at KHJ, KFWB, or KRLA."

The late 1960s took William to a familiar place of wanderlust. Before the decade declared "Peace Out," he skipped through a couple more Los Angeles stations. KBBQ and even KRLA, figuring he would bring a breath of fresh FM style to their formats.

The *Psychedelic Seventies* begin with William still Rockin' at KRLA. We'll soon see a different side of him. "Hair" continued its success on Broadway but did nothing to cover the streakers that heralded a "streaking epidemic" in 1973. That's a hint.

Seems everyone wanted to get naked back then; but for now ...

Today: With headphones hanging in the closet, William is somewhere in the North Carolina hills, "Spending my time on short fiction, and working on a couple of long-time-in-progress novels."

I should hope so! He has enough crazy stories to fill ten books. His favorite sign-off, "Yours 'til the wax melts, William F."

[*Image:* Courtesy of William; ridin' high, 2008.]

Waxin' the '60s:

Early decade artists kept hanging on to chart-toppers into the mid-Sixties, reworking their styles to combat the British Invasion. Though The Beach Boys topped KBLA's November 14, 1966 chart with "Good Vibrations," and the Supremes told us, "You Keep Me Hangin' On," at #2, Scots newcomer, Donovan, was hot on their heels at #4 with "Mellow Yellow."

THIS WEEK	LAST WEEK	TITLE	ARTIST
1	1	GOOD VIBRATIONS	BEACHBOYS
2	3	YOU KEEP ME HANGIN' ON	SUPREMES
3	4	WINCHESTER CATHEDRAL	NEW VAUDEVILLE BAND
4	6	MELLOW YELLOW	DONOVAN
5	2	I'M YOUR PUPPET	JAMES & BOBBY PURIFY
6	15	B-A-B-Y	CARLA THOMAS
7	5	96 TEARS	? & THE MYSTERIANS
8	12	STOP, STOP, STOP	HOLLIES
9	11	WHY PICK ON ME	STANDELLS
10	8	TALK, TALK	MUSIC MACHINE
11	13	A SATISFIED MIND	BOBBY HEBB
12	20	HEAVEN MUST HAVE SENT YOU	ELGINS
13	21	A HAZY SHADE OF WINTER	SIMON & GARFUNKEL
14	10	POOR SIDE OF TOWN	JOHNNY RIVERS
15	25	I'M READY FOR LOVE	MARTHA & VANDELLAS
16	7	HOORAY FOR HAZEL	TOMMY ROE
17	29	LADY GODIVA	PETER & GORDON
18	27	I'M THE ONE YOU NEED	MIRACLES
19	15	LOVE IS A HURTIN' THING	LOU RAWLS
20	23	DEVIL WITH THE BLUE DRESS & GOOD GOLLY	MITCH RYDER
21	30	BUT IT'S ALRIGHT	J. J. JACKSON
22	19	HAVE YOU SEEN YOUR MOTHER, BABY	ROLLING STONES
23	26	I GOT THE FEELIN'	NEIL DIAMOND
24	28	THAT'S LIFE	FRANK SINATRA
25	New	GO AWAY LITTLE GIRL	HAPPENINGS
26	24	BABY, DO THE PHILLY DOG	OLYMPICS
27	New	MAME	TIJUANA BRASS
28	New	PANDORA'S GOLDEN HEEBIE JEEBIES	ASSOCIATION
29	New	I'M LOSING YOU	TEMPTATIONS
30	New	TIME AFTER TIME	CHRIS MONTEZ

Hey hey, chickadees and chicadudes, we've got a special guest for you on BFYP-FM! Get your mojo workin' and listen for his howwwlllll.

"We gonna Rock & Roll ourselves to *death*, ba-by! You got the Wolfman Jack Show ..." takin' you *Higher and Higher* ...

Have mercy! >Part 3
Wolfman Jack
1938 ~ 1995
A Howling Great Time ...

At KUXL/Minneapolis in 1964, Bob Smith was relatively content with the station's growing success, and still controlled XEG and XERF broadcasts south of the Border. His taped *Wolfman Jack Show* attracted a cult following. Fans listened with incredulous humor, feigned outrage, and salacious grins.

"We got a night of Soul for you! C'mere baby! ... Shake it ba-by, let it *all* hang out. ... Hey babycakes, it's drinkin' time ...

While Bob Smith busted his moves in advertising, his inner wolf longed to connect *live ... you know ... the better to hear you with, my dear*. To make that happen, he'd need to pull out from under Mo Burton's umbrella and brave the rain of successes and bombs, on his own.

In early 1965, Bob set up a meeting with the power behind the Mexican border blasters' US setup. As "king of border radio," Harold S. Schwartz reigned from a lavish Chicago office.

Harold welcomed Bob—and his alter ego. He knew Bob's show from XERF and it didn't take much for Bob to convince him Wolfman should run on all three Mexican stations—XERF (Ciudad Acuña), XEG (Monterrey), and XERB (Tijuana). Bob's reputation for innovative and profitable sales on the show didn't hurt any either.

He'd teamed with a Minneapolis record shop owner, producing some of the first money-making oldies packages that included *The Lucky 40*, *The Big 30*, and *Wolfman's Blues Specials*.

He and Harold struck a deal and Wolfman finally finished his trek to Hollywood. His first reconnaissance trip included a reunion with his dear sister, Joan, who had moved her family to a ranch-style home in the Los Angeles suburbs. Which of course, made a great place to crash while he researched the SoCal radio industry.

Tapping into his innate sense for business, Bob wondered if he could program XERB to be perceived by locals as an L.A. station, not the border blaster it was, in Tijuana. Using the great audience connector of the Sixties—a little transistor radio—he scouted signals from Los Angeles to Bakersfield, which tips the top of the Southern California region, in rural, agricultural California.

His thought was to double the advertising base, letting the preachers sell until noon and selling L.A. retailer spots between black gospel and rhythm and blues shows, the rest of the day/night.

Location ... Location ... Location ...

Next on his list, "The number one thing, besides finding a cool place to live in L.A., was setting XERB up with a Sunset Boulevard* business address and making the station Rock." (*Bob's tribute to the glorified *77 Sunset Strip* TV show of his youth, which ran from 1958-1964).

His friend and longtime associate, Mo, obviously balked at Bob's decision to leave and set up on us own, in the West. Mostly because it interrupted his own empire-building plans.

It was Bob's turn and time to turn Wolfman Jack into a household name. He and Wolfwoman packed up the family and headed to "Beverly ... Hills that is ... swimmin' pools, movie stars"! Of course.

On a clear night, you could hear his plaintive aa*wooooo* all the way to, Arizona, Montana, Washington, Moose Jaw Canada, and Alaska.

Bob worked Wolfman's tale off, ensuring XERB's all-round success. Later citing it his greatest accomplishment, he thrived from 1966 to 1971 and declared it "a better soul station than anything else that had ever been on the air ..."

[*Image:* XERB'S howl echoed all the way to Berkeley in a far-out Hippie newsrag ad, *Big Beat World*, 1967. *BFYP* Collection.]

Part of that success came from patching old wounds and partnering again, with Mo Burton. Still flipping small failing stations into solid successes, Mo liked the idea of breaking into the Western markets. Teaming again with Bob, he took the background role this time, and they finished the decade on a high, in more ways than one.

Wolfman and Wolfwoman settled into a mini-mansion on Ferrari Drive, high in the hills. Life was good. Ah, there are no roses without thorns, though.

The hippies who made Sunset Boulevard cool, were now too stoned even for Wolfman Jack's taste. "I can stand a lot of strange stuff, but when people get all sloppy dirty, like they've got no self-respect, I want to be somewhere else."

Since somewhere else to send the hippies would take years of bureaucracy, Mo and Wolfman found a new home for XERB.

Sixth Street near Western Avenue once hosted a Fred Astaire Studio and stretched along three-quarters of the block. After a lavish upgrade in décor and equipment, XERB's official US offices housed a broadcasting studio "to die for."

The slick façade belied its Mexico connection as they slipped the border guards "la mordida," a "little bite," to allow their taped shows smooth traveling through customs. This served to keep the twenty-four-hour station humming for its rapidly0 growing fan base.

[*Image:* Big XERB flaunted its Hollywood address and resident Wolfman on its Monster Record Survey August 12, 1967 Soul. Cool shades. *BFYP* Collection.]

It didn't hurt that by rigging the towers in Rosarito Beach with directional reflectors, they effectively revved XERB's 50,000-watt transmitter to broadcast in the 150,000-watt zone. What a range!

Time for the Wolf to Howl in Public

After a Ku Klux Klan run-in back in Shreveport, Bob had kept Wolfman under wraps and out of the public eye. He knew that wouldn't last with XERB's popularity, though.

Hollywood is famous for its transformations and Bob decided this was the best place to truly bring Wolfman to life and give his fans a cheap thrill. Hiring a makeup expert to polish Lou's early interpretation of him, Wolfman prepared for his first California appearance.

A Little Richard performance in Santa Ana set the stage. But first ...

Due to the makeup artist's schedule, they began at three in the morning. After darkening Bob's skin, adding a big wolfy nose, and even more hair, they fitted him with fangs and long, midnight-black fingernails. Wolfman Jack was alive.

Still early though, he crawled back into bed with Lou. She woke up and he recalled, "It was a sight she wasn't prepared for. My ears rang from her screams for a real long time."

Playing his larger-than-life persona to the hilt, he arrived at appearances up and down California, in the largest limousine available. The show began with his first step out of the car. Preceded by a midget spraying perfume and scantily clad women tossing rose petals, Wolfman Jack made his entrance.

Wolfman especially enjoyed the central California gigs. Most of his fans had "never seen anything freaky-deaky like this." It was a more exhilarating high for him than any hallucinatory could produce.

Wolfman marveled that their shows never inspired problems, even with the "beautifully mixed" audience of black, white, and Hispanic.

Once he had mesmerized audiences in California, Wolf hit Las Vegas. After a week of shows in a side lounge, The Bonanza Hotel (precursor to MGM Grand) moved his show into the big hall. Some thought he was a little rough around the edges, but they still brought in standing-room-only crowds.

While in Vegas he teamed up with Don Kelley, leader of the Swinging Lads, who challenged Bob to polish his performances. He saw in Wolfman, the guy who could move beyond the solitary DJ-behind-the-mic-on-a-weekend-gig, and become a true entertainer.

Wolfman Jack was minutes away (in wolf/dog years) to his big break that would shove him into the national and worldwide spotlight.

They dumped his goofy sound effects, hired writers, and created a show to match the expectations of a paying audience.

Nothing great is ever easy ...

The process wasn't easy. To preserve the "funky essence" of Wolfman Jack, Bob often balked at the changes. As he said, "I can be as stubborn as a mule ... Fortunately, Kelley was a clever kind of muledriver."

The *Psychedelic Seventies* begin with a bang for Robert Weston Smith. Wolfman Jack comes of age, along with his audience, and we learn who he *really* is: black? white? big? small? Destiny awaits.

[*Image:* KPOI/Hawaii survey December 8, 1970; Wolfman Jack howls his way into a new decade under the balmy palm trees. *BFYP* Collection.]

We'll also meet Lonnie Napier and Frank Cotolo, two of Wolfman Jack's long-term employees and DJ friends. They stuck with him through the next few decades, as he won and lost, both personally and professionally.

Frank: "It was crazy. It was wonderful. It was fun. Wolf never cared to be called Bob, in private or public. All of us in the inner circle called him Wolf or Woof or Woofy, you know, but never Bob. That was 'gonesville,' you know?'

Lonnie on meeting Wolfman: "I walk in there and here's this dark, odd, paneled office with huge wooden furniture, and red velvet couches. It looked like a Mexican bordello."

Lonnie spent two hours waiting on those cushy couches for Wolfman to arrive, and when he did, "Here's this guy with these huge puffy sleeves, gold bracelets, Beatles boots and Elvis sunglasses, and this big ol' pompadour hairdo, and this goatee—this dark black goatee—and I was just blown away! I was like, in the presence of greatness—and I knew it!"

The evolving Wolfman Jack continued his West Coast and Hawaii appearances on stage and on air, until one ambitious and nostalgic filmmaker gave him a call. It was the right movie at the right time, for Wolfman's fame and fortune.

Today: It seems Wolfman Jack simply needed to finish his biography and then it was time to Rock on in Rock & Roll Heaven. The story of his death on July 1, 1995, is as famous as the story of his life. After a whirlwind tour to promote *Have Mercy! Confessions of the Original Rock 'n' Roll Animal*, Robert Weston Smith arrived home, and with a hug for his Wolfwoman, he died in Lou's arms.

The National Radio Hall of Fame acted quickly and inducted him into its hallowed halls the next year. (RadioHOF.org/wolfman_jack.htm)

Many musicians have paid tribute to Wolfman Jack in song, including Grateful Dead "Ramble on Rose," Todd Rundgren "Wolfman Jack," and everyone's favorite sing-along, The Guess Who "Clap for the Wolfman."

As with all those who touch many lives, there is no true death. Wolfman Jack remains a vibrant personality in the history of Rock and Roll broadcasting. He embodies the quintessential on-air DJ personality, who will never be forgotten as long as radio punctuates our airwaves.

But no one has ever howled like the real **Wolfman Jack**. A*oowwwwwwww*!!

Wolfman Jack in all his gravely glory can still be heard in captured airchecks around the Internet. A couple of my fave sites:

XERB 1090*

Yes, it still lives in archives. [And in this July 16, 1967 survey. *BFYP* Collection.] (*XERBRadio.com)

I'll leave you with some choice Wolfman Jack aircheck quotes ... ReelRadio.com:

"Hi sweet darlin's this is Wolfman Jack comin' to ya *live* from outer space! ... I think I must be higher now than I've *ever* been ... no, wait a minute here, that's not outer space, that's *Mexico*, man! I was lookin' out the wrong window. I know where I am now ... I'm down here with the dun-keys and the billy goats. ... Hey, dun-key, get outta here! That stuff don't wash out, ya know. Oh, dun-keys everywhere! I'm up to my neck in asses!"

"This is Wolfman Jack, skinny-dippin' in the oil of joy down here on XERB, the tower of flower power. Fifty thousand watts of soul power."

"C'mon everybody ... let's *boogie*!"

Special note: Various Wolfman Jack quotes from *Street Rodder* magazine (April, 1991), used with permission per Brian Brennan, Editorial Director, Irvine, California; StreetRodderWeb.com.

Is That All There Is ... ♪

(Epilogue)

Hardly! The 1960s decade of music and radio mayhem is *so big* that it transcends all that came after it. Surely, this little book of DJ memories cannot but tip the iceberg of '60s Rock & Roll and the Radio DJs who brought it to us.

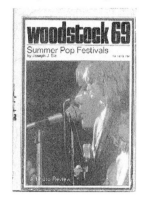

Even in its last six months, the 1960s music mystique soared at Woodstock (August 15-18, 1969), and rumors abound in October of a cryptic Paul McCartney "impersonator." (The reports of his demise were greatly exaggerated!)

[*Image:* Love reminiscing about life when concerts were truly fun? Find a used copy of 1970 paperback book by Joseph J. Sia, *Woodstock 69 - Summer Pop Festivals* (Scholastic Book Services). *BFYP* Collection.]

Effects of this decade reverberated through our music right down to New Year's Eve 1969. Our minds expanded with Zeppelin's "Whole Lotta Lovin'" and we felt Elvis's pain in "Don't Cry Daddy." (KGB/San Diego "Boss 30" December 30, 1969.)

The top hits of the 1960s reflected listeners' moods and minds. Rock and Roll, Radio, and the great and humble DJs from Wolfman Jack to Jack Vincent would never have existed without a *connection* to millions of enthusiastic radio listeners ... which led to a winding path back to your memories in *Blast from Your Past*. What do you have to look forward to? Plenty!

We're havin' a Blast now! Comin' up in *BFYP* Book 3, *The Psychedelic Seventies*, we swing into a decade of Peace signs, bell bottoms, midriff tops, lava lamps ...

Your radio tuned in to "Hey There Lonely Girl" (Eddie Holman), and we can almost hear the whisper from the back seat, "Let's make love, not war, Baby."

With the help of key Disc Jockeys, FM radio stations surfaced from underground to agitate the airwaves and finish a rebel decade. Cover your eyes and ears for what's up on the turntables next ...

The Psychedelic Seventies spans college campuses, love-ins with streakers and smiley faces, while boomboxes stream sounds of silence overpowered by a roar of war protests.

Ah yes, the boomboxes. With progressive speakers and pulling in more stations, they dominated the '70s radio party market. The small transistor radios transitioned through the boombox popularity with character. Literally.

What began in the '60s as advertising novelties, spread to a fun market in transforming transistor radios into character designs, from Gumby and Garfield, to major beer and soda brands, and teaming with Disney, just to name a few. Highly collectible now, the original ten dollar radios auction for up to a hundred-plus.

Coming to the end of the 1970s, we were doin' the Disco Duck! Agh! Kill me now! Never thought I'd say this, but thank goodness for Heavy Metal music.

Not to say we didn't love *Saturday Night Fever* and the BeeGees. But for the women, anyway, it wasn't necessarily the music that struck our fancy ... if only our boyfriends and hubbies could move like John Travolta!

I'd say, enjoy the moment ... *again* ... but I seriously hope you guys burned your leisure suits while we gals took our PMS out on the Disco ball! When it came to the music it wasn't all good ... but it was all memorable.

Blast from Your Past! Book 3, *Rock & Roll Radio DJs: The Psychedelic Seventies 1970-1979* ... coming in 2018!

[*Images:* Yep—they're all transistor radios from the 1960s and '70s; with exception of 45rpm record in background and Rock & Roll beer can in front, above. Below, they even went round, warm 'n' fuzzy. *BFYP* Collection.]

♪ Save the Last Dance for Me ... ♪

(Acknowledgments)

Like Dickens' *A Tale of Two Cities* (1859), the 1960s for those coming of age, told a tale of two very different personal and musical happenings. "It was the best of times, it was the worst of times, it was the age of wisdom, it was the age of foolishness ..." a hundred years later.

High school is a time—good, bad, and indifferent—that shapes the rest of our lives. "Coming of age" is not just a saying, it's a psychological and physical experience. My Rockin' thanks to the Universe for where and when I was born.

Which takes me to my high school chums. Not surprising, many remained in our rural area. Growing up Country was the best. *Remember when we ...?*

Life is bleak without a little (or lot) of help from our friends ... and family ... and even sometimes our enemies. (Think devil's advocate; though I'm more inclined toward devil's food chocolate cake.)

In the essence of your imminent boredom, I won't name everyone, but you know if you deserve a gold star and a big hug—or a big Santa-size lump of coal.

My "Three Mighty Muses," John F. Harnish, Patricia Bajnoczy, and Ron Connelly, wouldn't let me quit, even when I wanted to, during the crazy ups and downs of life that alternately halted and delayed my work. Without them, you wouldn't be reading this. They have my eternal gratitude.

It isn't only those living in the here and now who shape our accomplishments. My parents, Florence and Don, encouraged my inquisitive and adventurous nature, infused with the genes of perseverance.

My brothers, Donnie and Gary, inspired me to view the world with joy and excitement. Donnie and I played music together—Gary played the part of my Rockin' big bro to the hilt. I miss them every day, and I know they're beside me, with every Rockin' (or rocky) step I take.

I relied heavily on a few consistent and accurate as possible websites to augment our memories: ReelRadio.com, Airheads Radio Survey Archive, and 440: Satisfaction. They were my go-to sites for radio and disc jockey research, hosted by people who care about preserving our incredible era, as much as I.

Most of all—deep gratitude to the men and women who let me tell their stories. Their poignant moments gave "face" to anonymous voices flowing from our radio speakers of yore. Thanks for taking *Rockin' Rochelle* behind the mic to enjoy the magical moments *with* you ... again. Baby, you *know* what I like! ♪

What'd I Say? ... ♪

(Glossary)

Bubble Gum Pop – a genre of pop music a.k.a. bubble gum rock, bubble gum music, or simply bubble gum, glorified life and love; early bouncy tunes from 1954 to about 1965, and with a little more edge, through today (pop music).

Bubble Under – the radio industry term for songs that for whatever reason, just never quite made it up the charts, though might have a regional fan following.

Color Radio – rumor has it that this branding promo piece of history was the brainchild of programmer Chuck Blore at KFWB/Los Angeles. To combat the popularity of the new color televisions, Color Radio campaigns with cutesy jingles, spread east in various forms, like a viral YouTube fad.

ETs – electrical transcriptions were originally 16-20" dia. disks that held commercials & jingles; made of bare aluminum they're still called ETs even as they morphed into reel-to-reel tapes and other advanced forms.

Fishbowl radio studio – trendy radio stations of the day created "fishbowl" window studios that faced a major thoroughfare, visible to city street life. DJs not only wrestled with knobs, levers, turntables, microphones and telephones, they also endured the distraction of avid fans, obnoxious teenage guys (jealous) and pretty girls seductively parading by, giggling at the DJ's wink or nod.

Flamethrower – ever wonder what the radio industry calls those stations you can receive from hundreds of miles away late at night, when you're snuggled in bed with your transistor radio??? Yep—it's a flamethrower, generally with 50,000+ powerful watts of energy.

FM broadcasting – well, kiddies—and I am talkin' to the young'uns, the rest of you know what it means—I'm not going to get all techie, but it's a frequency band that carries information (predominantly music and speech) over electromagnetic waves, with better sound quality than the AM frequency.

Hooper Ratings – in the 1940s and '50s radio markets were measured by the C.E. Hooper Co. and set the early standard for ratings gathering.

Peanut whistle station – a low power radio station; not where an ambitious DJ wants to stay for long.

Red-light-green-light – known to some as a Chinese Fire Drill. How many times can you change drivers while your souped-up hot rod is idling at the red light, before it turns green? (Oops! Forgot to set the brake.)

Sources & Resources
(Bibliography & References)

HISTORICAL

1960s Slang Dictionary – Host-party.com/files/hp_1960s_Slang.pdf

440: Satisfaction – 440FUN.com/440sat.htm; "DJs, newspeople and unsung radio heroes"

Airheads Radio Survey Archive – Las-Solanas.com/arsa/surveys.php

Airchexx – Airchexx.com; "where classic radio lives"

Broadcast Pioneers of Philadelphia – BroadcastPioneers.com

Jack Levin: eBay Seller Extraordinaire of Vintage Radio Surveys – ebay.com/usr/rockandrollneverforgets?_trksid=p2057872.m2749.l2754

Keystone Record Collectors / PA Music Expo – RecordCollectors.org

Kip's American Graffiti Blog – Mark Groesbeck aka Kip Pullman KipsAmericanGraffiti.Blogspot.com/2010_10_01_archive.html

ReelRadio Top 40 Radio Repository – ReelRadio.com; non-profit aircheck archives

OLD TIME ROCK & ROLL – SING IT! LOOK 'EM UP ON YOUTUBE/STREAM

Benny Hill – "Transistor Radio" (1961); hilarious!

Bob Seger – "Old Time Rock & Roll"; 'cause no one says it better (1979)

Chuck Berry – "Rock & Roll Music" (1957)

Magic '60s Radio – Internet-Radio.com/station/magic60s; streaming the best!

Rich Bro Radio – Streamlicensing.com/stations/richbro/index.html; our *BFYP* DJ Rich Brother Robbin streaming the oldies

The Arrows – "I Love Rock & Roll" (1975)

The Beach Boys – "That's Why God Made the Radio" (2012)

The Guess Who – "Clap for the Wolfman" (1974); yeah baby!

RADIO NEWS

RAMP – Facebook.com/RadioAndMusicPros; Kevin Carter & Steve Resnik

San Diego Radio – SanDiegoRadio.org; Joe Nelson

YOU GOTTA CHECK 'EM OUT

Besides our "Historical" friends, more fun '60s sites:

All About Vinyl Records – All-About-VinylRecords.com; '50s, '60s &'70s

Classic Philadelphia Radio – PhilaRadio.com/airwibg1.aspx; (WIBG) airchecks!

California Historical Radio Society / Bay Area Radio Museum; BayAreaRadio.org/site

Do You Remember? – DoYouRemember.com; it's just too much fun ... all generations.

On This Day/History – OnThisDay.com/history/date/1960; start with 1960 and Rock On!

The People's History/1960 – ThePeopleHistory.com/1960s.html; pop culture & more.

Time Machine>> The 1960s – CollectorsWeekly.com/1960s; great collectors site.

Vintage Fashion Guild – VintageFashionGuild.org; for you retro fashionistas.

No format flip for BFYP! We're still spinning the vinyls with the Rockin' Redhead at 84.8-FM. This ain't your grandma's rockin' chair music!

♪ *Who ... Who ... Who wrote the ...*

Book of Love ... ♪

(About the Author)

The *Blast from Your Past* series is a perfect example of an oft-repeated phrase, "Timing is everything."

It came in an "Aha!" moment for author, LinDee Rochelle, in 2008, as she spoke with her favorite Rock & Roll Radio DJ, Bill Gardner, then in Phoenix.

They lamented the "good ol' days" of radio that planted a Rockin' seed in her mind. But she would have to go back ... way back ... and retrace a long and winding road.

Rochelle admits to a country-gal-gone-city upbringing, infused with varied eclectic music and creative tastes, influenced by her eccentric, dance instructor/artist mother.

As a 'tween, a healthy respect for classical (ballet) and jazz (tap and modern) soon gave way to a lifetime love affair with Rock & Roll. But for her, all music soothes the soul and lifts the spirit.

Rochelle came of age in the 1960s and Rocked her way through the '70s, much of it in administration at UC Berkeley. A fortuitous trip to SoCal led her to spend the 1980s surfing through San Diego, with her hangin' ten twin boys.

Swinging into the '90s Rochelle finally discovered she could make a living with her love of writing and editing. Published in regional magazines in Arizona and California, she eventually worked with a couple of small press book publishers before "retiring."

It took nearly a lifetime to ultimately pair her two loves, Rock & Roll and writing. In the *Blast from Your Past!* series she strives to leave a personal legacy for her descendants, as well as one for DJs, listeners, and an era that should never be forgotten.

Whenever possible Rochelle refreshes her muse in adventures along the ocean's edge, and boating, as far out to sea as the moment allows.

Rochelle maintains three online split-personalities, showcasing her expertise, talents and general eccentricities:

BlastFromYourPast.net (2008); even more DJ memories!
    Blast from Your Past Gifts: Cafepress.com/BlastFromYourPast

39AndHoldingClub.com (2012); BFYP's "little sister" where Age is *ATT*-i-tude!
    Club 39 Nifty Gifts: Cafepress.com/Club39NiftyGifts

PenchantForPenning.com (1985); the serious side of writing ... sorta

Come on in to the

𝓟𝓼𝔂𝓬𝓱𝓮𝓭𝓮𝓵𝓲𝓬 𝓢𝓱𝓪𝓬𝓴 ... ♪
1970 ~ 1979

Didn't see your favorite Rockin' DJ yet? Want to know who stuck around for the *Psychedelic Seventies?*

Check out *Blast from Your Past!* Book 3 DJs listed below—swing with us into the *Psychedelic Seventies* in late 2018! (♪ = recurring DJs)

Next up on your radio dial ...

William F. Williams ♪
    Best known KMEN/San Bernardino; KPPC/Los Angeles

David Leonard (music survey collector)
    Best known for his book, *Aircheck: The Story of Top 40 Radio in San Diego*

Jeff Prescott
    Best known KGB/San Diego, California

Evan Haning
    Best known KSLY & KVEC/San Luis Obispo, California

Billy Bass ♪
    Best known WMMS/Cleveland, Ohio

Lonnie Napier
    Wolfman Jack's friend & VP

𝓦𝓸𝓵𝓯𝓶𝓪𝓷 𝓙𝓪𝓬𝓴 𝓖𝓮𝓽𝓼 𝓕𝓾𝓷𝓴𝔂

Bill Gardner ♪
    Best known WIBG/Philadelphia; KVIL/Dallas

Andre Gardner
    Best known WZZD (formerly WIBG)/Philadelphia

Al Gardner
    Best known WIBG/Philadelphia

Neil Ross ♪
    Best known KCBQ & KDEO/San Diego, California

Randy Jackson with band, Zebra
    Best known for "Who's Behind the Door" (& more!)

Bob Buchmann
> Best known WBAB/Long Island, New York

Ron Riley ♪
> Best known WCAO/Baltimore, Maryland

Lee Gray ♪
> Best known WKLO/Louisville, Kentucky

Joey Reynolds ♪
> Best known WGRQ/Buffalo & WIBG/Philadelphia

Tom Donahue ♪
> Best known KSAN/San Francisco & KMET/Los Angeles

Raechel Donahue ♪
> Best known KSAN/San Francisco & KMET/Los Angeles

Alison Steele ♪
> Best known WNEW/New York, New York

Neale Blase ♪
> Best known at too many to mention!

Wolfman Jack Soothes our Souls

Shotgun Tom Kelly ♪
> Best known KCBQ/San Diego, California

Ed Sciaky ♪
> Best known WDAS & WMMR/Philadelphia

Rich Brother Robbin ♪
> Best known KCBQ/San Diego, California

Bruce Chudacoff
> Best known WLS/Chicago, Illinois

Dave Mason
> Best known WBBF/Rochester, New York

Frank Anthony
> Best known KCBQ/San Diego, California

Jim Higgs ♪
> Best known WKMI/Kalamazoo, Michigan

Dr. Don Rose ♪
> Best known KFRC/San Francisco, California

Jim Stagg ♪
> Best known WCFL/Chicago, Illinois

Frank "Mars" Cotolo
> Wolfman Jack's writer & sidekick

Jim LaMarca
> Often known as Wolfman Jack's PD at XETRA Extra Gold

Wolfman Jack, Winds Up the Decade

Rock On!

So, tell me, did you like our little stroll down Rock & Roll Radio's Memory Lane? No, seriously, *tell* me! Would love to hear from you: LinDee@BlastFromYourPast.net.

Share thoughts, comments, moments of memories, and your constructive critique. I'll listen. I'm retired ... what else do I have to do?

Speaking of sharing, please consider letting others know, through an Amazon review, how much you enjoyed one or more books of the **Blast from Your Past** series. You may not think those reviews matter, but trust me, they do.

⭐⭐⭐⭐⭐ Amazon reviews do more than simply share your thoughts and rate your enjoyment. Five stars urge Amazon to push a book a little further to the forefront of its category, providing an opportunity for more people to see it.

Less than five stars—even only one down, at four—sends a book plummeting to the bottom of the barrel, so to speak.

Yes, your review *counts*! Please—if you truly feel you can't honestly offer five stars, contact me. Tell me why—let me fix it. Thanks!

Did you receive this book as a gift or obtain from other than Amazon? Feel free to send your review to me, and I'll reply, and post it on my website.

Peace Out

Made in the USA
Las Vegas, NV
19 September 2021